The Call Within

Finding Purpose and Sparking Transformation

A Co-Authored Collaboration

of the Life Changing Energy Community

Compiled by Vickie Gould
Published by Morning Oak Publishing

The Call Within: Finding Purpose and Sparking Transformation
Copyright © 2025 by Morning Oak Publishing.
All rights reserved. No part of this book may be reproduced, stored in a retrieval system, or transmitted in any form or by any means, electronic, mechanical, photocopying, recording, or otherwise, without prior written permission from the publisher or individual authors.
ISBN: 9798992197303
Printed in the United States of America.
First Edition, 2025.

Dedication

To everyone who has ever felt lost, broken, or unsure of their path—This book is for you. May you find comfort in these stories, strength in your journey, and the courage to listen to the quiet call within.

You are never alone.

Table of Contents

Dedication 5

Foreword 13

Preface 14

Acknowledgments 15

Introduction 16

Symphony of Survival By Carl Gregory 19

Becoming Me By Jane Cooke 27

In My Skin By Elizabeth Wood 33

Awakening the Heart to Live a Life You'll Love By Jay Vince-Cruz 43

A Breath in & A Breath Out By Stephanie Harmon 51

Reconnecting with My Roots: Ancestral Healing and Inner Light By Lisa Ali
.... 59

The Healer's Journey: Transforming Stress, Trauma & Grief to Peace, Love & Joy By Gina Allgaier 67

The Universe Is Always At Your Heels By Carmen McKibben 75

Firewalking on the Sun By Ellie Epstein-White 83

Journey into Sound Healing By Harold "Rich" Bertram 91

Welcome to The Land Mahn By Margo Schaefer 97

The Year of No Regrets By Susan Fryman 105

Finding Purpose in Life's Challenges Through the Transformative Power of Sound By Mary Beth Cowardin 111

Time to Fly By Gretchen Melo 119

Lifelong Learning: A Journey from Crisis to Insight By Ellen Aresty 127

ALL THE PIECES By LoriAnn Bouchard 133

Believe By Carolyn Soto Bell 139

Survive, Thrive, PTSD, and Addiction By Jennifer Pechumer 145

A Walk Through the Trees to the Sea By Jill Perrin 153

From Darkness into Light By Mary Sue Dale 159

Life Changing Transformation By Kerry Martin 167

Sharing the Light By Vicki Wissig 175

Breaking Generational Cycles: Reclaiming My Emotional Expression and My Identity By Ashley Cantor-Birnbaum 181

A Healer's Journey By Susan Bloom 189

IF YOU CAN'T SEE THE LIGHT AT THE END OF THE TUNNEL... MAYBE YOU ARE THE LIGHT By Teresa Kamiya 195

From Grief to Peace: A Journey of Healing and Transformation Through Holistic Practices By Rashida Sheffield 203

Out of the Shadow By Jennifer Penick 209

From Broken to Fueled By Theresa DeLorenzo 217

A More Complete Sense of Self By Carrie Van Acker 225

Transforming My Veterinary Practice – A Journey to Holistic Healing Through Island Life, Music, Medicine, Yoga, Animals, & Self Love By Eve Harrison..233

Harmonize Your Heart and Heal Your Soul By Kimberly Lim....................241

The Search for Meaning: My Journey from Law Enforcement to Spiritual Coaching By Valerie Holden...249

Waking up to Ancient Frequencies By Mayuri Radha Das.........................257

Trust the Path By Sylvia P Mason..265

Breathing Through the Pain: My Journey from Barely Surviving to Enthusiastically Thriving By Karen Lynn Warwick......................................273

Death Endurance Rise By Marie Hamilton 281

A Journey Through Shadows to Light By Marcella Hutchens.....................289

The Missing Piece By Brooke Stone 295

Introduction and A Dark Night of the Soul By Kimberly Measel 303

From Failure to Featured By Bobby Gray 311

Embracing The Journey through Spirituality and Sound By Kristin Whitcomb 319

Out of the Darkness of Domestic Violence and Into Consciousness, Forgiveness and Compassion By Joyce Martin 327

Belonging By Becky Diver 335

Unseen, Undetected, and Unbelievable Truth By Tresa Mazurek...............341

Finding My Freedom Through Fasting By Jazmin Briggs 349

Reclaiming My Kefi By Bessy Goulianos 357

Releasing Cinderella By Jill Briansky 365

Something in the Water By Catherine Devine Zagorski 373

Finding my Light By Laura Degelmann 381

WARRIOR GODDESS By Carla Cunningham 389

My Healing Journey By Jennifer Morris 395

Unapologetically Auténtica: On a Journey to Empowered Radiance By Karen L Ramos 401

Dear Reader, ... 409

Foreword

We all experience moments in life that challenge us to the core—times when the world feels heavy, and the path ahead seems unclear. These moments can feel isolating, as if no one could possibly understand the weight we carry. But if there's one truth the authors of this book have learned, it's this: healing doesn't happen in isolation. Transformation often begins the moment we realize we aren't walking alone.

The Call Within is a shared space where vulnerability meets hope, and where struggle leads to growth. Each of the 52 authors in this book has faced their own crossroads. They've known loss, uncertainty, and hardship. But through it all, they chose to listen to that quiet voice inside—the call that urged them to keep going, to heal, and to embrace their unique journey.

This book is a reminder that no matter how difficult life feels, someone else has been there too. And while our paths may look different, the human experience connects us all in ways we sometimes forget. Whether you're just beginning your healing journey or well on your way, I hope these stories serve as a reminder that your inner voice—your call within—can lead you to places you never imagined.

I believe the timing of this book's release is no coincidence. A new year offers a chance for renewal, reflection, and possibility. There's something beautiful about starting fresh, about stepping into the next chapter with intention. I invite you to approach these stories with an open heart, allowing the lessons, insights, and moments of grace to resonate in your own life.

Thank you for picking up this book. By doing so, you're not only honoring the journeys of those who wrote these words, but you're also taking a step toward your own healing.

This book shares deeply personal experiences involving trauma, loss, and mental health struggles. Some stories may bring up difficult emotions. We encourage readers to honor their feelings and take breaks if needed. Reader discretion is advised.

Preface

It's incredible how a simple idea can grow into something far more meaningful than expected. *The Call Within* began with the thought that the stories we hold inside could not only heal us but also reach someone else who needs them. If even one person feels less alone after reading this book, then sharing these stories has been worth it.

What unfolded through this project became more powerful than we could have anticipated. When we were invited to contribute our journeys, many of us thought we were simply writing about moments of hardship, perseverance, and healing. But the process revealed something deeper—a collective act of courage, honesty, and vulnerability. We didn't just write about transformation; we lived it. In sharing these stories, some of us found more of our own healing. The act of writing became a release, a way to make sense of our experiences, and a path toward something lighter. This project reminded us that writing can be profoundly therapeutic—it allows us to lay down pieces of our pain and, in doing so, set ourselves free.

This book isn't meant to offer all the answers. It doesn't claim to show the perfect path to healing. Instead, it stands as a reminder that growth often begins with listening to the quiet voice within—the one that nudges us forward, even when the next step feels uncertain. We believe that call exists in all of us. Sometimes it's faint, and sometimes it's impossible to ignore, but it's always present, waiting to be heard.

As you move through these stories, we hope you'll recognize reflections of your own experiences. Perhaps the struggles you face won't feel as isolating. Maybe you'll find comfort in knowing that while healing is personal, it doesn't have to happen alone. Perhaps you'll be inspired to put pen to paper too and write your own healing story.

Thank you for holding this book in your hands. By doing so, you're not just witnessing the journeys within these pages—you're becoming part of a greater movement of hope, healing, and connection.

With gratitude,
The Authors of *The Call Within*

Acknowledgments

Bringing *The Call Within* to life has been an incredible journey—one that wouldn't have been possible without the collective energy, vulnerability, and courage of the 52 authors who shared their hearts and stories. Your willingness to open up and trust this process is what gives this book its power. Thank you for trusting me—and for trusting yourselves—to share your stories with the world. Thank you for showing up with authenticity and grace.

To the Life Changing Energy community, you inspire me every day. Your belief in healing, growth, and raising the vibration of the world is the reason this project came to life. I'm grateful to each of you for being part of this journey and for the light you bring.

A big thank you to the Life Changing Energy team, especially my daughter, Stephanie Lyskawa for all your dedication and late nights. The work you do behind the scenes makes all of this possible, and I'm lucky to have you for more reasons than this project.

And to you, the reader—thank you trusting us with your heart. By reading these stories, you're not just supporting the authors, you're stepping into the circle of healing and transformation. I hope these words remind you that you're never alone, and your own story matters more than you know.

With love and gratitude,
Vickie Gould
Founder, Life Changing Energy

Founder, Brighter Healing Foundation

Introduction

At some point in life, we all face moments that change us—whether we're ready or not. Sometimes it's a slow unraveling, and other times it hits like a thunderclap. These moments shape us, stretch us, and call us to look deeper within ourselves.

The Call Within is a collection of stories from people who faced those moments head-on.

Each of the 52 authors in this book has walked through their own fire—loss, illness, grief, and the kinds of struggles that often feel impossible to share. But through these experiences, they found something unexpected: healing, clarity, and a renewed sense of purpose.

This book holds more than personal stories—it carries pieces of the human experience that we all recognize. It's a reminder that even in the toughest moments, there's always the potential for growth. And maybe most importantly, it shows that no matter what we're going through, someone else has been there too.

The Call Within is also part of a bigger mission from the Life Changing Energy community. At Life Changing Energy, we believe in raising the vibration of the world one healer at a time — one healed heart at a time. The proceeds from this book will go directly to Brighter Healing Foundation, a 501(c)(3) non-profit dedicated to helping provide holistic healing tools, education, and resources to people who need them most.

Wherever you are in your journey, I hope these stories meet you where you need them. I hope they remind you that even in the hardest moments, something beautiful can emerge.

This book discusses themes of trauma, grief, suicide, and mental health challenges, which some readers may find distressing. Reader discretion is advised.

As a collaborative effort, featuring contributions from a variety of authors, each story has its own unique voice, personality, and literary style. The chapters range from formal and informative, to personable and conversational, to those that feel like texts, social media posts or streams of consciousness. As a result, every chapter offers a distinct tone and perspective, reflecting the diverse experiences and insights of the contributors. We encourage you to explore the chapters with an open mind, but if a particular chapter doesn't resonate with you, feel free to move on to the next one—there's something here for everyone.

Symphony of Survival
By Carl Gregory

Put your seatbelt on, we're going for a ride

It was a plunge into a world unseen, a world where sound itself became a force that could heal, hurt, or haunt. Long before I could make sense of words, before I could even understand what I was hearing, sound was shaping me—just like it shapes you. We often take it for granted: the way a voice can soften a blow or harden a heart, the way a simple tone can convey love, hate, or fear. But I didn't fully grasp its power until I stood face-to-face with it, using it as a tool to unravel the tangled mess of trauma. Come closer. I'll show you. But hold on tight—my journey is a bumpy ride.

It's a Boy

My story begins like everyone else's, cocooned in darkness, my existence muted and blurred. It wasn't long before everything shattered. My entry into the world was no gentle lullaby. It was chaos—a sudden eruption of panic and urgency, like a bomb ticking down to its final second. I wasn't supposed to survive. I don't remember it, but I can almost hear it now: the frantic voices of the doctors, the shrill alarms of machinery, the desperate pounding of my mother's heart as they struggled to bring me back. I can imagine the tight grip of silence as everything hung in the balance, then, somewhere deep inside, the sudden, raw explosion of sound as I gasped my first breath.

It must have felt like being ripped from the void and thrust into a battlefield, and in a way, it was. "It's a boy!" someone called out, but it wasn't a joyful declaration. It was a statement wrapped in disbelief and relief, every syllable trembling with the residue of terror. I didn't understand any of it, of course, but somehow, I felt it. That chaos, that brush with death—it imprinted itself on me.

As I grew through childhood, I became quiet, almost eerily so. My world was a storm of noise: doors slamming, voices rising and falling in sharp, jagged peaks. Arguments would erupt out of nowhere, loud and violent, shaking the walls. I learned early on that it was safer to stay hidden in the corners, where I could blend into the shadows and absorb every sound and vibration without drawing attention to myself.

The Thin Blue Line: Cover Now, Officer Down

After some college, I entered the world of law enforcement. Police work is a life of contrasts—long, uneventful hours followed by sudden, gut-punch moments of sheer panic. They say it's 90% boredom and 10% chaos, but what they don't tell you is how that 10% can tear through your very core, leaving your heart pounding long after the dust has settled. Some sounds from those moments will cling to you forever, branded into your memory like scars. I learned this firsthand one bleak, unforgettable night—a night that began with routine and ended in the kind of fear that most people will never know.

The shift started uneventfully, just like countless others. I was going through the motions of my job, the familiar drone of my partner's voice fading in and out over the radio. It was one of those calm nights that lull you into a false sense of security. But then, without warning, the static hissed violently to life, and a voice cut through—jagged, raw, and desperate. "Officer down! Officer down! Cover now!" The words hit like a sledgehammer, sending shockwaves of dread through my veins.

It was my partner's voice, but it was twisted, unrecognizable under the strain of terror and pain. My body tightened, and a cold sweat broke across my skin. My partner's voice had always been steady, composed, and unshakable. Hearing it splinter and crack under the weight of fear twisted my gut into knots.

My mind raced through worst-case scenarios, every second stretching into an eternity as I made my way to him. The radio buzzed with panicked chatter from officers scrambling to respond. But it was his voice that rang above it all, slicing through the noise like a blade. I couldn't shake the way it cracked—each syllable sharp with desperation.

The scene was chaos. I headed directly toward the madness, willfully, quickly, and without hesitation—a blur of movement and shadows. But above the confusion, I heard it again—his screams. They pierced the night, raw and primal. I turned and spotted him, locked in a brutal struggle with a towering figure. My partner was pinned against the concrete, the suspect relentless—a beast of a man driving him further into the ground with every strike.

Time warped. The world narrowed to the rhythmic thud of flesh hitting flesh, the ragged gasps of my partner fighting for air, and the deafening rush of cortisol in my body. Training took over. Adrenaline turned me into a machine of pure instinct. I charged forward without thinking, driven by that sound—the sound of someone I cared about being torn apart.

There was shouting, grunting, a tangle of limbs and uniforms, and then, finally, silence. My partner lay there, gasping, his chest heaving with the effort to suck in air, his leg twisted into shapes it should not have been. His eyes were wide, wild, still caught in the primal grip of survival.

Later, after he was transported to the hospital, I stood in the aftermath, staring at the debris and personal items scattered across the scene. My heart hammered against my ribs, my breath sharp and uneven. I tried to focus on the voices of my fellow officers, the chatter of the radios. But all I could hear was his scream, looping over and over in my head. His voice, shattered and broken, tore through the night like the cry of a wounded animal.

In the locker room, long after the shift ended, I sat on a cold metal bench, staring blankly at the walls. The world around me continued its rhythm—the soft murmur of voices, the clink of lockers opening and closing. But for me, time stood still. All I could hear was that scream, echoing, reverberating, carving itself deeper into my soul with every repetition.

The Thin Red Line: Unknown Aircraft Down

Finishing my career and honorably retiring from law enforcement should have been the end of the madness. But it was merely a shift in the terrain—a trade of one chaos for another. Emergency management and firefighting called to me, offering a way to stay in the fray without the same brutality, all while I pursued my doctorate degree. But danger has a way of finding you, no matter where you go. I learned that during my first night on duty in a small, isolated mountain town—a night that plunged me straight into a new kind of fear.

I hadn't even settled into my new surroundings when the call came in: "Unknown aircraft down in remote terrain." My gut clenched as the words sank in. Images of flaming wreckage, twisted metal, and mangled bodies filled my mind. What kind of aircraft? How many passengers? Was anyone alive? The questions buzzed like angry wasps, but there was no time to think. I grabbed my gear and headed into the frozen darkness, my breath fogging in the icy air as I raced to the scene.

The command post was a bleak, wind-blasted clearing on the edge of a mountain road in the middle of nowhere. I squinted through the gloom, searching for any sign of the wreckage high up on the mountain. And then I saw it—a faint, pulsing light high on the jagged slope. My heart leaped. A distress signal? A survivor's flashlight? I had no way of knowing. Then a new sound emerged—a soft, haunting beep that sent a chill down my spine.

It was barely audible over the howling wind, a weak, intermittent pulse that seemed to come from nowhere and everywhere at once. I strained to hear, my ears aching from the cold. Was it an emergency beacon? Was someone up there, trapped and clinging to life? The sound teased me, taunting me with its vagueness, refusing to reveal its secrets. And then came the worst realization: I couldn't reach it.

The mountainside was treacherous, the terrain too steep and icy to navigate in the dark. My radio was useless this far out, and my phone was out of range. I was cut off, stranded in a desolate, freezing wilderness with nothing but that maddening beep to remind me how powerless I was.

Hours passed. The cold seeped into my bones, numbing my fingers and toes, but the sound never stopped. Each beep felt like a countdown, a reminder of every second slipping away. I had no idea what was up there—a plane filled with passengers, a private jet, a military craft. I only knew that every beat of that mechanical heart might mean the difference between life and death.

Finally, a Blackhawk helicopter roared overhead, its searchlight sweeping over the treacherous terrain. I held my breath as it hovered over the wreckage, its blades chopping furiously to hold position in the wind. The Blackhawk rose quickly, and then the verdict came: it wasn't a plane or an aircraft. It was a fallen satellite, its lonely beacon flashing aimlessly into the dark. No passengers. No survivors. Just an empty piece of metal.

Relief washed over me, but it was tinged with something darker—an emptiness, a sense of having faced down a ghost. The sound faded, but its echo lingered, haunting me long after I packed up and headed down the mountain. It wasn't just a beep. It was a siren of helplessness, a call to action that had led me nowhere.

I was left with a feeling that there was more out there for me—a way to help people without feeling helpless.

The Sound That Called Me

Long before I knew what trauma was, sound was shaping me. In the womb, I imagine the muffled rhythm of my mother's heartbeat, the low hum of her voice, and the cadence of the world beyond her body. Sound was my first connection to life—a constant, grounding presence even before I could name it. But it wasn't all soothing. There was the yelling, the arguing, the loud machines, and the doctors' frantic voices at my birth.

That connection deepened as I grew, but it wasn't just the comforting sounds that marked my journey. It was the contrasts—noise and silence, chaos and calm. Unknowingly, I carried this relationship with sound into my career in law enforcement. It was a world of sharp contrasts: the static crackle of the radio, the piercing blare of screams, and the moments of eerie, heart-stopping silence that followed. Sound could warn you, save you, or haunt you. For me, it was the screams that stayed—the primal cries of fear and the shouts of desperation etched themselves into my soul. No matter how many years passed, those echoes never truly left me.

Later, when I transitioned to emergency management and firefighting, sound took on new shapes. The roar of flames, the steady hum of water pumping through hoses, the pounding thud of my own heartbeat in moments of danger—it was all a symphony of survival. Yet, amidst the adrenaline, there was a quieter sound that stayed with me: the whispered prayers of those I tried to save and the soft sobs of those I couldn't. I can still hear someone saying to me, as they were fading away, "Just hold me and speak to me."

But it wasn't until the world came to a standstill during the pandemic that I truly understood the role sound had played in my life. The silence of lockdown was deafening, forcing me to sit with my own echoes—the unresolved trauma, the memories that refused to fade. It was in that silence that I realized I wasn't just carrying my own wounds. I was carrying the sounds of every person I had tried to help, every moment of chaos I had survived.

When the lockdowns lifted, I stepped into the field of mental health therapy. As an Advanced Certified Clinical Trauma Specialist, I worked with clients whose pain mirrored my own—those haunted by echoes they couldn't silence. Despite my extensive training, I felt something was missing. For many of my clients, words failed them. Their trauma was too raw, too deep to articulate. I longed for a way to help them express what they couldn't say.

That's when I discovered Music Integrated Therapy. Through music, my clients began to find a voice for their pain. The vibrations of a single note could capture what entire sentences couldn't. Yet, even as I witnessed breakthroughs, I saw the need for something more—a way to anchor my clients after they had poured out their emotions, to help them find peace in the aftermath of release. They needed a beginning and an end to their trauma feelings.

I immersed myself in learning how sound could do more than evoke emotion—it could heal. I began introducing sound healing to my clients after my journey through sound training. What I witnessed was transformative. The gentle tones of Crystal Bowls, tuning forks, and Tibetan Bowls didn't just soothe; they created a space where trauma could unravel, where the body and mind could find harmony.

But the most surprising and unexpected transformation was my own. As the vibrations filled the room, they resonated within me. The echoes of my past—the screams, the sirens, the roar of flames—began to soften. Sound, which had once been a source of chaos, became a source of calm. Through these sessions, I wasn't just guiding my clients toward healing; I was healing alongside them.

I came to understand that trauma isn't just a story we carry—it's a resonance, a vibration, its own frequency that lives within us. Sound has the power to reach where words cannot, to shift those deep vibrations of pain into frequencies of hope and connection. From the womb to the fireground, from screams to silence, sound has been the constant thread in my life. It led me to my calling, to a place where I could transform the echoes of chaos into a symphony of healing. Sound taught me to listen—to my clients, to myself, to the spaces between the noise.

Through its vibrations, I found my purpose. And through its resonance, I've helped others find theirs.

A Moment of Thanks

I was given an opportunity to share a glimpse of my journey with sound and how it has made an everlasting imprint on me, changing me forever. The stories I shared aren't the most dramatic, dangerous, or eventful I've experienced, but I felt they convey my journey well. By sharing these moments, I have made myself vulnerable, revealing some of my innermost feelings and emotions. This is not an easy thing for me to do, but I do it with an open heart, hoping you find that sound is part of your journey too.

People have been by my side all along the way, and I could not have done it without them during the times they were in my life. Acknowledging that many of them have, in one way or another, moved on from my life, I still want to thank each one of them for being there when I needed them, whether they knew they were helping me or not.

A special note of thanks goes to a wonderful person—caring, thoughtful, loving, and always encouraging me to be a better version of myself—my partner, friend, and wife, Yulia. Another goes to my son, Wyatt. We never know the roads we will travel or the sounds we will hear. I promise you, until my last breath, you will always be able to call me for anything—I will hear your sound. Always follow Tecumseh's *The Fear of Death* and have your song; I have mine.

I love you both.

About Carl Gregory:

Carl Gregory, MS, AMFT, is an Advanced Certified Clinical Trauma Specialist with extensive experience in law enforcement, emergency management, and firefighting. Throughout his career, Carl has supported individuals across all life stages—including military personnel and first responders—helping them navigate trauma's challenges. His journey into therapy began during his law enforcement career, where he earned a master's degree in counseling with a focus on Marriage, Family, and Child Therapy, and pursued a Doctorate in Emergency Management (ABD).

Carl's therapeutic approach emphasizes accountability and authenticity, drawing on his personal experiences with trauma. He connects deeply with clients, serving as a collaborative partner in their healing journey. Carl is trained in multiple therapeutic modalities, including EMDR, CBT, CPT, Prolonged Exposure Therapy, Solution-Focused Therapy, ACT, Motivational Interviewing, DBT, Music Integrated Therapy, and Sound Healing. His compassionate yet direct style empowers clients to face and process difficult emotions, fostering growth and resilience.

Becoming Me
By Jane Cooke

I grew up in a family that was unsupportive. I never seemed to be good enough, smart enough, or worthy enough. The sadness and feeling of inadequacy that were part of my everyday life became part of my character. I carried that damage into my marriage to someone who was unstable himself and had severe addiction issues.

My creation story starts during the orientation session at the court-ordered rehabilitation clinic where my spouse was being treated after getting a drunken driving ticket.

In a room of approximately forty people, the counselor asked, "By a show of hands, how many of you truly believe that if your significant other does not make it out of rehab, your life is over?" I was the only person in the room to raise a hand. My only thought was that I was eternally grateful I had chosen to sit in the very back row so most people could not see my humiliation and stupidity.

That single question cracked open a long-buried truth: I was living for someone else. I felt so unworthy of love, I didn't know how to live for myself. Sitting there in that moment, I realized my life could no longer go on this way. I needed to rediscover my worth, but I had absolutely no idea where or how to begin.

To the counselor's credit, he calmly went on with the orientation without singling me out or asking why I felt the way I did. He simply explained the signs of codependency. He made a good case for everyone to believe that everything would turn out exactly as it was supposed to.

I did not believe one word that came out of his mouth.

I left the meeting shortly before it was scheduled to end because, of course, I was not interested in any therapy session or conversation about my choices. I sat in my car for quite a bit of time trying to puzzle through what had just happened. The thoughts running through my mind were chaotic and desperate. They took on every hue of darkness and flooded my mind with screams of inadequacy and failure. I lost all hope. All I wanted to do was slip farther into the deep, dark hole and stay there where I could manage the pain by ignoring the truth of my circumstance.

However, there was one light in my life: my twelve-year-old daughter.

As I drove out of the parking lot, my mind racing with one bad idea after another of how to end this nightmare, it started to rain. It wasn't a hard rain, but more than a mist. The humidity it brought with it was like a shroud, dampening everything around me. I'm not sure how long I drove around trying to come up with a solution; yet, eventually, I decided I just wasn't strong enough to make it through this and that everyone would be better off without me. My daughter could be raised by someone who could actually show her how to be happy and healthy. That wasn't me.

I decided to take my own life.

Yet, even though I was in the midst of an extreme emotional crisis, I knew that committing suicide was not really the answer, and the thoughts that everyone would be better off without me did not make sense. So, I decided to get help.

I spotted a phone booth outside a closed liquor store. It was one of the old booths with four glass walls, a hinged doorway, and a ratty telephone book hanging limply from a chewed-up chain. The doorway was half ripped off its hinges and totally useless. The light in the booth flickered on and off erratically. This was not the "good" part of town, and I should not have even entertained stopping. Yet, it truly did look like a shining beacon of hope on this dark, rainy night and offered a bit of protection from the weather.

I stopped and scrambled for some change to use in the booth. I got out and ran to the booth, trying to keep from getting completely soaked to the bone. I begged all the powers that be that the ratty phone book would at least have the page listing the Suicide Prevention Hotline. The odds were against me, but as I said, I was desperate for some kind of relief from the agony rampaging through my mind.

I found the number! With trembling hands and deep resolve, I managed to get the coins into the slot on the phone and dial the number. I was prepared to bare my soul to the rescuer on the other end of the line and get the help I needed to survive the night and get back home to my daughter.

Never in a million years was I prepared for what I heard.

Beep, beep, beep…beep, beep, beep…beep, beep, beep.

A busy signal.

It was the last straw. In what felt like slow motion, I slid down the glass of the phone booth and landed in a heap in the puddle of muddy water on the floor of the booth. I clung helplessly to the phone receiver, listening to the busy signal. The rotten stench of old sweat, dirt, and mildew attacked my senses. The rain pelted my body, and the wind caused the broken door to moan with the type of agony that was ravaging my soul. As the busy signal droned on, the despair felt endless, as if the world had confirmed my worst fear: I was utterly alone in my struggle.

Beep, beep, beep…beep, beep, beep…beep, beep, beep.

People tell me the busy signal should have eventually stopped and the phone should have disconnected. All I know is that I sat in that phone booth for several hours, listening to the busy signal. I would like to tell you that I worked everything out in my mind and that I knew exactly what I should do. I would like to tell you I picked myself up, redialed the number, and spoke with a counselor. I would like to tell you I experienced a revelation and that my life was laid out before me and everything worked out fine.

I would like to tell you a lot of things.

All I can tell you is that I don't remember having any brilliant thoughts—no aha moments, no call to action to make everything all right. No bright lights leading me to inner peace and ultimate knowledge. What I do remember is that, at some point, I could no longer tell what were raindrops falling on my face and what were tears falling from my eyes. At some point, the chaos in my mind quieted, and I was no longer in a state of pure panic and terror. At some point, the beep, beep, beep became more of a reminder that I had choices, and less an insistent accusation of all my failures.

At some point, as the rain fell and I sat in that booth, I felt a small shift. The chaos in my mind softened—just the tiniest of changes, barely perceptible—and was replaced by a glimmer of strength I hadn't known I possessed. I picked myself up from the floor of the phone booth, hung up the phone, wiped off as much of the muck and mud as possible, got back in my car, drove home, and hugged my daughter.

The road to recovery has not been smooth and effortless. It has not been without a few pitfalls along the way. And it has definitely not been short and sweet. Yet, the person who walked out of that phone booth on that dark, rainy night was a completely different person than the one who walked into it. No better, no worse—just different. I became me.

I am now a grandmother, and my grandsons call me the "exotic grandmother" because I talk to them about energy. I tell them that the energy they put out into the Universe is the energy that gets returned to them. Before the phone booth, I was a victim and could only see the darkness and futility of life. After the phone booth, I made a conscious effort to change my thinking and to put positivity and light into the ether. I have been on a journey of self-discovery and open-minded exploration.

In the ensuing years, I studied many of the healing arts. I am a mindfulness practitioner, an energy guide, a crystal healer, and a master sound healer. I work with light and sound. And with every crystal, every sound, I could feel myself reclaiming the lost parts of me, slowly replacing pain with hope and anger with peace. I was learning that I could change the energy around me, and that life didn't have to be a battle. Healing was real, and it was mine to discover.

Thanks to my studies and realizations, my mission in this life is to try to make a positive difference in the lives of every individual I meet and in every situation I encounter. I do my best to avoid assigning guilt and fault to every action that is not perfect as defined by the rules in this plane of existence.

As I've continued my healing path, I now use these gifts to help others. I know that there is quite a bit we can do to heal our little corner of reality. I have shifted from a place of self-doubt to a place of confidence, compassion, and personal empowerment. Every session, every conversation that I co-create with another, feels like I'm giving a part of that phone booth revelation to someone else—a way for them to break free from the pain and feel alive again. And sharing these tools isn't just healing for them; it completes my journey, making all those dark moments useful and perceptive.

Wow! I sound like some kind of demented, metaphysical version of Mary Sunshine. And that is a laugh. I still hold a corporate job, make plenty of mistakes, and have even been known to lose my temper and use a few cuss words. I get sad and happy for no good reason. And there are days when I just don't want to get out of bed because it means I have to do something I don't really want to do. The difference is that I no longer assign negative aspects to these normal, daily feelings and emotions. If I do not want to experience a particular emotion, then I use my tools to change the energy and simply do not play the blame game. And, quite honestly, sometimes it works better than at other times. It seems that the more open you are to change, the more easily it is to manipulate it.

Everything that exists is made of energy. And all energies work in coordination or conflict with each other at any given time. Using the energetic properties of a crystal to assist in calming the mind or the audible energy of a singing bowl to instill peace just reinforces the fact that everything is energy. We may find ourselves angry, sad, or depressed; yet, if we do not want to feel those things, we can adjust the energy surrounding us to get us more aligned with the energy we want to feel.

It may sound complicated; however, it truly is the easiest thing for us to do because we are naturally attuned to energies that support us the most. Think about the last time you were sad and wanted to not be sad any longer. Did you listen to a favorite song? Did you eat a food that always puts you in a better mood? Did you visit friends or family that made you feel better? Did you take a walk in nature and feel the sunshine on your face? That is ALL energy!

So, I invite you to dip your toe into the "energy game." Use energetic tools like crystals, sound, and light to play with the energy fields that surround you. Pay attention to what your thoughts are when you are in an emotional state—both positive and negative. Make a conscious choice to change any energy that you no longer want to experience and embrace those energy patterns that make you feel like the amazing, talented, precious, unique being that you are. Revel in your brilliance. Embrace your divinity. Shine your light!

My journey of discovery and growth, like yours, is a testament to the power of energy, light, and love to transform every corner of our world—one heart at a time.

I have ultimate faith in your ability to accomplish anything you identify you want in your life because you are energetically designed to be absolutely amazing. I guarantee it. Be still. Listen to your soul. Use your power. Align your energy.

Beep, beep, beep.

About Jane Cooke:

Jane Cooke is a gifted writer, energy guide, and retired Learning & Development professional. She also holds certifications in hypnotherapy, mindfulness, life coaching, crystal healing, and sound therapy. The books and articles she pens always provide an open-hearted insight into the incredible power of the human mind, body, and soul. The workshops she offers assist individuals in aligning with their own magnificence and embracing their innate brilliance. Her mission in life is to be a positive influence for everyone she meets and for every situation she encounters. She has often been described as being too creative and is fully invested in the belief that anything is possible. She is fascinated by quantum physics and most things that are fantastical and imaginative. She is a gypsy and loves traveling and immersing in new cultural environments. Find Jane on social media:

- Email: jcooke114@gmail.com
- Website: janecooke.com
- Facebook: https://www.facebook.com/jane.cooke.180

LinkedIn: **https://www.linkedin.com/in/jane-cooke-05a1991/**

In My Skin
By Elizabeth Wood

My seven-month-old son needed me on Sunday morning, August 17, 2008. Like many times before, I picked him up and perched him on my left hip.

He's not warm.

I wrap my right arm around his chunky back. *Warmth.* I alternate sides, back and forth, checking for feeling. I feel nothing on my left side.

It's not him. It's me.

I pinch my right forearm with my left thumb and pointer finger. *Ouch.* Then the left forearm. *Nothing.* Left forearm again. The skin turns red, yet I feel no pain, no sensation.

Slowly, I set my son down on the white carpet and pick up the phone.

My best friend, Shannon, answers.

"Oh, my gosh!" she says, not asking any questions. "I'll be right there!"

She's at the front door a short while later, knocking before I can finish fumbling with my slip-on sandals. A family member arrives to care for the children. I kiss my son and two-year-old daughter goodbye and pause to look at them—really look at them—before I go.

I study their sweet faces and their hands waving goodbye so their images will be etched in my mind.

Will I feel the warmth and softness of their hugs again?

At the hospital emergency room, a male doctor walks in wearing a crisp white coat. Part of me is convinced he'll know how to fix me.

I'm wrong about this.

"Hello! What brings you here today?" the doctor asks, though his concerned expression suggests he already knows. "You're numb on your left side?"

"Yes," I say. "I'm numb on my entire left side… right down the middle. My scalp, my teeth, my arm, my leg—everything!"

His eyes widen. Mine do, too.

He's never heard that one before. I'm horrified. I want to scream but say nothing.

The doctor jots down a few notes and approaches the hospital bed to conduct a neurological exam.

"Point with your right hand, then touch your finger to your nose," he instructs. "Now, the left."

I do both without any challenge.

"Good," he says.

Next is the temperature and sharpness test. A metal object feels cold and sharp on the right side, but not on the left.

"I don't feel it," I say. "It's like my skin is dead on my left side. I can move my arms and legs and speak, but I can't feel it on the left side."

The doctor runs his hand through his hair. More notes are written.

"Have you had any health issues lately?" he asks.

"A sore throat that started two days ago," I reply. "It still hurts on the right side of my throat, but not on the left."

He smiles weakly.

"I don't want to send you home like this," he says. "Let's do a CT scan."

The scan is quick and over before I have a chance to worry. I'm led back to the hospital room, where my friend is sitting quietly. She looks at me eagerly, hoping for instant results.

The doctor returns a few minutes later with good news.

"It's not a brain tumor," he says. "Nothing showed up on the test. I'd like to keep you here overnight to monitor you and get you in for more testing tomorrow."

A nurse takes my temperature and blood pressure, then assesses my numbness for any changes.

As part of her routine, she poses this question: "What is the most important thing we can do for you today?"

"Make me better," I reply without hesitation.

As Sunday afternoon turns into Sunday evening, I'm wheeled to a room on the cardiac-care floor. I appear to be the only patient under the age of 60.

I don't belong here. I should be at home, reading bedtime stories to my kids.

Instead, I've become a prisoner in my 28-year-old body, a body I no longer recognize or trust. I yearn to escape it.

Thankfully, I was unaware that my condition would get worse—much worse—before it would improve.

On day three, I wake up numb on the right side, too.

It's accompanied by extreme exhaustion, a continuing throat infection that doesn't respond to antibiotics and other symptoms.

I'm sent home with a name for my symptom—paresthesia, or numbness of the skin—and a recommendation to see a family doctor and a neurologist.

Tens of thousands of dollars in medical tests reveal nothing remarkable, yet the numbness persists.

Dozens of doctors, mystified.

Neurologists and specialists of all kinds poke and prod me but conclude there's nothing more to be done unless new symptoms surface. I'm left to wait—to see if this will subside or worsen.

Each passing day chips away at my hope that my sense of touch will return—that I'll feel sensations like warmth, coolness or softness again.

Friends and family check in, asking, "How are you?"

I appreciate their concern, but the question fills me with anxiety.

It's a relief to know my children can feel my hugs. It's maddening that I can't feel theirs. I feel alone in this skin that has forgotten how to feel.

> Something's got to change.

I want to shed this skin, but that's not an option. I want to demand an answer, but one doesn't seem to exist.

Instead, I do what I can.

I make changes based on recommendations from a new family doctor.

Organic food. Herbal supplements. Acupuncture. Prayer. Talk therapy.

One morning, weeks after implementing dietary changes and supplements, I wake up and realize I can really wake up. The heavy, invisible blanket draped over my body for months—the one I'd come to accept as normal—is gone.

I HAVE ENERGY!

It feels like pure oxygen is being pumped into my body. I'm in awe. I feel alive again despite the lingering physical numbness.

When I wake up about a week later, I roll to one side and realize I can feel some sensation in my lower body.

MY FEET! MY LEGS! They feel the sheets!

I squeal, swishing my legs back and forth, savoring the sensation.

Thank you. Thank you. Thank you.

Feeling the sheets was everything I needed to understand that I could feel better.

As I'm writing out my to-do list, I include, "Reduce stress."

Something clicks. My past experience with yoga reminds me that it connects me with a sense of peace, the opposite of stress.

That's precisely what I need.

I book a class at a fitness center.

On Monday night, I'm late to yoga class. The room is dark. The music—a soothing blend of wind instruments—is turned up to drown out the fast-paced song being played outside of the group fitness room. Sweat lingers in the air from the fitness class before this one.

I lay down my yoga mat, which makes an audible unsticking noise as I slowly unroll it. Unrolling it slowly seems to prolong the mat's agony, so I rip the rest of it open, like I would with a bandage, and sit down on it.

I'm convinced that all eyes are on me, the latecomer, but I scan the room and see that everyone's eyes are closed. Everyone except for the instructor, who has one eye open and it's looking right at me, the high-strung newcomer in this sea of serenity.

"Is this your first time?" asks the instructor, a woman with the best posture I've ever seen. It appears that she's asleep yet speaking to me.

I probably don't look that peaceful when I'm actually sleeping.

"No," I say softly, shaking my head.

I look up at the ceiling fans and lose my balance. The room seems to be spinning. Thankfully, I'm sitting down. I put my hands on the ground to prevent myself from tipping over.

What am I doing here? I don't belong here.

"Welcome," the teacher says, fully opening her eyes.

I breathe deeply and smile.

"Love yourself where you are today," she says.

Her words seem to be a message meant just for me.

She guides us through downward dog, triangle and other yoga poses familiar to me. She tells the class that she's in her 60s and has stood on her head each day for decades.

"Before our final meditation, we will prepare for headstand, for those of you who'd like to try it," says the teacher, her unspoken calmness surrounding her.

She demonstrates a headstand, then walks around the room, offering encouraging words and spotting the regulars brave enough to attempt this maneuver. Some succeed.

I shake my head to decline when she walks by.

Not today. Not yet.

Over time, my tree pose—that is, standing on one leg with my arms above my head—becomes steady. Depending on the day, I can maintain my balance for the entire duration the teacher suggests—it's about 45 seconds per side, but that can seem like 20 minutes at times.

Holding the poses allows for a deep strength to build in my muscles. It's a rush to feel anything, even discomfort, awakening in the muscles below my skin. I especially enjoy savasana, the last part of class that involves lying down and being still.

I notice that with regular doses of yoga, the way my body and mind respond to stress is changing. I experience—*really* experience—peace and joy like never before.

During the still, quiet moments on my yoga mat, I gradually set aside fear and worry. I breathe and remember who I am beyond the thoughts and emotions I experience.

And I'm aware that I'm gaining a new sense of connectedness with myself and others. I'm learning to trust my intuition and myself.

Yoga helps me, and so does talk therapy.

Both remind me of organizing closets. They involve being present with what's arising, connecting with clarity, and then knowing (and sometimes doing) the next right thing.

I continue practicing yoga weekly. It is a must-do, even when I travel.

When visiting my parents over a holiday weekend, I look up yoga classes taught by my high school friend, Jennifer, and attend one.

Jennifer's yoga class introduces me to a faster pace than I'm used to, but the physical movements are familiar. The breathing patterns are identical. Deep breath in. Deep breath out.

After the class, we discuss our love of yoga.

"I'm terrified of the headstand, but I really want to do the headstand," I say.

She points to the wall and offers to spot me.

I kneel down next to the wall and do the pre-headstand movements I've practiced for many weeks. Shakily, I bring one leg up, followed by the other, and Jennifer catches my legs and helps me sustain a safe headstand position.

"You're doing it!" she says. "You have great balance. You can do this on your own. You just have to believe."

On the next Monday, during headstand time at my usual yoga class, I raise my hand for assistance. The teacher comes over and stands next to me.

Carefully, I sit back on my heels, cradle my elbows with my hands, lower my head and push off of one foot followed by the other into my very first unassisted headstand.

Time stops. I remember to breathe.

I feel warm all over, like the sun, radiating joy and doing what was once impossible.

I am ecstatic.

Taking vitamins and standing on my head were not *the fix*.

However, during this part of my life journey, I became better at living.

I learned how to set healthy boundaries. I learned how to listen to my heart. I learned how to cherish the sweetness of life.

As a result, some relationships grew stronger, while others unraveled.

My perspective softened on how things "needed" to be in order to be happy.

With my own permission, I became free to be who I was all along. I became comfortable in my skin.

I learned that living well doesn't mean having an answer for everything. It involves embracing life, challenges and all, with openness and curiosity.

It feels good to feel good.

And just how good is it possible to feel? I intend to find out.

About Elizabeth Wood:

Elizabeth Wood helps adults and teens connect with ease and create sustainable changes in everyday life. She specializes in working with people who've experienced challenging life circumstances (e.g., trauma, chronic illness, loss).

She is an experienced 500-hour yoga teacher, certified iRest® teacher, Ayurvedic Health Counselor and Reiki Master Teacher.

A writer and former journalist, Elizabeth aims to share the ancient wisdom of yoga and other practices in ways that are accessible and applicable to modern-day living.

Elizabeth lives in central Ohio and enjoys spending time near water, hiking, traveling and being with family and friends.

She offers classes and retreats as well as individual sessions for in-depth study. Connect with her on social media @elizabethwoodyoga and through her website, www.elizabethwoodyoga.com.

Headshot

Image credit: Marcy Harris-Ortiz

Awakening the Heart to Live a Life You'll Love

By Jay Vince-Cruz

I was content with life … but did not feel at peace within. I became numb to that part of me—the part that was hidden and filled with shame since my adolescent years. With each passing year, it became easier to ignore that part. I grew so accustomed to life as it was because there were many aspects that felt good. I couldn't complain, as there was much to be grateful for: over 16 years of marriage, wonderful family and friends, a beautiful townhome, and two furry cats. I was grateful to have full-time employment as a pastoral musician. I was in good physical health. I felt financially secure. I had even traveled abroad on several pilgrimages. I had everything I thought would make me happy, yet there was a quiet ache inside, a sense that I was living on borrowed peace. My life was full, but I wasn't truly alive.

As some say, things are not always as they seem. Deep down, something was wrong. A part of me felt incredibly alone and paralyzed. Each day, I wrestled with the fear that the real me would be rejected, and it became easier to keep my true self locked away, even as it suffocated my spirit. I felt the fire of my spirit dwindling, fading to its last embers. This became all the more apparent during the time when the world was masking up in 2019. As I wore a literal mask each day, it felt like my soul wore one too—hidden from the light, trapped behind walls I'd built for protection but that had become my prison.

I believed others would judge me. I was afraid I wouldn't be loved for who I am—afraid for my safety if the truth was known—afraid I would no longer be welcomed within the circles of family, friends, my Filipino culture, and my Catholic church community. Truth be told, I was judging myself. I wasn't open to giving others a chance to understand me. I was making choices from a place of fear instead of empowerment.

It was easier to love everyone else but myself. It was easy to say yes to volunteering my time and talent for charities. Easy to say yes to anything family and friends might ask of me. Easier to be distracted with longer hours at work than to face what truly mattered. I adjusted my behavior and choices, caring far too much about what others thought of me. Behind the smiles and the busy schedule, there was a part of me, unseen and forgotten, that yearned to be acknowledged.

At times, I wanted to choose me and say yes for myself, but there were so many competing thoughts: *That's not how I was raised. That's not what the Church teaches. That would be selfish and disordered.* Some might say I was a people pleaser, which was more about wanting to fill a void of love and acceptance. Thirty-plus years later and 16 years of marriage seemed too late. Uncoupling would raise a host of other questions. People are often happy when they hear of an engagement, marriage, or the birth of a child, but sharing news of a marital relationship ending naturally prompts questions like "Why?" and "What happened?" as though the experience were shameful and contagious. I did not want to be pitied or receive condolences. Nor did I want those more inquisitive than caring to ask questions. I could not imagine changing course. It just felt too late.

Ironically, I don't think there was any mistake in working full-time for the Church. After the financial crisis of 2008, I was "right-sized" out of a technology position at a major financial services firm after ten years of service. I was glad to receive a severance package and welcomed unemployment compensation. This afforded me time to look for work while learning a new instrument—the organ. With the job search, I knew my heart wasn't drawn to another technology position.

One weekend, while attending a conference in Chicago for my church, I heard the Spirit calling as I showered in the hotel room. I remember the water falling on me, and the message was vividly clear: *"Be open."* The liturgical conference was named *"A Knock at Midnight,"* and I felt just that—a knock on the door of my heart. As the water washed over me, I let go of the thoughts and questions circling my mind: *Am I good enough as a musician? Will the income be enough?* I surrendered all that weighed on me as the water made its way down the drain. In releasing those doubts, I felt space open within me to seek employment with the Church. I told God: *If this is your will, help make it happen.* And in reply, I felt a sense of co-creation. Feeling spurred to take action, I began looking online.

After returning home to New Jersey, I visited a church that had recently posted a job opening. Though I discovered that the position had already been filled, I remained open.

Three days after that awakening moment in the shower, I received an email from a pastor at a church where I had previously served as a substitute pianist. The pastor asked if I knew anyone interested in a full-time church musician position. My immediate thought: *Um, me!* I felt hopeful with that door knock. A week later, I interviewed. The process was intimidating; a long-time professor from Westminster Choir College and a parishioner were part of the interview and audition panel. Other candidates with music degrees were also vying for the position. I had to let go of fears about whether I was good enough. Within a month of that shower awakening, I was hired and accepted the offer to serve as a full-time Director of Sacred Music. I was filled with gratitude and awe!

There was no mistake in finding myself leading singers to exhale and make room for an inhale, using their breath to give God praise and thanks. No mistake in helping the assembly sing with their whole hearts or in preparing children and youth for the sacrament of reconciliation. I was helping others connect with God, yet I wanted the same for myself—a personal relationship with my Creator, to live authentically, to let my whole heart sing.

I needed to turn inward for answers and direction.

I was blessed to have a number of 'angels' whom I allowed into my innermost circle. Some suspected, while others intuitively knew my truth—the truth I kept hidden, unwilling to admit even to myself. One of my spiritual guides invited me to speak it aloud. I couldn't. I didn't have the breath or the wherewithal. I also thought to myself, *What's the point?* Saying it wouldn't change anything. It wouldn't undo the choices I had already made. I felt like I was standing at the edge of the water, deciding whether to plunge in or retreat. If I let enough time pass, the urge would fade, and my mind would rationalize staying silent.

But one day, I could no longer accept a life of contentment. I wanted more, at least for a fleeting few seconds. I wanted to take off the figurative mask that seemed to protect me but was, in reality, a facade. Could I surrender this mask, to make room for something more?

After additional prodding, I gave in. I thought the words I was about to say wouldn't matter or change anything. In a matter-of-fact tone, I said, "I'm gay." I paused, stunned by my own words. A strange, unfamiliar feeling washed over me. I asked myself, *Did I just say that?* Then, I repeated it, this time with greater confidence and intention: "I am gay."

Again, that strange feeling came over me—a feeling of rightness, of authenticity. In that moment, it was as though years of silence lifted. I felt a surge of peace, my spirit reawakening with each word. This was the truth, and it was freeing.

It was an unforgettable, life-changing moment when I mustered the breath and dared to say who I am. Like taking a plunge into cold water, the feeling was invigorating. A part of my heart that had been silenced now had a voice. I was no longer at war with the inner dragon that divided me. Saying those words aloud felt like standing on the edge of a cliff—terrified and exhilarated. But as soon as I leapt, I knew I was flying. I felt alive!

Words from the Ho'oponopono practice became my healing mantra: *"I'm sorry. Please forgive me. Thank you. I love you."* I couldn't take back the words I had spoken. I couldn't unsee the truth.

So, here I am. But now what? What kind of life do I want for myself? What do I want to create? Do I continue to embrace and love this inner dragon—my whole self?

I allowed my heart to speak once again as I put pen to paper:

I want to be me ... just to be me.
    I want to be free to tell the whole world, so I can be ... just to be me.

After much discernment, I grew in my desire for my external reality to match my inner truth. I knew I had to take steps to shift this by having difficult conversations. I wanted to be free to accept and love myself as I am—to live in my truth, to live with integrity, and to accept and love the world as it is.

It became clear that my next step was to share this with my spouse. That experience was full of tears. I didn't want to break her heart, but ending that relationship was necessary for me to begin anew. One step at a time, everything else began to fall into place. The fears I held were far worse in my mind than they were in reality. I can't say I felt fearless, but I had enough courage to exceed my fears. Family and friends were loving and supportive—thank God! I had to let go of what was. Every choice became a step closer to freedom, each one lifting the weight of old fears and allowing me to live fully as myself. With each conversation, I felt a greater sense of freedom—free to be me. I found true love within myself and then found true love with my best friend, Dom.

As much as I loved the ministry work I was doing for the church, I could not stay. I resigned from the full-time position to make space. The church had been my spiritual home, filled with joyful and memorable experiences. But leaving was the right choice for my well-being—for the freedom to be me, to live in my truth, and to love as myself. That said, I'm still happy to visit my Catholic spiritual homes; they remain an integral part of my spiritual growth and development.

And, just as I once picked up the organ as a new instrument, I found myself drawn to crystal singing bowls and the Life Changing Energy community. As with any faith journey, I took it one step at a time, following where the Spirit called me. I'm grateful for the opportunities to work for myself (surrendering the 'security' of an employee position) and to build Quantum Light Wellness, an EESystem Center, with Dom (embracing an adventure). In creating Quantum Light Wellness, I was creating a space where authenticity, compassion, and healing could thrive—a place where I, and others, could embrace who we are.

While there are countless unique circumstances in our musical spiritual journeys, the healing process for awakening the *I am* in one's heart is universal.

8 Steps I Took to Awaken the *I Am* in My Heart

1. **Breathe into and out of your heart.** ♥ Be present to gain clarity.

2. **Connect with your heart.** ♥ Create sacred space through silence or nature. Close your eyes and ask: *What would make my heart sing?*

3. **Direct your attention and ears to your heart.** ♥ Listen for the Divine whispering in your heart.

4. **Express what is in your heart with your voice.** ♥ Notice subtle changes in your body and voice as emotions run through, aligning with your true, best, and highest self. Make choices from a place of empowerment, not fear.

5. **Follow and trust in the Divine leading your heart.** ♥ Faith is a journey taken one step at a time. Surrender what no longer serves you.

6. **Give yourself grace.** ♥ Offer grace to God/Divine/the Universe too.

7. **Heal with love.** ♥ Time does not heal; love heals. Love transcends all, including fear and judgement. Practice

Ho'oponopono: *"I'm sorry. Please forgive me. Thank you. I love you."*

8. **I am who I am.** ♥☐ Affirm your truth. Speak positive affirmations:
    I am love.
    I am light.
    I am truth.
    I am enough.
    I am worthy.
    I am healing.
    I am beautiful.
    I am grateful.

We are here to learn to love and be loved. Our hearts want to sing! When you awaken, follow, and love with your whole heart, you will live a life you'll love.

About Jay Vince-Cruz:

Jay Vince-Cruz, a native and resident of New Jersey, loves life (and music) and the life he is co-creating with his amazing partner Dom Campbell building something more beautiful than either of them could have imagined. He loves helping others transform their lives - mind, body, heart and spirit - from the inside out.

Jay serves as Co-Director for Quantum Light Wellness Center whose holistic offerings include a 24-unit Energy Enhancement System invented by Dr. Sandra Rose Michael (as featured on USA Today, Fox News, NBC News, yahoo!news, The Globe and Mail) located in Hillsborough in central NJ.

He brings his unique self with co-facilitating educational workshops and leading sound baths as a certified expert Sound Healer with Life Changing Energy. He also enjoys conducting energy scans as a certified expert Bio-Well practitioner trained by the inventor Dr. Konstatin Korotkov. Jay sends infinite waves of healing love and light to all!

A Breath in & A Breath Out
By Stephanie Harmon

In loving memory of Thomas Mackenzie

We come into this world taking a breath, and we exit this world taking a breath. Our whole lives consist of a breath in and a breath out: a breath of peace, joy, courage, happiness, and connection; a breath of grief, fear, rage, judgment, anger, and disconnection; a breath of ecstasy, pleasure, love, and accomplishment; a breath in darkness and a breath in light. A breath of holding on, and a breath of letting go.

I have seen a few very close people to me take their last breaths here on this Earth. It changes you in ways that I cannot put into words. The last breaths of my Nana in my early 20s brought me fear of death, which equated to a serious fear of living an authentic life. The last breaths of my father in my 30s brought me closer to myself, intuition, love, and gratitude. But the death of Tom was profound. I did not know then that my own breath would become a lifeline, guiding me through the darkest hours and helping me uncover hidden layers of myself.

I had searched my whole life for real love. I had been through the heartache of losing loved ones, the traumatic loss of my father, friendships that did not serve my highest good, working crazy hours in corporate roles that never aligned with the contribution I wanted to make to humanity, illness, sexual trauma, divorce, and the painful process of finding self-love. In many ways, I was working toward exiting the matrix; I just wasn't quite aware I was doing so yet.

Shortly after losing my father unexpectedly, I started seeing a medium regularly. After my first visit, I made the hard decision to file for divorce. My father showed up for me and validated what I already felt was happening in my marriage. He said, "Little girl, you are on a journey to find out who you really are and what self-love is. Continue to do the work and know that the man you have been looking for is coming." He described him as tall, strong, handsome, and a salt-of-the-earth kind of guy. My father said, "You will both teach, learn, and show one another what real unconditional love is. Just look for the ducks."

Look for the ducks? What the hell does that mean?

In the months leading up to meeting Tom, it was hard to miss all the ducks that were coming out of the woodwork. I was greeted many mornings by ducks at my car, heard quacking constantly, and saw ducks showing up in odd ways in life—on book covers, screensavers, or plastered everywhere in someone's house. I started to believe this was more than coincidence. Every time I saw them, I would take a deep breath in and out, somehow knowing I was destined for greatness.

I knew the moment I met Tom that there was something different. My heart and stomach felt at peace. Tom was tall, strong, handsome, and a salt-of-the-earth man whose nickname happened to be none other than "Puddle Ducks." Dad was spot on.

It all happened so fast, cosmic in nature. I remember telling Tom on our first date what my father had said during that visit to the medium nine months before meeting him. I felt that if he thought I was batshit crazy, then he wasn't the one for me. But he didn't. From that moment on, we grew close in a way I had never experienced with anyone. There was no judgment. We taught, learned, and evolved together.

Tom would take me on regular adventures to places and activities I had never experienced. He was amazing at finding the best food, drinks, beaches, trails, and historical spots. For the first time in my life, I felt safe to truly be myself and speak my truth. I felt like I could finally take a deep breath and let it all go.

Time was going by so quickly. Winter was almost over when COVID reared its life-changing head into the world. Tom had been a cancer survivor since childhood and was due for his usual annual physical and scan in March 2020, but the world shut down, and it was postponed. During the shutdown, Tom started to experience stomach discomfort and likely many other symptoms he didn't share. He never complained. However, he had discovered a growth in his lower abdomen that required follow-up.

It was the week of July 4th when I woke in the middle of the night to find Tom in the fetal position, groaning in pain. I rushed him to the ER but couldn't accompany him due to COVID restrictions. Then came the call no one ever wants to receive. The doctors confirmed that the growth Tom had felt in his lower abdomen was a large, sneaky, and very aggressive cancerous sarcoma. His medical team believed the sarcoma had developed as a result of the radiation he received during his childhood cancer treatments. The growth had blocked many essential organs, requiring several surgeries before any treatment could even begin to keep him alive.

I stayed on FaceTime with him as much as I could. To this day, I can't imagine the fear and pain he endured—not just physically, but also on mental, emotional, and spiritual levels.

Tom came home and began his uphill battle against cancer with extremely aggressive treatments. He nearly died during one of these treatments, which left him unable to speak, open his eyes, or move his body. It was terrifying. His oncologist consulted with top experts at Dana-Farber and Sloan Kettering, but even they were running out of solutions as the cancer continued to defy treatment. Through it all, Tom continued to "fight the good fight," as he would say.

Despite the aggressive treatments, the cancer spread relentlessly. Tom found ways to be grateful for his life experiences, speaking often about all he had accomplished in his 34 years. He seemed to find a semblance of peace, but I was consumed by fear. I had to constantly remind myself to breathe. Around this time, I discovered breathing and meditative practices, and I began seeing the repeating numbers 152 everywhere. The only connection I could make was that it was the time I was born.

We met with the oncologist after Tom's final treatment and scan to see if this round of treatment had shrunk the cancer. It wasn't the news we had hoped for. The cancer was getting bigger and continued to spread. His oncologist suggested palliative care and exploring clinical trials. Tom decided he was done with treatment and wanted to live his life to the fullest with whatever time he had left. We still hoped for a miracle—through a clinical trial or simply the universe's grace.

In the weeks that followed, Tom experienced a burst of energy, and for a brief moment, life felt almost normal again. It was truly a gift. Breathwork was teaching me to stay present and soak in every moment, and that's exactly what we did. We went on adventures, tried delicious food, and spent time with the people who truly mattered. October was wonderful, and I felt a flicker of hope.

But November brought new challenges and frequent hospitalizations as Tom fought to stay alive. On my birthday, he was in the hospital. Despite this, I woke up to a text from him with instructions for my birthday presents. He even had flowers waiting for me when I visited that day. I asked him how he managed it, and he simply said, "I have my ways." He never lost his sense of humor.

Tom returned home just in time for Thanksgiving, his favorite holiday. He enjoyed his meal and time with his stepmom and father. But his immune system could no longer fend off even the smallest threats, and he landed back in the hospital that evening, gravely ill. It was then that we had the tough conversation about hospice.

Tom expressed his wish to spend his final days at home, and I vowed to do everything in my power to honor that. Hospice trained me in administering medication and managing his pain. He seemed at peace with the situation, often speaking about rest and spending time together.

At night, Tom would ask me what I was looking at. I described a woman who appeared vividly in my mind's eye, with specific traits, likes, and hobbies. Tom said she sounded like his mother, who had passed away from cancer years before we met. This brought him comfort and awakened something inside of me that I had long suppressed to conform to societal expectations. I had experienced similar visions of loved ones on the other side during earlier moments in my life. She was here for him.

One afternoon in early December, Tom said he wanted to visit his Meme one last time. She was 99 years old and had played a big role in raising him as a child. Christmas was approaching, but Tom hadn't been able to get out of his recliner in days; his body was reaching its limits. Tom's aunt, knowing how much this visit meant, arranged for the fire department to help fulfill his last wish. By some grace, Tom walked into his Meme's house and had a final, meaningful visit with her.

When we returned home, I knew it wouldn't be long. That evening, Tom spoke to me about his confidence that I would be okay. I promised him that I would. We shared a beautiful kiss and held hands until he fell asleep. As I sat beside him, I watched the rhythm of his breath, each rise and fall a reminder of the preciousness of life.

On the morning of December 30, 2020, Tom was transported to hospice. Despite my deepest efforts, I couldn't keep him comfortable at home anymore. He understood and sought the relief hospice could provide. When we arrived, Tom looked at me and said, "This is the room my mother passed in." We both found comfort in that connection.

The nurses worked to ease his pain, and Tom was able to let go of any lingering worries or regrets. We had heartfelt conversations, and he seemed lighter, ready to rest.

On New Year's Eve, Tom's aunt and uncle came for a final visit. Before they arrived, Tom encouraged me to go out and have dinner with my mother. It felt surreal—sitting at a dinner table, knowing the person I loved most was preparing to leave this world. What do you even talk about in such a moment?

After two hours, I returned to find Tom in a deep sleep. I pulled up a recliner next to his bed, held his hand, and began speaking to him. I told him how much I loved him, how grateful I was for his presence in my life, and shared some of my favorite moments we had experienced together. Over the course of his illness, we had already spoken about everything—but now, everything felt final.

As I sat by his bedside, I watched his chest rise and fall, each breath slower than the last. I closed my eyes, trying to memorize the sound, willing myself to keep breathing even when Tom no longer could. At one point, I drifted off to sleep and woke to find him looking at me. I knew in my heart what that look meant.

I told him I loved him deeply, thanked him for all his love, and assured him that it was okay to let go. I promised I would be okay. In that moment, Tom took his last breath. He passed at 1:52 a.m. on January 1, 2021.

In the quiet aftermath of Tom's passing, I would lie awake at night, feeling the gaping emptiness in the room and within myself. The darkness seemed to press against my skin, forcing me to sit with it, to let it wash over me without fear. Tom's passing made me confront my deepest fears and emotions, leading me down a path of self-discovery and holistic healing.

Through breathwork, energy medicine, meditation, and self-reflection, I found a new way to embrace life, uncovering a more authentic version of myself. For those brave enough to embark on this journey, it is never what it seems, and you never know what you will find. I didn't know what I was searching for, but it found me. And what I found, I became.

I learned how to explore my edges and dive into the darkness that lurks beneath the surface. It was there that I discovered an untapped power within me. I began healing all the pain I had carried. I started to see my patterns, my truths, and the truths about the world. I unraveled everything I had been taught and conditioned to believe about myself and life.

I learned to truly forgive, to feel gratitude, to be sorry, and to love even more deeply for all my life experiences. What was revealed to me was that Tom and I had chosen this journey together to learn certain soul lessons. It has been almost four years as I write this, and I am still discovering gifts within myself that I wouldn't have found without this experience of unconditional love, pain, cancer, and breath.

I am sure you're wondering if I still see ducks. The answer is—yes, all the time. They show up in the most unconventional ways. This past spring, I was taking a walk in my neighborhood and came across a bench with a very pronounced duck pillow on it. These types of synchronicities happen every single day if we are open to receiving them. Our loved ones are only a thought away.

This story isn't just about love and loss; it's a testament to the strength that resides within all of us, waiting to be uncovered. This journey serves as a reminder that even through the darkest and most challenging experiences, we can discover parts of ourselves we never knew existed. These discoveries guide us toward a more authentic, fulfilling life of self-discovery and transformation.

About Stephanie Harmon:

Stephanie is a spiritual and psychic medium, reiki master/teacher, and sound practitioner. Stephanie provides intuitive guidance/coaching, cupping therapy, reiki for dogs, spiritual decluttering, etc. She integrates the healing of crystals into her healing modalities.

Stephanie also uses a cutting-edge device to measure your energy to see where there are energetic blockages in real time and how effective a healing session can be.

Stephanie believes in speaking your truth, living a life of authenticity, loving yourself and others unconditionally, and living your purpose while empowering others to do the same.

Website: www.harmonyinhealing.me

Reconnecting with My Roots: Ancestral Healing and Inner Light
By Lisa Ali

As I entered the bustling airport terminal, fluorescent lights reflected off the tile floor. My heart was in my throat as my eyes searched the crowd for faces that felt familiar yet unknown. As I descended the escalator leading to the baggage claim, there they stood. My heart began to pound as I saw them for the first time. *Is this real?* Faces that were both familiar and unfamiliar, eyes that reflected a history I had longed to know but never touched. Though I'd never met them, an inexplicable sense of belonging anchored me to that moment, as if the spirits of my ancestors were there, witnessing and waiting alongside us. I couldn't breathe; my breath caught in my throat, overwhelmed by a mixture of joy, pain, and fear. *What if they don't want me? What if I am not enough? What if they reject me?* My mind raced as a lifetime of unspoken questions hung in the air.

We stood silently, connected by an unspoken bond that transcended the years apart. This was the moment I met my biological siblings. My little sister stood there with tears in her eyes, waiting for me to step off the escalator so she could run into my arms. I wrapped her in the warmth of my embrace, holding on to a person I longed to know. My little brother, more cautious than my sister, walked forward with open arms and embraced me. My doubts dissolved, allowing my joy to surface, though there was so much sadness for the time lost. As we embraced, I realized this grief wasn't just about our separation; it was about something much more profound.

As I processed this moment, I felt an undeniable pull, not just toward my siblings but toward something bigger. There was a sense of connection I had never felt with anyone in my life. I thought, *How can you love someone you don't know? How can you feel a connection with a stranger?* But they were not strangers; it was something greater. It was an ancestral presence, almost as if the spirits of those who came before me were watching, guiding, and witnessing this reunion. I could feel their energy; ancient, steady, and patient. Joy, grief, and healing surged all at once. Finally, there were faces and stories that mirrored my own in ways I had longed for. The sense of belonging I craved all my life was here, in the arms of my two siblings. I was home, but the healing had just begun.

As a transracial adoptee, I've faced challenges in developing my identity, finding a sense of belonging, and navigating the world while grappling with indescribable grief. Meeting my biological siblings opened something in me, a deeper wound I hadn't fully realized: the grief of lost ties to a connection I never thought I would experience. As a counselor, healer, and energy mover, I had spent years helping others heal while feeling disconnected from my own roots. The reunion revealed that my path to healing needed to extend beyond my professional life. It showed me that ancestral healing was necessary, a calling to reconnect with the past to fully embrace my present.

This story is about family, connection, and healing; but it's a different kind of healing. Meeting my siblings didn't just bring answers about my family; it created a spark in my soul that ignited a journey to heal generational wounds that had followed me unnoticed throughout my life. The disconnect I had always felt wasn't just about being a transracial adoptee. It was about the loss of identity, belonging, traditions, and ancestral roots. These roots carry a legacy that demands recognition and healing. This story is about reclaiming those roots, how I began to heal the traumas of generations past, and how this process transformed my understanding of myself and how I move through the world today.

To bring you to the here and now, I must take you back briefly. I was a secret baby, born to a white woman in the 70s, a mix of Black, Puerto Rican, and Caucasian heritage. My birth brought shame to my mother's family, leading to my adoption at three months old by a fantastic family. I now understand I had a bigger purpose in this world, and being given up for adoption was the first part of my story. Knowing this does not negate the feeling of incompleteness I carried throughout my life. It was a quiet hum that resonated in the fiber of my being, a persistent feeling of disconnect—a void.

Growing up as the "brown girl" in a predominantly white community left me feeling like a visitor in my own life, navigating a culture and identity I could never fully claim as my own. Despite my accomplishments and success as a counselor and healer, the void remained. I often felt like I was drifting through life like an untethered balloon. I had friendships but lacked real connections. While I felt loved, a massive void lingered within me—a constant reminder of unfinished work.

My journey into spiritual healing, including meditation, crystal work, and chakra alignment, was my way of seeking connection, but it never fully addressed the core grief I was experiencing. I couldn't understand why these modalities weren't working for me. As a healer, I questioned why I couldn't find healing within myself, deep within my cellular being and soul. I yearned to be part of something greater, something profound, something ancient. Have you ever felt that sensation? It's instinctive and visceral, a pull deep within your being.

I could sense the tug of ancestral energy long before I encountered my siblings, before I grasped the deeper connections, and before I understood what I was being called to do. As I stood face to face with my sister and brother, the void slowly began to close. Everything came into focus. The missing pieces weren't just about family; they were about ancestral connection. Seeing their faces, I realized I didn't just see them; I saw my ancestors, lineage, and history. Images of generations past passed through me.

It was a spiritual awakening, a jumpstart into the journey I had unknowingly been preparing for my entire life. Reuniting with my siblings was more than reconnecting biological ties; it propelled me into healing ancestral wounds and aligning my path as a healer with a deeper purpose.

At that moment, as I looked at them, I realized this grief wasn't just about our separation; it was about something much deeper. I knew then that I needed to find a way to heal this deep wound beyond traditional therapeutic modalities. The need to heal differently came to me. I knew I needed to lean into the healing of my cellular being, and I knew it would take more than I had done before. I realized that the healing I sought and needed wasn't just about me; it was about reconnecting with and liberating the energy of past generations.

Before meeting my siblings, I had attended a few sessions with a Reiki healer, which were amazing; however, after the emotional intensity of meeting my siblings, I found myself feeling unbalanced. The levels of pain in my body increased, and the flare-ups of chronic pain became indescribable. I had tried so many healing modalities before, but when my friend invited me to a sound healing session with various instruments, the crystal bowls sang an ancient song that my soul instantly recognized. It was as if my ancestors themselves were humming through the vibrations.

Lying there with a garnet at my feet to ground me in my root chakra, I could feel the song of my ancestors. It was an ancient sorrow, an ache that surged from the bottom of my feet to the top of my head; a release. That release during the sound bath convinced me that this was the next step in my healing process and the next step in how I would move forward in my work to heal others. I began to manifest what needed to be done.

The H.E.A.L. Path (Harnessing Energy for Ancestral Liberation) became my sacred framework, a blueprint for healing that honored the souls who came before me and acknowledged the resilience they passed down. At that moment, the H.E.A.L. Path manifested into the universe.

I embarked on the first part of my healing journey. *H* stands for honoring your ancestry. I began by creating daily rituals to honor my ancestors. Part of this healing process involved acknowledging the pain of being given away and being a secret. For the longest time, I believed my ancestors couldn't know me. Creating an altar specific to those I knew in life and those who gave me life became the first step in embracing who I am. Lighting a candle and offering a prayer of gratitude has become a comforting ritual for me. I feel a deep connection to those who came before me, and I believe that releasing the pent-up energy of sadness, anger, and pain is slowly healing me.

The second part of this daily ritual involves journaling, which has always been challenging as I tend to get lost in words. I began writing letters to my ancestors, sharing my thoughts and feelings while asking questions and expressing gratitude. This allowed me to process the flood of emotions that meeting my siblings had set into motion. I often wrote about the grief I held throughout my life as a teenager and young adult. These were the times I felt the most lost, with a deep desire to belong. Journaling in this way helped me release the pain of being "given up" and fostered compassion toward my birth mother.

Writing this letter took me back to the moment I held my daughter for the first time. The same connection that swept over me when I met my siblings was there when I looked into the face of this precious child I had just given birth to.

The *E* in H.E.A.L. is engaging in energy alignment. Each sound healing session became a profound journey into ancestral memory, where the vibrations moved through my body like waves of ancient wisdom, releasing generations of stored pain. This is where the most release and healing happened for me. Each sound healing session shook loose feelings buried deep within me, emotions I didn't even know I had been holding on to for years. The release of this energy was refreshing and body-altering.

The grief I once felt began shifting into gratitude—gratitude for the life I live, the humans I love, and the gift my biological parents gave me. With every strike of the mallet, the vibrations moved through my body like waves, continuing to shake loose generations of trauma and grief that didn't belong to me alone. With every hum of a chord, I felt the ties of generational connection knit into a sense of calming peace. With every tone, I felt the energy shift, and I felt lighter. The healing was happening not just for me but for those who came before me.

I have always used mala-making and affirmations as tools to heal myself and my clients. The *A* in the process stands for affirm and intend. After the reunion, I felt called to create a mala, using it as a symbolic tool for healing. Each bead represented a specific intention: forgiveness, courage, and connection were just a few. I chose a mix of mookaite jasper, known for understanding emotional and behavioral patterns passed down through generations; moonstone, to help cope with cycles of change; and smoky quartz, for grounding. Each bead became not just a physical object but a vessel for ancestral wisdom and healing intention. With each bead strung, I felt a piece of my lineage being threaded back together, bringing us back into alignment.

Lastly, the *L* in the process is letting go with compassion. Over the years, I've realized I haven't shown myself enough compassion. While I give so much energy and compassion to others, I often fail to extend the same kindness to myself. Meeting my siblings and seeing their bond stirred up memories of times I felt disconnected and unsure of my identity. This reunion forced me to look back and offer compassion to my inner child.

Now, as I light a candle on my ancestors' altar each morning, I am learning to let go of ancestral pain. This stage is ongoing but profoundly powerful as it symbolizes the release of old wounds. As I continue to move forward, I feel deeply connected to my ancestors in ways I never had before. This connection has become a guiding force in my life, and the H.E.A.L. Path framework has become a cornerstone of my work to honor my ancestors and help others do the same.

Meeting my biological siblings started a lifelong journey of healing. It wasn't just about reconnecting with immediate family but also about unearthing and addressing the generational wounds that have shaped my family for decades, maybe even centuries.

Healing is not a singular act but an ongoing process that involves honoring our past, aligning our energy, affirming our intentions, and letting go with compassion. Each morning ritual now feels like a sacred conversation with those who came before me, their wisdom flowing through me to my daughter, creating a tapestry of resilience and love that will echo through generations.

Know that you carry the light and strength of those before you. Healing isn't just for yourself—it's for your family, both past, present, and future. As I continue to heal, I have begun to pave the way for my daughter and those who come after her. In honoring my ancestors, I honor myself, and in doing so, I create a legacy of liberation, love, and wholeness that will echo through time.

About Lisa Ali:

Lisa Ali is a Licensed Professional Counselor, holistic coach, and healer with over three decades of experience supporting individuals on their path to wholeness. A Colorado native and mother of one, Lisa specializes in working with attachment struggles, adoption-related grief, and ancestral healing. Her approach integrates traditional mental health therapy with holistic modalities such as energy work, chakra alignment, and sound healing. Guided by the belief that humans inherently possess the wisdom needed for self-healing, Lisa serves as a compassionate vessel, walking alongside her clients as they unlock their inner potential. Her extensive experience includes guiding individuals through complex emotional landscapes and facilitating transformative experiences using an integrative, culturally attuned approach. Lisa is deeply committed to helping others reclaim their power and navigate life's challenges with resilience and grace, fostering a safe space for profound healing and personal growth.

The Healer's Journey: Transforming Stress, Trauma & Grief to Peace, Love & Joy

By Gina Allgaier

I believe everyone is in recovery from something. My name is Gina. I am a mother of four sons, in recovery from the deaths of two of our children.

When I was pregnant with the twins, Drue and Jake, I knew before the doctors there were two babies. But something felt off. One baby seemed to have less energy. I realized before the doctors that something was very wrong. Two weeks before their due date, we learned our sweet baby Drue had a congenital heart defect and likely would not survive.

We were blessed to spend four days with him, but Drue left us, and my heart, mind, and soul felt ripped apart. A seismic inner shift occurred. People say time heals the pain and you move forward. The pain did subside, but I did not yet understand that deep grief doesn't just end, and if not properly processed, it stays with us, buried inside, waiting to be acknowledged and felt before we can heal and release ourselves from suffering.

When our youngest son, Koby, arrived, he brought back some of the light that had left with Drue. Mistakenly, I thought I had processed Drue's death and healed. And then tragedy struck again. When our oldest son Tristan was 21 years old, he died from fentanyl poisoning during his struggle with drug addiction. Suddenly, I became an angel mother of two beautiful boys, plunging back into the deep abyss of darkness, pain, and suffering.

Eventually, I realized that years of grief, stress, and trauma had taken their toll on my mind, body, and spirit. My sleep quality was poor, and most of my front teeth had been replaced with crowns from excessive grinding. My blood pressure was rising despite regular exercise, and I had developed chronic neck pain. The joy for life I had previously embodied was gone.

To cope with devastating, life-changing, indescribable losses, one must have a willingness to live, tremendous resiliency, and create a pathway forward to regain inner peace. Yes, my soul felt cracked open, but through the pain, I reached inward, determined to honor my sons by learning to live again. Leaning into my faith, connecting to a greater purpose, and leveraging energy healing techniques have created my path to peace. Each heartbreak carved out a space within me that I would eventually fill with a profound understanding of love, healing, and the powerful, unseen connection I share with my sons in spirit.

Eternal Energy

Science tells us that a mother and her children remain connected after birth for decades through a process called microchimerism because they each carry cells from the other. Perhaps that, at least partially, explains the sense of knowing when something was horribly wrong with each child. Perhaps it explains the sense of connection that remains.

The days leading up to Tristan's death, my mind and body were on high alert, as if I knew something awful was going to happen—the same way animals sense the energy of impending storms. The night before his death was confirmed, just after midnight, I lay down to sleep. At some point, I woke up feeling a pulse of energy and a white shard of light pass through my forehead. The next morning, I knew in my gut, in my soul, he was gone.

This was the first of the energetic experiences I believe I had with Tristan's transition. My forehead was sensitive to the touch at the spot where I felt the piercing light. Later in the day, I had a sense of knowing in my mind, telling me where to find him and a sign to look for. He was gone, but there were other experiences in the days that followed.

The thought of life without your children is agonizing, almost unbearable. When Tristan left this world, I wondered how I could survive without him in it. And yet, I feel like a part of him is still with me, guiding and supporting me. There have been countless instances of butterflies, owls, and feathers appearing at the exact moment, or shortly after Tristan comes into my mind, or after I ask for a sign.

Once Tristan transitioned to spirit, I saw who I believe was baby Drue, for the first time ever, in a dream. Two of my sons are no longer here in physical form, and yet, in some ways, I feel like they are both present with me on a subtle level. Is it my imagination? My mind making meaning of the worst possible reality? Perhaps. But I hear so many other parents speak about the messages and signs they receive from their children who have passed away that I now believe an energetic connection remains after your child or loved one leaves this world. Every feather, every butterfly feels like a gentle reminder from them, telling me that they're still here, guiding me on my journey.

Releasing Stuck Energy

The moment Tristan's death was confirmed, I released that gut-wrenching, guttural sound—the one in the movies a parent makes when a part of them leaves this world. Later, I felt a thud in my lower back as if I had been punched. The pain was a dull ache that stayed with me for the next six months. I tried exercising, stretching, visiting the chiropractor, and receiving massages, but nothing helped. The ache in my back felt like a physical reminder of the grief I carried. No matter how much I tried to release it, the pain stayed, echoing the intense sadness in the canyon of my soul.

Then I began hiking. Long hikes, with the intention to climb Mt. Rainier—a mountain Tristan loved. I wanted to do this to honor his life. The training became my mission, connecting me to a sense of purpose. As I hiked, I started to feel lighter, more at peace. Each step toward healing was a step away from the heaviness of despair, and fragments of the joy I'd once known started to surface. The sadness began to lift, and as I prepared to head to Mt. Rainier for the climb, I realized the pain in my lower back was gone.

Early in the grief journey, friends gifted me a private yoga session. It felt as if I was slogging through water trying to flow through the sequence. At the end, as we moved into savasana, the floodgates opened. I cried—hard. The relentless agony of losing my oldest child, the fear and heartbreak of watching the grip of addiction turn him into someone I didn't recognize, his death, and then learning to adjust to our new reality without him in it—all poured out of me.

Later, I realized I was also still grieving the loss of baby Drue, as well as processing other personal traumas that had never fully been resolved. That experience, there on my mat, of complete release, was a pivotal moment in my healing journey. Another shift had occurred inside my body, mind, and soul.

Kellie J. Wright, a personal transformation coach, guided me through the wisdom of her book *Internal Journeys: A Spiritual Transformation,* which she describes as downloads received while on her own recovery journey. Her book offers readers a way to connect back to themselves through a process of self-realization. Kellie was instrumental during the first 18 months of my grief journey, helping me transform suffering into a small measure of peace.

Tristan's death due to the disease of addiction led me to create a non-profit, Speakup About Drugs, with the mission of educating people about the dangers of illegal and illicit drug use and providing skills to improve well-being. I recalled that as Tristan's addiction spiraled, it was like he innately knew what his body and mind needed to heal. He began cooking nutritious foods, tried to regulate his circadian rhythm, spent time connecting in nature, longed to return to mountain biking, and practiced yoga. He ran out of time when he chose to ingest what he thought was a "party drug" that turned out to be unknowingly laced with deadly fentanyl.

But that part of his journey led me to wonder whether clients' recovery rates would improve if they were riding bikes, running, hiking—moving energy through their bodies. We formed Ride4Recovery, a mountain biking group, and many participants seemed to achieve or sustain sobriety. Perhaps creating an active lifestyle and moving energy through the body and mind could help people who were struggling with addiction. I wanted to know more.

Trauma and ACEs

I attended a conference about research on ACEs (Adverse Childhood Experiences), where the number of traumas people had at a young age were measured and correlated with a variety of health and behavioral issues in adulthood, including addiction. Higher ACE scores were associated with a greater risk of chronic disease, mental health issues, and social challenges.

Listening to this information, I wondered: If higher ACE scores heavily influence future health outcomes, why is it that some people who experience horrific trauma seem to move forward in their lives, while others with similar experiences succumb to mental health and chronic disease struggles? And why do some people who don't appear to have high ACE scores still end up experiencing adverse mental health effects?

The answers get complicated, but regardless of nature and nurture, moving energy through the body and mind does seem to help people self-regulate their nervous systems. It shifts them out of the fight, flight, or freeze response that occurs with traumatic events, helping to build resiliency. Techniques like breathwork, yoga, meditation, and sound healing are just a few tools that can be used to activate the parasympathetic nervous system and calm the body and mind.

When we pause, pay attention, and notice—without judgment—what is happening in and around us, we can choose how to move forward, calmer and with clarity. These are some of the techniques I offer others, and I regularly witness or hear about their positive impact on healing journeys.

Healing Through Transformation

On a whim, I decided to join a sound bath experience at a local yoga studio. I didn't know anything about sound healing and had no idea what to expect. It was amazing! Listening to the sounds from the instruments being played, my body responded to the frequencies. My toes and fingers tingled, and I felt like energy was flying off my body. What was this? I wanted to experience it again!

The self-love transformation coaching, yoga, and sound bath experiences were my introduction to energy healing. Biking, hiking, and even running became integrated into my regular routine. This was starting to make sense to me—a pathway to healing and creating resiliency outside of the traditionally accepted protective factors acknowledged in the field of addiction or prescribed by doctors at the time.

My transformative journey of healing deepened as I studied to receive multiple certifications through Deepak Chopra's training program, including Yoga Instructor and Wellbeing Coach. The training focused on meditation, breathwork, and the ancient Ayurveda healing system, equipping me to pair philosophical information with physical practices to promote well-being. With each hike, deep breath, and sound bath experience, I felt my body begin to soften, like a deep exhale, and my mind cleared. I was finding my way back to myself.

Another "A-ha!" Moment

Another "a-ha!" moment came when I read Bessel van der Kolk's book, *The Body Keeps the Score,* which explains that trauma causes energy to get stuck in our tissues. Until we acknowledge the trauma, sit with it, and feel it, the pain and suffering remain in our tissues. We must let the emotions move through us to heal.

Paul Denniston, creator of Grief Movement Training, uses movement, breath, and sound to move the stuck energy through the body. Paul's coaching has been another instrumental key in my own healing, equipping me to guide others.

Once I began to understand the importance of moving energy through the body and mind, becoming a sound healer was an intriguing next step. I am not musical but am fascinated by the ability of frequencies to entrain with our cells, calming the breath and thoughts. I registered for the course, again not knowing what to expect. But just like that first sound bath session, the training with Vickie Gould at Life Changing Energy was a transformative part of my personal journey.

Sound healing provides me and others a calming experience that improves well-being. Specifically, my tense neck releases when I play the crystal bowls. My blood pressure has stabilized, and my sleep has greatly improved. Clients say sound baths calm their nervous system, and some have experienced hips, knees, and stiff backs releasing during sessions as their body and mind deeply relax and the stuck energy moves through.

Combining Tools for Healing

As I grow in my practice, I am learning to combine different tools and techniques to activate the parasympathetic nervous system and shift the mind from busy beta brainwaves to the restful awareness of alpha brainwaves—and even transcend to the deeper meditative theta state. Trauma, I've learned, doesn't just exist in the mind; it lives in the body. Releasing it is like finding freedom, finally feeling peaceful again in my own skin.

I am excited to continue discovering ways of combining movement, breath, and sound with ancient wisdom and modern science to facilitate healing from stress, trauma, and grief. These practices create transformation, prevent and reduce rates of addiction, and help others thrive, living healthy, recovered lives.

Healing from Grief and Trauma

Healing from grief and trauma is an ongoing journey with no time limit. The tools I now have led me from wondering how I would survive the loss of two children to thriving and moving forward. I am deeply connected to love and purpose, helping others live the best versions of themselves.

Yes, life is full of stress, trauma, and grief, but it can also be filled with peace, love, and joy. I believe that while grief and trauma shape us, with the right tools and support, we can use the pain as a foundation to learn, grow, and become wiser versions of ourselves. Through our experiences and hard-won wisdom, we can serve others and achieve our higher purpose in this world.

About Gina Allgaier:

After a 26 year career as a Sales and Marketing Executive with Kraft Foods, Gina Allgaier founded Speakup About Drugs, a non-profit dedicated to reducing the rate of addiction and overdose deaths. As a mother who has experienced the devastation of child loss, Gina used energy work to heal her mind, body, spirit and created an active lifestyle grounded in purpose to transform her own deep pain into peace and reclaim joy.

Certified through Chopra Coaching as a Yoga Instructor and Wellbeing Coach, through Life Changing Energy in Sound Healing and Reiki, and as a Grief Movement Guide, Gina enjoys using movement, breath and sound to help others move stuck energy through their body and mind to improve wellbeing and live the best version of themselves. Gina and her husband live in Bentonville, Arkansas.

The Universe Is Always At Your Heels

By Carmen McKibben

I remembered parking the Tacoma truck in the garage, realizing I had successfully taken it back from my ex, who had no intention of taking financial responsibility. I gripped the steering wheel tightly as the weight of everything I'd been through began to lift. This was more than a truck—it was a symbol of reclaiming my life and my strength. I felt the Universe at my heels, nudging me to recognize my worth and take the next step. I started to feel lighter as the rush subsided in my body. Opening the middle compartment, I saw handwritten notes that I knew were placed there to provoke me. Notes like "I love you" and "miss u more" were written in colored markers. I deserved more and could achieve what I worked for; however, a level of healing had to take place. Poetic justice does not always make the heart peaceful.

A few years earlier, the Universe was near me when I dealt with a severe liver disease. I escaped the 72-hour notice the doctors gave before my body would begin to shut down. The Universe said it was not my time to leave this Earth. I survived and began my physical healing. I still remember going outside for the first time since my hospitalization and how happy I was to smell gas fumes in the city air. My body slowly began its restoration after facing a life-threatening disease; however, my mind was not quite there yet.

After leaving a toxic relationship and surviving a health scare, I sought the help of a life coach. The end of the relationship was a healthy outcome, yet I still felt inadequate, blaming myself. I worked with the life coach for about two years before meeting my current partner on a dating website. On our first date, my partner asked me if I would consider relocating to his home state with him. His question was so abrupt that I second-guessed my decision to have coffee with this guy. I advised him that we should first see how our relationship progressed before making such a decision. Two years later, we married. Six months after our wedding, we moved to Washington State.

After the move, we began pursuing our family-building goal. I was 32 years old and wasn't concerned about barriers to conceiving. We adjusted to our new surroundings, created new friendships, and built new careers. Yet, we still had not gotten pregnant. Five years passed, and I decided to discuss it with my primary care physician (PCP). At the PCP visit, I was told that losing weight might help achieve pregnancy. That conversation added pressure that wasn't helpful in my journey to conceive. I tracked my periods to calculate ovulation times and ensure my partner and I scheduled time to try. It became another overwhelming job. At 38 years old, I sought a fertility doctor. Because of my age, the doctor advised that my only option was in-vitro fertilization (IVF). The cost presented was well over $25,000, which became a barrier, as my partner and I didn't have the funds.

Arriving home, I felt defeated. We had to figure out how we could begin treatment without the funding. Fear set in as our dream of parenthood seemed further away. Things started to look bleak, and I forgot that the Universe provides. When I shared the news with my parents, they offered to pay for the first IVF treatment. I hesitated to accept their generous offer; however, having a child was also a dream for my parents. I was their only child, and they wanted to become grandparents. In mid-summer 2019, I began my treatment cycle.

I walked into the treatment not knowing how my mind and body would react. I had heard the treatment could cause my hormones to go a little crazy and that my mood might feel the impact. I went through invasive processes, including daily hormone injections and weekly blood work. The injections and medications caused severe migraines and digestive issues. Frequent blood work left my arms bruised from repeated pokes, and the daily injections caused bruises throughout my abdomen. The treatment process was uncomfortable; however, it was necessary to achieve pregnancy.

In the fall, I became pregnant two weeks after the embryo transfer took place as part of the procedure. Some medications were stopped, new ones were introduced, and periodic blood work continued. By December, I was nearing the end of my first trimester. We decided to wait until the trimester ended to publicly announce the pregnancy. Two days before the end of the first trimester, I noticed a blood spot.

I was worried and called the fertility clinic. I was advised to observe if additional blood appeared or if it stopped. The clinic nurse told me that if the bleeding continued, I should go to the hospital. Panic set in, so my husband took me to the ER. It felt like a nightmare, sitting through a long wait in the waiting room. I kept getting up to check the bathroom, looking for any change in the bleeding. Finally, my name was called, and I quickly followed the ER staff to a patient room in the back.

As soon as I mentioned bleeding, I was sent for an ultrasound. And then, another period of waiting. I prayed and hoped; however, my intuition told me the baby had not survived. When the ultrasound technician began the scan, I could see the screen, but there was no evidence of movement. The technician wasn't allowed to share her findings with patients, but when her eyes met mine, I knew. The baby didn't make it. Once the ultrasound was completed, the technician returned me to the patient room where my partner was waiting.

After 45 minutes, the doctor came in and confirmed that no heartbeat was found. I froze. Sitting in the ER, numb and broken, I felt my dreams crumble with every word the doctor said. I didn't even hear him explain that I would pass the baby over the next few days. When he asked if I had any questions, I simply shook my head. His voice sounded like an echo, distant and unreal. When he left, my partner asked me something, but I couldn't hear him.

I was numb for a moment, and then a wave of sadness hit. All the efforts, the injections, and the hope—it was all gone. I was sinking, wondering if this was the life I was meant to live or if the Universe had completely forgotten me. The sadness quickly turned to anger, and I screamed, thinking how unfair life was. I didn't understand why we had lost the baby. I kept repeating, "We lost our baby." Within a few days, I had to undergo an emergency D&C, as my body was unable to reject the remnants of the fetus.

A few weeks after the D&C procedure, I was overwhelmed by heavy grief and depression. It was difficult to accept the outcome, especially after following the fertility clinic team's instructions so closely. I questioned my existence and felt like I had failed to provide a child for my spouse. The grief and depression ran so deep that I no longer wanted to continue living. I remember grabbing my blood pressure medication and considering an overdose. At that moment, the Universe gave me a quick shake, and I realized where my thoughts were leading me. I contacted a friend to talk about how I was feeling, and that conversation gave me a glimmer of hope.

In March 2020, the COVID pandemic forced all local fertility clinics to shut down indefinitely. At that point, we stopped pursuing additional fertility treatments. By May 2021, my partner and I decided to relocate back to Arizona. My father's health had declined due to diabetes and heart disease, and I had started new employment, working from home. After moving to Arizona, I began searching for a new fertility clinic in the Phoenix area. Yet, even with this transition, something was missing—I still felt incomplete.

The Universe then introduced me to an opportunity to attend a healing retreat in Sedona, where I experienced a sound bath session. The sound bath took place outdoors, where retreat attendees lay on yoga mats under a beautiful, ancient tree. As I lay on my mat, my eyes traced the tree's branches and leaves. I felt each note of the singing bowls vibrate through my body, dissolving the weight of my grief and filling me with quiet peace. A sense of relaxation overtook me during the sound bath, lifting the heaviness from my chest. My gaze softened, my eyes closed, and I breathed in the natural surroundings. By the end of the session, the tension in the back of my neck had disappeared. I felt less worry and more focus.

Sound baths allowed me to reconnect with my musical roots from childhood and young adulthood. When I was immersed in music during those years, I felt balanced, unafraid to take risks or face new challenges, and free to embrace my creativity. Sound healing didn't just help me relax—it helped me believe. It became a tool to visualize the life I wanted, allowing me to feel the love and possibilities the Universe had held for me all along. I began to trust that my dream of motherhood wasn't lost, only waiting for its time to bloom.

After the retreat, I continued to incorporate sound baths into my lifestyle. Sound baths and meditation became my rituals of gratitude. With each note, I felt myself aligning with the Universe, grateful for the lessons—even the painful ones—that had brought me to this point. I learned that true gratitude is more than an attitude; it's an energy, a way of being that connects us to the Universe's love and guidance.

In 2021, I underwent two more IVF treatment cycles, but they did not result in a pregnancy. I focused on losing weight to improve my chances of conceiving and maintained my sound bath practice. I changed my eating habits and exercised more. Each treatment cycle was painful and uncomfortable, filled with uncertainty at times. Yet, sound baths were instrumental in helping me manage the stress and anxiety of these treatments. They also helped me articulate my manifestations more clearly. I had to believe that conceiving a child was possible and release any fear that created barriers to my family-building dream.

I began to let go of control, allowing the Universe to guide me. In doing so, I discovered a profound sense of freedom. Each sound bath taught me to release fear, trust in the flow of life, and believe that the Universe would always be there, guiding me forward. With the sound baths, I could visualize more easily—seeing a baby in my arms surrounded by family. After my fourth IVF treatment cycle, we became pregnant with Eliam. Today, Eliam is a vibrant toddler, curious about life's surroundings and full of joy as he plays with his ball.

Healing begins at different times in a person's life. My healing journey began in my thirties, and it continues as my soul learns lessons and evolves. Life had given me warnings to start my healing journey earlier; however, I resisted listening. That is one major lesson about healing: a person must be humble enough to listen when the Universe speaks. In my twenties, during my involvement in a toxic relationship, the Universe advised me to seek healing support, but I ignored the signs and spiraled downward.

Another lesson I've learned is to trust the Universe. As I faced each setback—from the D&C to my struggles with depression—I began to sense something larger, a presence nudging me to continue and seek the light. Despite the darkness, I held on, trusting that the Universe was guiding me, even when I couldn't yet see the path. The Universe will always have the best intentions for you. When I failed to place trust in the Universe, fear set in, and I took actions that were unhealthy for my soul, body, and mind.

In my healing journey, I worked on building a relationship with the Universe. As I nurtured that relationship, trust grew between us. With trust, our bond became solid, harmonious, and filled with genuine love.

Another vital lesson I've learned: let things, places, people, and circumstances flow in their rhythm. When the Universe knows you trust it, the things, people, and experiences surrounding you will flow in and out of your life at the right time. The Universe has allowed me to encounter new people, places, and opportunities that I believe are in my present for a profound reason. I've learned to live in harmony with the Universe, knowing that each trial brings me closer to my purpose. My journey isn't over, but with the wisdom I've gained, I understand that every challenge brings a gift. I'll continue to follow the Universe's whispers, trusting that I'm always exactly where I need to be.

A final lesson in my healing journey is to always embrace gratitude. I know this may sound mundane, as we see the word *gratitude* in signs, books, and slogans everywhere. But do we truly embody gratitude in our energy? I had to go within, change my energy, and set the intention to genuinely practice gratitude. Sound baths and meditation have become powerful tools, giving me the inner strength to honor gratitude on a deeper level.

During sound bath experiences, I see beautiful golds and yellows when I close my eyes and focus on gratitude. I often find myself smiling as I tell the Universe how thankful I am for the lessons so far and for the reassurance that the Universe has never left me alone. She is always at my heels. Life's journey is full of unknowns, but if we listen closely, we can hear the guidance of the Universe—ever-present, nudging us toward healing, growth, and purpose.

May you, too, find the courage to trust that even in darkness, the Universe is always there, guiding you forward.

About Carmen McKibben:

Carmen McKibben is passionate about holistic wellness healing techniques including sound bath healing and meditation techniques. Carmen's health journey includes anxiety and unexplained infertility diagnosis for over 10 years. The practice of sound bath techniques provided beneficial outcomes for Carmen as she navigated through fertility treatments including in-vitro fertilization (IVF).

Carmen became a certified sound bath practitioner founding New Moon Abundance Healing to provide sound therapy to help clients with inner healing. When inner healing is conquered, the restored self has the clarity to create manifestations of abundance for an enriched life!

When she is not focusing on her holistic business, Carmen is an AZ real estate agent. She is a doctoral student focusing on infertility and mental health. She enjoys outdoor activities, gym workouts, and meditation retreats in Sedona. She loves connecting with family including her husband, 2 labs, 1 husky, and her miracle son Eliam!

Firewalking on the Sun
By Ellie Epstein-White

"It's cancer," the doctor stated, sounding the bells of alarm loudly as if striking a gong. The words hung in the air, shattering the calm. It felt like a sudden, unexpected winter storm, one that we had no way to prepare for. Mom embodied strength, but I could see the weight in her eyes, the sudden cloud of fear and uncertainty settling over our family. It was barely a month from the time we lost my mom's father that Mom received her breast cancer diagnosis, making it a bleak November 1995. She had this misconception that since she inherited her father's diseases, she wouldn't get her mother's. I was initially kept in the dark about Mom's cancer diagnosis since she wanted to "spare me" from feeling scared of losing her at such a young age, especially after the recent loss of my grandfather. Like everything hidden, I became aware of my mom's illness as it was unearthed and brought into the light.

Mom treated cancer like a subject for a dissertation for a PhD. Her course of study was to research everything possible on cancer so that she could best gauge the course of action for treatment. This degree of study on cancer was like a full-time job. Mom consulted articles, books, doctors, friends, and those who had experience with the disease. She reached out to everyone she could think of to obtain doctor recommendations and find the best care for her course of treatment.

Assessing her plight, Mom was unclear about how to proceed with her "cancer therapy." She was plagued by whether to get a lumpectomy with radiation therapy or a mastectomy. Due to her history of horrible rashes with sun exposure, Mom had major concerns about undergoing radiation therapy, worrying that her skin would have terrible reactions to the radiation. She tried to get as many opinions from doctors as possible but found the answers disconcerting and often unhelpful. Even the radiation oncologist was unable to determine if her skin problems would flare up due to radiation therapy. One female doctor provided an interesting perspective on how to perceive cancer but left Mom's concern regarding radiation unanswered, stating that she'd intuitively go for the mastectomy, as she'd want to eliminate the part that "betrayed" her. The idea of "being mad at her breast" never entered our radar. Mom's mind raced through options, but each consultation added another layer of confusion. No one had a clear answer, and she couldn't shake the feeling that she was left to decide her fate alone.

During her cancer odyssey, Mom became slightly disheartened by the medical establishment, wondering if she could trust the doctors with her life. How could she trust her doctors if they didn't take charge and take care of things? She felt that the doctors didn't care about her well-being or treat her any differently because she had a life-threatening disease. She calculated the days, waiting for her test results from her biopsy. Taking life by the reins, Mom pushed the doctors for answers. Time was running out for her to decide on treatment and have surgery. The biopsy confirmed that the lump was approximately 1.2 centimeters, a relief because anything under 2 is considered stage 1 cancer. Mom felt confident that she could "beat it" and that "it's not a death sentence."

Regardless, every night, the anxiety crept in, a quiet terror that made every small ache and twinge feel like a sign of something worse. It was like firewalking, trying to stay grounded as fear burned under her skin, feeling like she was swallowed by the sun. Nighttime brought out "fear demons," coming in storms of scary dreams, Mom's rendition of Dante's Inferno. She called these "fear episodes." One "fear episode" came after reading a recommended book, *Dr. Susan Love's Breast Book*. This book gave Mom a whole new understanding of cancer. She realized that once breast cancer metastasized, it was curtains. Cancer was difficult to treat at this stage. Dad tried his best to console Mom during these "fear episodes." Dad, the mathematician in the family, tried to remain optimistic, saying, "The statistics are with us—they are on our side."

Yet, Mom was imprisoned by the fear that the cancer would metastasize. With breast cancer, they didn't give a five-year "cure" pronouncement because it could metastasize, growing slowly over the five-year period and then suddenly appearing. Mom hoped to celebrate her 60th birthday and live to surpass the age her mother reached when she died. Cancer doesn't disappear or get less intense, as "experiencing grief" might "after a death." Mom began to realize that she might live in fear for the rest of her life, as they call it in the books, "living with cancer." We learned to adapt and get used to this way of life, appreciating each day we're given.

Both Mom and I acted like warriors, attending to life as if everything was "normal." To tame my mind, I focused all my energy on what I could control and buried my pain in my schoolwork and swim team. Eventually, my time was consumed with school as I slowly fell down the rabbit hole, drowning in an overload of homework. Mom juggled life by taking "sick leave" from her station as coordinator and professor of Women's Studies at the University of New Hampshire. Mom was Wonder Woman, chugging away with her duties as mother, wife, sister, daughter, and friend. She did not let cancer become an obstacle and kept life moving by attending plays, concerts, lectures, events, and meetings while juggling doctor appointments. Mom played her part as "supermom" to keep everything as "normal" as possible at home. She managed to handle the myriad problems that arose and take care of me. It was Mom who cheered me on and shuffled me to my swim practices and meets. Swimming was aquatic Kundalini yoga, allowing me to find "home" through the power of breath. Each swim practice granted me respite, a chance to escape and drown out fear. But every time I resurfaced, reality awaited me.

At my core, I was scared to death that Mom would not defeat the disease and die. My 13-year-old self felt like a cat curled up, hiding underneath a couch, weathering a severe thunderstorm. So, I decided to use my writing to "heal my way through" my problems. This sparked the idea that I could "heal my mom" and "bring her back to life" by creating a "sacred healing ceremony." Mom attributed my "inspiration" for ritual to Penny, who conducted a "Croning Ceremony" for Mom's 50th birthday. Ritual allowed me to bring together all parts of my life into one whole. I thought that a "healing ceremony" could channel all my energy into a higher vibrational frequency that could help facilitate a safe place for healing to occur. Having planted the seed, I brought this ceremony into fruition by enlisting the assistance of a couple of Mom's friends, Penny and Lucy.

Using a lifeline, I reached out to Lucy by letter, expressing my concerns regarding my mother's health. I confided in the one person I felt represented "faith" for "counseling my fears." Lucy was a practicing nun, feminist, and professor at the University of Louisville, devout in the art of prayer, and her light glowed with the wisdom of a "spiritual" nature. My letter suggested that we "heal my mom back to life" by performing a sacred healing ceremony for Mom.

My idea was to facilitate healing in the "sacred space" of our family home while being in the oasis of our tribal community of family and friends. Lucy responded to my letter enthusiastically, helping me spin the fabric of positive energy into the situation, praising my idea for a "healing ritual" and calling it "wonderful." Lucy had recently read an article called, "Artists as Healers: Envisioning Life-Giving Culture," which spoke powerfully to her. The article conveyed the "ceremonial" aspect of "art" as being potent enough to raise energy, consciousness, and vibrations. The "art of ritual" enhances and augments action into a collective consciousness of vibrations and binds the participants together in a shared space of spiritual community, creating an opportunity for a haven of healing.

Lucy thanked me for informing her about my mother's condition, stating that she was very concerned, yet hopeful that with Mom's "intelligent approach to the matter," and with everyone's support, Mom "will be fine." Lucy happily offered me suggestions for crafting my own healing ceremony for Mom, although she would not be physically present.

It was mid-December 1995, and the weather mirrored the chaotic storm of our lives. Due to weather, the healing ritual needed to be postponed from Saturday to Sunday. The circle was cast in the living room of our house. To begin the ceremony, I lit sage in an abalone shell. This ritual was rooted in the "spirit" of Native American tradition. Honoring each of the four directions and calling upon the elements of the universe, we blessed Barbara Anne White.

All the participants knelt in a circle around Mom, passing around the burning sage for everyone to sniff, smudging the energy of the space. There was only the sound of silence as the shell passed from hand to hand. I explained the items gathered for the altar: the crystals (amethyst), candles, feathers, herbs (sage and lavender), and the homemade potpourri.

Penny said a prayer while Mom rested in the middle of the circle supported by pillows handmade by her friends for her 50th birthday and Penny's hands. The circle was connected by holding hands, and I held my mom's hand. Words poured like medicine to help "heal" my mother from cancer as I read from my "Algonquin Wisdom" poem:

> *"We honor Barbara as daughter, sister, mother, wife, friend and call upon the elements of the universe to bless her. We thank Barbara for everything and pray that Great Spirit blesses her. May the spirit of wind carry away worry and fear. May water purify and leave your path sparkling. May Earth support and energize you. May fire transform imagination to enlightenment..."*

A long bell of silence sounded as people sent healing energy, essentially the life-force energy of Reiki. Mom felt bathed in the power of healing: love, light, and good thoughts. We were extra sensitive to the beauty of the season, and everything was intensely beautiful: the bright lights, the colors, the flowers, the snow outside. Even the house glowed with beauty: the Christmas tree was lit, candles flickered, the red roses and yellow mums, and one of her friend's bright blue and yellow African outfits. When the energy bath of the circle was complete, everyone gave Mom their blessings. With each blessing spoken, I felt a shift in the room—a warmth, a peace that hadn't been there before. It felt like our collective breath was filling the space, holding her up, bathing her in light. Mom was whole like the moon, no matter what phase she was in.

In the closing ceremony, everyone chanted and held their hands in toward Mom, transferring their healing energy: "As we spread our hands over you, we send our love." Even the smells were wonderful: the flowers and potpourri, cinnamon and citrus from the warm punch Mom made, the sage. For our ceremonial sound component, Enya accompanied us on the stereo as I had not yet been introduced to singing bowls. The sound was ever-present as Enya bathed our home in beautiful music, which we all thought went perfectly with the vibe of the sacred healing ceremony. All the major people in Mom's tribe attended the ceremony. Mom reported that she felt part of the effectiveness of the ceremony was that everyone sincerely wished her well. In that circle, as I held my mom's hand, I felt our hearts beat together, each of us sending hope into the air, willing her body to respond. It was a moment that brought us all closer, binding our hearts in a shared purpose.

Mom's immune system was already compromised: being sick and fighting cancer. She was in the safe space of her home, where she could start facilitating the healing process for her body. Perhaps, the sense of beauty in the air was heightened because Mom's life was being threatened by cancer. I hoped that this healing ritual would "lighten" her load and "inspire" the world to create health and well-being for my mother. I hoped that the "yellow brick road" to her full recovery from her dis-ease would lead her to the emerald city of her heart, home in her heart-space. Her body has the wisdom to heal itself with the help of all worlds of medicine.

Soon after the healing ceremony, Mom decided upon a reasonable course of treatment for her cancer. Both Mom and her doctors concluded that her cancer didn't call for the removal of her lymph nodes, a practice under debate in the medical world. The lump had been removed during the biopsy procedure, so Mom didn't require any additional surgery. Mom walked into the sun, opting to pursue radiation therapy along with hormone therapy. Research trials were still underway to determine which course of treatments was best and most effective. Mom thought there was still much to learn about women's health as medicine was not always designed for women's health and bodies.

As time spiraled on, we became confident in her course of action and could see the storm of cancer starting to dissipate and drift out to sea. Mom was thankful to all gods, goddesses, and powers when radiation was over, and she was blessed with the wealth of health again. Watching my mom grow stronger, I felt a profound gratitude, not only for her recovery but for the lesson that healing is both a science and a sacred art. Mom chose to live, so she did. Gracing me with her physical presence as I blossomed into an adult, Mom dreamed of seeing the first female President of the United States, believing this vision will ripen into reality during my lifetime.

My thirteen-year-old self realized the power in sacred ceremony and seeing wonder in everyday miracles. I witnessed how "healing hands" can "save" one person at a time. In the simple act of holding space for someone else's pain, I discovered my own path. Healing, I realized, isn't just about treatment or science—it's about love, belief, and the courage to create a sacred space for hope. Mom brought me to my first "sound healing" concert, guiding me down the "Healer's Art" path. Like Dorothy in *The Wizard of Oz,* I skipped along, carving out my own yellow-brick road, and discovering that "home lives within my heart." The voice of Oz turned out to be yoga, guiding me "home" to myself and integrating all the pieces of my life together like a puzzle. Dancing to the drumbeat of my inner-sky soul-song, I breathe out joy to nourish the garden of life. Sat Nam.

About Ellie Epstein-White

Ellie Epstein-White feels a sense of purpose in sharing her writing as a way of healing herself while inspiring others to take their own Hero's Journey to find joy in life. While being an avid yoga and meditation practitioner and loving being immersed in the art of sound, she is employed by the NH Department of Safety.

Ellie is a member of the Good Energy Healing Club facilitated by local author and natural health intuitive, Hilary Crowley. Having participated in a variety of "healing art" programs, Ellie holds both Reiki and Sound Certifications. She studied "minerals and rocks" and Usui Reiki Ryoho with author, teacher, and crystal expert Nicholas Pearson.

Ellie loves spending time with her cat, Robin, and family and friends. She hopes to lead those who are in her "field of light" in "off-the-mat Yoga," and use this chapter to spark new beginnings for both herself and others.

Journey into Sound Healing
By Harold "Rich" Bertram

Hello, I'm Harold "Rich" Bertram, and my path to the metaphysical has been as enlightening as it has been fulfilling. As a devoted practitioner, I am honored to hold the titles of Reiki Master and LCE Certified Expert Sound Healer. My spiritual healing journey is one woven with discovery and transformation, allowing me to nurture others on their own paths to holistic well-being.

First, I am grateful to you, the reader, in that you are taking time to take a glimpse into my life's journey as a Spiritual healer and how I became who I am today.

My journey began with subtle sparks of curiosity and experiences inspired by my mother, who was very spiritual. She was a talented, multilingual artist and seeker of the unknown, who believed in an unseen energy connecting us to all things. This energy, she said, is something we instinctively sense from birth and are drawn to explore for growth and connection. While her ideas seemed unusual to me as a child, they resonated deeply. Through her and others, I discovered auras, crystals, pyramid energy, meditation, astral projection, music, and more, shaping my path of self-discovery.

I am sure, as many people can probably relate, life has its own lessons, and they are not always pleasant or exciting. Life, death, love, sorrow, regret, to name a few, can be game changers along our journey. It is with this thought that I fast forward a bit on how this was for myself. We all have our highs and lows in life. From loss to love: I lost my mother but gained a soulmate and a son. Now, we're in California, close to family, raising our child together.

It was there I had found a job that would be a good vehicle to meet the demands and fulfill life's needs to provide for my family. For 20 years, I worked as a commercial heavy equipment technician and compliance inspector, a job that became physically exhausting and mentally draining. Over time, it took a toll on my body—trigger finger in my left hand, numb fingertips—and left me feeling disconnected from my spiritual practices and community. What once brought meaning was overshadowed by stress, division, and the relentless demands of life.

Then heading to work early before the sun came up on the morning of October 10th in 2015, the unexpected happened. While driving, my thoughts on work with the changing colors of the horizon in my view, I was approaching an intersection and caught movement out of the corner of my eye. Yup, that moment where time seems to go in slow motion. A speeding car ran the red light, and nothing I did to avoid what was about to happen worked as we met in a crash of twisted metal and flying debris. It seemed like an eternity before I could register what had just happened. I couldn't move my legs pinned under the dash, and my body was pressed against the driver's door and unable to open it. I tried to see out the shattered windshield and passenger's side window to no avail. I just sat there with my thoughts racing through my head—my family, how bad was I hurt, will I be able to provide for them, what is taking the emergency vehicles so long? Was this my fault? Finally, I was extracted and on a flat board, my wife talking in the background to an officer, telling me I'll be okay, and it wasn't my fault. I was hit by a drunk driver, and they never applied the brakes. It was while I was being loaded into an ambulance that time seemed to return to normal, and pain seemed to set the pace.

After chiropractic treatments and ACL replacement surgery on my left leg, I believed life would slowly return to normal. I returned to work. The trigger finger and numbness in my hand worsened to a point where I couldn't open my hand for the first few hours of my day. I would need a regimen of ibuprofen and aspirin every morning to get them working. My left leg would give out without any warning at random times like it was not even there. This gave way to not being able to confidently use ladders or walk stairs without fear of injury. My self-confidence was fading.

I kept in touch with my mother's best friend, Bev, who was very much family and a big part of my life growing up. During these times, she often gave me advice. I would often find myself traveling to visit her. We would speak of my mother often and share again those days of the exploration of the unknown and different energies and practices we both shared in our lives. She encouraged me to return to what I loved to do and had a gift for. She often spoke of how proud my mom was, that I was an empath, that we shared the love of music and art, and of course that my crafting skills were inherited. She would often scold me, telling me to do what I love to do, that I should be authentic to myself. After my father passed away, those words became stuck in my mind as I gathered my mother's and father's belongings to bring home.

I often shared Bev's thoughts with my wife. My wife and I always wanted to start a business that involved crafting, and she encouraged me to start crafting in my spare time. My physical injuries were not getting better. I returned to seeking out how to expand my knowledge on healing and met a Reiki Master who worked with me as we shared our knowledge of what we had learned on our individual journeys. We became great friends, and after some time and a lot of practice and study, I became a Reiki Master. While practicing Reiki and combining what I learned in the past with Crystal Healing, working with Auras and Pyramid energy, I began to feel a shift inside me. I started to see common practices and crossovers. But moreover, it gave me great joy to help others and apply what I had learned to help them, which in a way, helped me. That awareness and drive was back in force; I felt grounded and aligned. My confidence grew with it. I'd share my experiences with Bev, and she would cheer me on. She would parallel my wife in encouraging me. Soon, I found myself once again around like-minded people and community. I attended a drum circle at an event and left with a feeling focused and excited. Soon afterward, when going to community events, I began to practice drumming for guided meditation and spiritual events. This sparked something inside me, the connection of sound and the raising of energy.

During this same time, I began crafting. I combined my work skills and my crafting and spiritual skills. I started crafting metaphysical items, combining Reiki, apothecary, moon water, crystals, and stones into custom one-of-a-kind products. After some time, I began to share them with the community and got very positive responses. Soon, I started making custom items for other people and was getting wonderful results. With the nurturing support of my family, I embarked on an exciting new venture in May 2021, and Tri-Moon Bazaar was born—ushering in a vibrant space for holistic discovery and spiritual growth.

Soon a new lesson in life was to present itself, the lesson of balance. Working my current job while balancing Tri-Moon Bazaar, continuing to practice healing with Reiki, and spending quality time with my family was a true challenge. I loved that I got to not only help people heal but also craft with energy. However, one of these things was not like the others. My current job was becoming more demanding. Looking back, I realized I was robbing Peter to pay Paul in the form of hours, often sacrificing family time or rest.

I also learned that a spiritual healer and metaphysical crafter was not widely accepted by those in my sphere of influence in the world of my current job and, for lack of a better word, among "Muggles." I had to walk on eggshells regarding my views to maintain an acceptable persona at work. There were several times I had to bite my tongue to stay professional in the workplace and in interactions that presented themselves in that environment. I was sure I had scars forming on my tongue. I felt closeted, like Rich the mild-mannered co-worker by day and Rich the spiritual healer responding to the Reiki signal behind closed doors. I would share my frustrations with my wife and Bev. My wife supported me, and Bev continually told me I needed to be true and authentic to myself. I knew this to be true, but how could I take that step? Would I risk everything I had accomplished so far? Security versus my calling and doing what I love—it was a true struggle that played in my thoughts every day.

Then, in February 2023, I made a spontaneous purchase—a set of seven 432Hz crystal bowls that resonated deeply with me. As soon as they arrived and I played them for the first time, the very hair on my arms stood on end, and I knew I was in love. The tipping point came one day when I saw an ad that read, "Life Changing Energy," offering accredited certification and education for sound and energy healers. Out of curiosity, and always looking to learn more about energy healing and my newly acquired bowls, I clicked the link and discovered a new world. I shared this experience with my fellow Reiki Master and best friend, which resulted in her acquiring her own set of bowls. Soon we were learning the LCE courses and practicing together. After some time, we performed our first sound bath for the grand opening of a new business in South Pasadena, which was a huge success. I shared my new adventures with Bev, who delighted in hearing how well I was doing and how I was helping so many people. My friend and I created "Flowing with Crystal Sound" and, to this day, we perform sound baths twice a month in South Pasadena.

After the grand opening performance, I visited Bev for a weekend as I often did. We shared views, personal discussions, and casual walks to connect with nature. However, this visit was different. She sat me down and asked what was stopping me. Why did I hesitate to do what I loved?

I asked her what was behind her questions. Her face softened. She said, "Do you know how much your positive energy affects others around you? You have these wonderful gifts, and I have been blessed to see you help others who believe in what you do. I have seen the change in you these past few years. I could not be prouder of you, and I am sure if your mother were alive today, she would say the same. You need to be proud as well. Let others see the real you. Stop hiding. Be authentic to your beliefs and who you are. Do what drives you and inspires others to do the same. Be available to be seen by those seeking help, and bring hope to those in need. You heal the world, one person at a time, by showing others it can be done—through what you do, what you love, and the energy you share with them."

Her words hit hard, and it was one of the longest drives home I have ever had.

After much reflection and discussions with my family, I retired from my job to become a full-time business owner and sound healer. I felt a huge weight lifted from my shoulders, which showed in my self-esteem, my crafting business, and "Flowing with Crystal Sound." I began to feel whole again as I continued to practice and learn. Gradually, my injuries healed. I gained full use of my left hand and feeling again in my fingers. My leg had not given out in months. I was performing public and personal sound baths and receiving personal bookings with great success. The gratitude I felt was overflowing, and I was finally able to share openly with those around me.

On July 23rd, 2023, Bev passed on. I knew in my heart that her questions and advice during our last visit were her final gift to me. That priceless legacy, filled with love, lives on inside me in everything I do.

I continue to learn, grow, share my gifts, and pass on the lessons to this day. I am proud of myself and everyone who shares the journey of being a healer—a journey of connection to the energy that binds us all.

This especially rang true on June 6th, 2024. I was blessed with the opportunity to perform a sound bath for the United States Department of the Interior as "Flowing with Crystal Sound," via a hybrid format. As I sat and talked with my friends beforehand, I imagined 20 or 30 people attending online to experience it. It was an amazing energetic experience to know I was playing for people across the United States. I poured my heart and energy into the session, intending to reach every attendee. Afterward, I learned that 182 people had attended. I was told they loved the energy they received, and it was heartfelt and life-changing.

Through these experiences, I discovered what my mother and Bev had always seen in me and tried to teach me all those years ago. I learned the importance of balance and harmony in our lives.

I now truly believe we all have the potential to tap into our own inner healer and connect with the universal energy that surrounds us. My goal is to help people awaken their own healing capabilities and find peace within themselves. I want to share with as many people as possible—healing the world one person at a time by showing them it can be done.

About Harold "Rich" Bertram:

Harold "Rich" Bertram is a seasoned practitioner in the metaphysical arts, dedicated to the art of healing and spiritual growth. As a Reiki Master, proudly within the lineage of Dr. Mikao Usui, and a LCE Certified CMA Expert Sound Healer, Rich harnesses the vibrational power of crystals, Tibetan sound bowls, tuning forks, and more to create immersive experiences in sound baths, guided meditation, and Metaphysical Crafting. Co-founder of Flowing with Crystal Sound and co-owner of Tri-Moon Bazaar, his commitment to community and knowledge-sharing shines through and believes every moment is a chance to learn and grow, seeing each person as both a teacher and a student making a meaningful impact one sound wave at a time.

Welcome to The Land Mahn
By Margo Schaefer

I have been a career flight attendant since 1996. During a flight in January 2004, at the top of descent into Boston, I used the aircraft lavatory. I excreted 90 percent blood and very scanty urine. Unbelievably, I felt no pain; however, I realized I was seriously ill. I did not know why this was happening nor what the source of this incredibly shocking sight could be. Cloaked in panic but staying calm and acting quickly, I rang the pilots in the cockpit and informed them that, in the event my body could not withstand the depressurization of the aircraft or should I faint during descent, they should be prepared to alert paramedics upon arrival.

Thankfully, I completed the flight unscathed but deeply concerned. Upon arriving at our hotel, I anxiously informed my crew members that I would seek the advice of the emergency room team at a local hospital. In the bone-chilling winter night air, I sat alone in the back seat of a taxi while a stranger drove me to the nearest ER. My diagnosis was a severe bladder infection. I became flush with uncertainty. What? How could this be? I had no pain, no fever, no discomfort. Additionally, I was cleared to continue my three-day trip as scheduled. I took the risk and finished the route.

Immediately upon returning to my hometown, I sought the advice of my primary physician. I was instructed to complete three urine tests during three consecutive weeks. Alarmingly, each test result showed no indication of an infection, and again, there was no pain associated with the issue. At that moment, faced with the unknown threatening my life, I had no idea that this event would confirm my calling, where healing others would become my lifelong journey.

Nearly two months later, there was another episode of excreting 90 percent blood with scant urine during a flight. Landing close to midnight, I quickly collected my bags and drove an hour to arrive at my hometown hospital emergency room. My mind raced as I awaited triage and was eventually referred to call a local urologist to seek an evaluation with the urology department the next morning. I was extremely worried and tense all through the night, not knowing if a potential blood clot might end my life. I sat wondering if I should phone my family to inform them that my bladder episodes had become more serious and possibly life-threatening. The thought that I might not wake up flooded my mind with fear. I had no one to call, however, as my parents were on a Caribbean cruise, my sister was busy working, and I didn't want to alarm my grandparents because I didn't have a proper diagnosis for the cause of my medical episodes.

This second episode of blood excretion, strangely enough, occurred during the same week that I was to meet up with my family in Florida. The plan was to accompany my sister on her flight to Fort Lauderdale, utilizing the flight attendant jump seat as the flight was fully booked. This type of flight travel is common within the aviation industry; however, on the day of our intended flight, I wasn't aware the flights were at capacity due to annual Spring Break travelers.

My sister and I arrived at the airport early Thursday morning, well in advance to check in for the Fort Lauderdale flight. Upon checking in, I was told there were no open seats to Fort Lauderdale until the following Tuesday. I quickly explained to the agent that I needed a flight going to Florida that same day. I further explained that I had no checked luggage or carry-on. Additionally, I was willing to pay full price for a last-minute booking to ensure my seat on the flight. Surprisingly, at that moment, the agent looked up at me and said she had just received a message saying a passenger would not make the Fort Myers flight on time. This seat had become available just four short minutes prior to departure. Hastily, the agent listed me on the Fort Myers flight. Once again, I confirmed I had no luggage to check and therefore had enough time to board this flight.

My sister was puzzled by my consideration of a flight heading to the west coast of Florida rather than the east. After all, the plan was to meet up with our parents in Fort Lauderdale. This meant I would have to find my way across the state to meet up with everyone upon landing. With four minutes remaining before flight departure, I said, "Yes!" and requested to board this flight.

On board the flight, my assigned seat was adjacent to the parents of the person who couldn't make the flight. I quickly sat down, buckled up, and stowed my handbag while the aircraft door was closed for an on-time departure. I introduced myself and shared that Fort Lauderdale was my destination and that I had a lengthy commute upon arrival in Fort Myers. The couple informed me that, due to Spring Break, finding a rental car would be extremely difficult. They urged me to skip waiting in line at the counter, exit the airport terminal, and flag down any rental company courtesy vehicle to ask for help locating an available car.

I took their advice. I swiftly found the area where the courtesy vehicles idled as they waited for customers to board. A senior-aged gentleman opened his van door and asked, "Honey, how can I help you?" I responded with urgency in my voice, explaining that I needed to rent a car and drive to the opposite coast. He informed me his agency had only two cars remaining and that he could try to get me to the facility before a scheduled tour group of forty people arrived. He expeditiously drove me to his car rental company, where I was able to rent one of the only two remaining cars available.

Feeling relieved that I was able to overcome the unexpected transportation delays, I was still continuously troubled about my developing medical issue. With what felt like a brick in my stomach, I began the three-hour drive to reach Fort Lauderdale in the hopes of meeting my family without further delay. During the drive, I phoned my parents to inform them of my whereabouts. Making light of the situation, I humored myself and greeted them with a lighthearted Caribbean-accented, "Welcome back to the Land Mahn." After all, they were just returning from the islands.

My parents were stunned to hear that I had driven alone across the state to meet up with them and my sister in Fort Lauderdale. Frustrated with their own travel delays, they were stuck in Miami traffic and couldn't arrive at our original time in Fort Lauderdale. They then inquired about my sister, and I didn't have a clue. She was supposed to arrive in Fort Lauderdale two hours earlier, but we later discovered her travels were delayed as well.

Miraculously, we all arrived in Fort Lauderdale within twenty minutes of one another. We couldn't believe it, given the individual scenarios we each encountered. Once we regrouped at the Fort Lauderdale airport, we continued our drive to South Beach Miami and arrived at our hotel mid-afternoon. At this point, our family stress began to fade as we were finally all together in the same location, at the hotel reserved by my father's work conference group.

Unbeknownst to us, and much to our chagrin, our assigned hotel room was under construction. We were greeted with the constant head-banging sound of a jackhammer on our balcony, breaking apart concrete, while plastic tarps covered what was supposed to be our oceanfront view. My sister and I decided to leave this uncomfortable scene in search of a calmer environment. Walking through the hotel lobby, we made our way to the front desk to seek more information.

While walking through the lobby, I noticed a stately gentleman sitting at a computer in the hotel business lounge. Needing to check my work email, I asked him if I could be next in line to use the computer. He graciously offered me the computer he was occupying. I informed him that I could wait thirty minutes so as not to rush him, but I would like to use the computer immediately after him. He kindly insisted that I sit down and check my email as he stood up and began to walk away.

Upon opening my email, the attachments wouldn't download. I noticed in the mirror in front of the computer that the same man was still nearby. I quickly reached out and asked for his assistance with downloading the email attachments. He took time away from his busy schedule to help me.

Meanwhile, my parents arrived in the lobby area and requested that I conclude my work, shut down the computer, stop talking to the man, and join them for dinner. I quickly asked my parents and sister to wait for me, as I needed a few more minutes to check my work emails. As the gentleman continued to help me, he shared that he worked within the medical community and was there for work. I thanked him for taking the extra time to assist me with the computer task and wished him a good weekend ahead.

I joined my family in the lobby, and just before exiting the hotel for dinner, I noticed a conference poster promoting the Urology Cancer Convention. A sense of wonder came over me; I was sure that the sign was there for a reason—it had to be. Suggesting it was most likely a coincidence, my family and I continued out the front revolving door of the hotel. They still didn't know about my second episode, as it had occurred while my parents were on the cruise and my sister was regularly tied up at work.

I was terribly upset at the thought of my family rushing me off the computer and ending my conversation with the one individual who might have been affiliated with that conference. My heart sank. While at dinner, I was silent. My mind was engulfed and numb, contemplating an opportunity I may have missed.

The next morning, I struggled to find the right time to tell my family that my bladder issue was becoming more serious and potentially life-threatening. Although I built up the courage to inform them during breakfast, I found it inappropriate to discuss my medical condition at the breakfast table and decided to wait until later that afternoon.

After breakfast, I exited the hotel restaurant and heard a voice say, "How's my favorite flight attendant doing today?" Normally, seeing no one dressed as cabin crew, I would have continued on my way, but it occurred to me that it might be one of my father's colleagues or maybe even the company president. Turning around, I was thrilled to discover it was the same gentleman who had helped me the day before.

I kept walking, not wanting to interrupt his time, but he called out again, saying, "Wait, I can help you." I was stunned—shocked, even. I asked him if he was a doctor and if he was a urologist. He answered yes to both questions and insisted that I go to St. Louis, where he could help me.

As we walked, we arrived at the same sign in the lobby that had caught my curiosity the day prior—the one promoting the Urology Cancer Convention. I asked him if he was there for the conference, and he replied, "Yes, and the class can wait." He then jotted down his contact information and full name: Dr. Jaime Landman. He assured me that he and his medical team in St. Louis would help me survive my rare cancer type, pheochromocytoma.

A weight lifted off my shoulders as a sense of hope filled my soul. I then went to find my parents in the hotel room and informed them that, yes, the man I had met the previous day at the computer and the conference sign in the lobby were both part of a connection meant to help me. When Dr. Landman looked me in the eye and said, "I'm here to help you, and we will get through this together," I felt a sense of relief I hadn't known in months.

Dr. Jaime Landman had me prepped for an eight-hour surgery three months after my first medical event, which had occurred during the top of descent into Boston. While I was being prepped for surgery, my parents and sister were being prepared for the harsh reality: I had a rare cancer type with only a five percent chance of survival. The surgery would be challenging, as the cancer was attached to both my left adrenal gland and within my bladder, located along the aorta.

However, Dr. Landman assured my family that he had seen a beautiful aura around me and had made time for this surgery so that I could go on to help others restore their vitality through holistic health care. I promised myself that if I survived this challenging surgery, I would dedicate my life to helping others find harmony, strength, and healing.

Throughout my recovery, I kept that promise in my heart. I resolved to spend my available time promoting vitality and balancing life's constant stressors. I learned and witnessed that a sky-high attitude can take you to 35,000 feet. A confident attitude and lofty ego can help us achieve personal goals, such as obtaining our most lucrative job, creating status within our careers, or retiring with a sound financial plan.

However, a sky-high personality stretches to the universe by setting aside ego and being present to listen, observe, and support others along our path. My journey to becoming a holistic health care practitioner was shaped by providing patience, kindness, and respect for humanity, embracing others' time schedules regardless of age, color, language, nationality, or religion. By setting aside ego and cultivating a personality that stretches to the universe, I found my true calling.

About Margo Schaefer:

Margo is a charismatic, personable professional, with multiple skill sets. She understands the importance of restoring body balance, and is committed to helping others seek balance in their daily life through holistic health care modalities such as acupuncture, nutrition, sound healing, traditional Chinese herbs, and tuning forks. She has completed Tuning Fork and Sound Healing certification with Life Changing Energy and Yoga with Breathwork teacher certification from YogaBody Barcelona Spain.

She has Bachelor of Business Administration in Human Resources, Bachelor of Professional Health Science, and Masters in Traditional Chinese Medicine. Formerly, an acupuncture student professional organization student membership Director.

She led a lobbying effort to congress to help strengthen the national identity, acceptance of acupuncture into the Veterans Administration hospitals, and protect herbal access. She has helped many people suffering from a wide range of conditions, including chronic pain and anxiety. She can be reached: mzmargo@yahoo.com

The Year of No Regrets
By Susan Fryman

I remember the day I told my friend, "This is going to be the year of no regrets." It was a clear, sunny day. Days like that hardly ever happen here in Southwestern Ohio, but when they do, everything seems brighter and clearer. We were training for another marathon. That kind of training takes thousands of hours and miles together. Some people say that during marathon training, you talk about everything except the marathon. That's so true. We talked about anything and everything: our hopes and dreams, our successes and failures, and even what we wanted to eat.

But on that clear day, before I let my brain get in the way, I stepped out of my comfort zone. I allowed myself to say what was welling up inside me. I didn't let my brain stop me with all the "you can't" reasons. I said it: "This is going to be the year of no regrets."

Did you notice that I wasn't even brave enough to say I was going to live a *life* of no regrets? Nope, just a year. Surely, I could live that way for one year, right?

That was such a difficult concept for me. I had spent my entire life full of regrets and missed opportunities. I never felt good enough. I had always let doubt and comparison rob me of my hopes and dreams. I never felt qualified. I don't even know why I carried those thoughts about myself. The constant negative messages I fed myself were holding me back.

But on that sunny day, I finally listened to my outside supporter instead of my inner critic. *This is going to be the year of no regrets.*

Before we get to that day, I need to tell you about what brought me there— about the times I silenced my outside supporters and only listened to my critics, both external and internal. On the surface, my life looked great. I had graduated as Valedictorian of my high school class. I completed college in three years with a double major, graduating Magna Cum Laude. I had a job that utilized my degrees. I was in a relationship. I had just bought a condo. Things were *great*.

I was miserable.

I had always lived the life others wanted for me. The truth was, I had no idea who I was or what I wanted. I was living for someone else. In fact, I wasn't really living at all—I was barely existing.

The "dream job" was toxic. Each morning, I dragged myself out of bed and into the shower, only to sit in a chair and cry. I cried in my car on the way to work. I cried in the parking lot. I cried at my desk. Some dream job.

Not long after that, my relationship ended. One morning, he walked up to me and said, "You know, I don't think this is going to work out." I was stunned. Not long before, I had signed the paperwork for the condo he wanted, depending on him to help pay the bills. How was I going to manage it all on my own? Some dream relationship.

That day, I looked him in the eyes and said, "Then you need to get out of my house." As soon as he left the room, I sank to the floor and sobbed. My inner critic pounced, whispering, "You can't do this. You're a failure. You'll never get it right."

I went to my boss at my toxic job and asked if my position was secure. I explained that I was now solely responsible for the condo. He looked me in the eyes and said, "Of course."

Not long after that, he looked me in the eyes again—and fired me. Some dream job.

Everything I thought I was supposed to be doing with my life was gone. Jobless and alone, I was crushed by waves of regret. I began to realize that I had spent my whole life meeting everyone's expectations but my own.

When I came home the day I lost my job, there was a message on the answering machine from a stranger. It was an older woman calling her friend, leaving her phone number. I thought, *You know, that lady is going to be worried when her friend doesn't call her back.* So, I called her.

"Ma'am, you don't know me, but you left a message on my answering machine today. I just wanted you to know it was a wrong number."

She thanked me and said, "Have a blessed day."

I started sobbing. "Oh, thank you. I've had an awful day. I lost my job today."

That stranger became my outside supporter. She said, "Oh honey, they didn't deserve you. There's something so much better out there for you."

She was right. A stranger's words spoke louder than my critics.

I began to surround myself with outside supporters. I worked to listen to their words instead of my inner and outer critics. It didn't happen overnight. In truth, it took years, and I'm still working on it. The journey wasn't linear—sometimes, it felt like there were more valleys than peaks. But let me tell you something: I lost the things I thought I wanted in order to find myself.

I would love to tell you about some of my personal outside supporters and how they helped me discover and continue to walk my path. I won't include their names, but I hope they recognize themselves. I am forever grateful to them.

There aren't enough words to describe how my walking friend changed my life. She continues to support my hopes and dreams today with wisdom like, "If you act like a horse, people will treat you like a horse." Because of her, I believed I could run a half marathon—and then a marathon. Because of her, I got my passport. Because of her, I took my first international flight. Because of her, I went to Venice, where I met the man who is now my husband. Her belief in me showed me that I could do what I once thought was impossible.

Another dear friend from yoga class believed in my potential. I had always wanted to take yoga teacher training, but my inner critic told me I wasn't thin enough or flexible enough. One day in class, this friend walked by my mat, and I asked if she thought I could do the training. Without hesitation, she said, "Of course you can." Because of her belief in me, I completed not only my first teacher training but have since trained both in the United States and internationally.

My yoga mentor encouraged me to teach. Initially, I thought I would take the teacher training just to learn more, not to actually teach. During the training, we were required to attend 30 hours of classes led by other teachers. I regularly attended a beginner's class at the studio. One day, the teacher asked if I would substitute for her. Before my inner critic could say, "You're not good enough," I said yes.

A local business manager believed I could lead. My husband works at a local running store, and the manager asked if I would teach a weekly yoga class there. Before my inner critic could interfere, I said, "Sure." I taught that class for two years before COVID put a halt to our meetings. Some of the students from that class still regularly attend my yoga classes today.

I have completed most of my yoga training at a school in Southwest Ohio. I've trained with those teachers locally, in India, and in Bali. They have taught me to seek out the lessons in my challenges. They encourage me to look deeply within myself, knowing I already have the answers I seek. Once I discover those answers, they encourage me to lean into my true self and share it with others. I've been honored to teach at their school, both in Ohio and in Bali.

I also have a dear friend who encourages me to pursue my dreams, no matter the cost. Another reminds me that there are two kinds of people in this world: those who care only about themselves and those who care about others. I have friends who remind me that I have so much to share with the world and encourage me to go out and do it. I have friends who believe in my teaching, who push me to think big, and who remind me that I am truly special. Most importantly, I have friends who help me quiet my inner critic and recognize my own worth.

At first, it felt like a constant tug-of-war inside me, with my insecurities fighting against every word of encouragement. Slowly, though, I let my supporters' words sink in, replacing my doubts with possibilities. It's amazing how the brain begins to rewire itself when you allow yourself to see what your supporters see in you.

I have become my own inner supporter. Now, when I see opportunities that excite me, I take them. Even if my heart races, my breath shortens, and my palms sweat, I move forward anyway. I have completed eleven marathons all over the world. I was even married during a half marathon. I've traveled the globe to train and teach, living in India and Bali for two months.

I have found myself, and I am unapologetically bringing my authentic self to the world. I'm not perfect, but I've learned that life is truly a practice. We aren't perfect at it, but that shouldn't stop us from living.

Most importantly, I've realized the harshest lies and words often come from within. The negative stories we tell ourselves can keep us stuck. That's why it's crucial to seek out and listen to our outside supporters.

If you're thinking you don't have any outside supporters, I encourage you to step back from your critics—both inner and outer. Often, those critics drown out the quiet, supportive voices around you. Remember, a supporter could be anyone: a stranger's smile, a kind word from an acquaintance, or even an accidental voicemail from someone you've never met.

Do you remember when I said, "This is going to be the year of no regrets?" What if I told you it's time for all of us to live a life of no regrets? Let's not look back—let's get started. Surround yourself with people and things that remind you of your strength, your dreams, and your potential. Let them help you quiet your inner critic until you become your own best supporter.

Take that first step toward a life of no regrets.

About Susan Fryman:

Susan Fryman of The Waking Owl is a 500 hour registered yoga teacher, Reiki Master and Master Sound Facilitator. She is certified in multiple styles of yoga, meditation, pranayama, sound therapy and Thai Yoga Massage. She has been trained and has taught locally and internationally.

Susan loves to continue to learn and is currently studying to be Yoga Therapist and a Doctor of Ayurveda. She continues to live in that condo in Cincinnati, Ohio with her husband and their cat. She seeks to bring her style of yoga and healing to the world.

Finding Purpose in Life's Challenges Through the Transformative Power of Sound

By Mary Beth Cowardin

Have you ever experienced a time when life feels off kilter? A time when nothing seems to be going right and getting through the day is simply put, hard? That's how I've often felt these past few years. As I navigated these challenging periods, I miraculously found the beauty of sound baths to help calm my mind, soothe my soul, and give me reassurance that everything will all be okay. I had no idea these sessions would become my journey to discovering peace—and even a new purpose—amidst such profound upheaval.

I'm a tough cookie. Most things don't rattle me. I take adversity in stride and seek the best in situations. I believe when life gives you lemons, make lemonade. Throughout my career, I've been praised for my achievements, advanced professionally and experienced success. However, in 2021, the earth beneath me started to crumble, and only recently has it felt like life has taken a turn for the better.

My world exploded in January 2021 when my dad experienced an unexpected life-threatening illness. While on a golf outing to one of the West Coast's most beautiful, rugged courses, this dream trip quickly turned into a nightmare. After lunch the first day, my dad went to his hotel room. Soon after my uncle found him lying on the floor in a fetal position. They rushed him to the nearest hospital. After a few days in this small, primitive facility, they transported my dad to a larger hospital in Medford, Oregon, several hours away. The flurry of diagnoses he received during those days brought an emotional roller coaster of highs and lows. My stepmom flew to be with him thinking he had an irritable bowel issue and they'd be home soon. By the time she arrived, the diagnosis had completely changed, bringing with it a much grimmer outlook.

Fortunately, one doctor took special care studying dad's x-rays and identified a blood clot around his heart. When the doctors opened him up to remove the clot, they discovered dead intestine tissue caused by blocked blood flow. As a result, they removed 18 feet of his intestine. They kept him in a medically induced coma, with his chest still open. Three days later they operated again and closed him up. The emergency gastro-intestinal bypass surgery saved his life.

He and my stepmom stayed in Oregon for weeks before being permitted to travel cross country home to fully recover. Recovery wasn't easy. In the first three weeks at home, my dad ended up in the ER five times with complications. It was a trying time. The pandemic prevented us from visiting him in the hospital, making the situation harder. The good news is after months of proper rest and medication, my dad improved. I'm happy to report that today he has regained much of his strength and stamina and is back to normal.

Just as life's storm seemed to calm, another test came my way. My best friend from college, who successfully beat ocular melanoma six years earlier, learned what every cancer survivor dreads. Cancer had returned. At her mid-year checkup, doctors found several lesions on her liver. My heart sank at this news. Despite knowing there was a strong possibility her cancer might return one day, I was in disbelief, honestly, in denial. My friend was one of the strongest, smartest, most disciplined people I've ever met. A few weeks after her upsetting diagnosis, she and her husband came to dinner. When she left the room, her husband shared her prognosis of having 14-24 months to live. We sat in stunned silence. There's no possible response in such a moment, and we had to put on brave faces knowing she would return at any moment.

For months, I watched her struggle with a blunt, unfriendly doctor and listened to her stories of terrible service at the cancer hospital my husband and I had supported for years. That spring, she went in for surgery, only to be sent immediately back to recovery because the doctors couldn't agree on a treatment plan. Determined, she researched her disease, reached out to medical professionals across the world and found her own clinical trial, without her own doctor's help. She and her husband traveled to Philadelphia for treatment, using a service designed for military veterans that flew them by private plane. I'll never forget the day she texted me a photo of them standing beside a small plane on a sunny day, ready for her first treatment. That picture was a symbol of hope. She finally found a doctor ready to fight alongside her.

I am grateful to have amazing people in my life, many of whom share a passion for fighting cancer. For the past 15 years, I've co-captained a cycling team, Girls with Gears, who rides to raise funds to support life-saving research at The Ohio State University's James Cancer Hospital. A fellow team member is involved with the Karen Wellington Foundation, a non-profit with the mission to bring joy to women battling cancer. Through this foundation, she gave me and my friend a memorable afternoon of pampering. While the spa treatments were a delightful gift, it was our heartfelt conversation afterward that made the day truly unforgettable.

With the treatment area all to ourselves, we spent hours talking. My friend shared her few fears, her conversations with God, and her promise to dedicate her life to helping others if she survived. During our chat, I mentioned an upcoming yoga retreat and asked if she'd like to go. She was hesitant in her reply, likely wondering if it is smart to commit to something a few weeks away given the uncertainty surrounding her life. True to her "can-do" attitude that I've long admired, she said "Let's do it." So, I registered us.

The Tuesday afternoon before this event, she texted me that she was being admitted to the hospital, despite feeling completely fine. The test results from that day's doctor visit showed signs of liver failure. Her doctor immediately admitted her to The James Cancer Hospital. Unfortunately, the stay extended through the weekend, and she could not go with me to the yoga retreat. Not wanting to go by myself, I asked my husband to join me. Like the good trooper he is, he agreed, despite knowing he'd likely be the only man in the room. I'm forever grateful he joined me that day.

Being inside this geode built in the woods high on a hill during winter felt surreal—like sitting in a Jetson's-style spaceship, suspended among tall trees. Not being a yogi myself, I tried some of the moves, yet most of the time I sat on my mat enjoying the peaceful atmosphere and the chance to think about my friend and what she's endured. The instructor closed the retreat with a sound bath. I had never experienced the beauty of crystal sound bowls before. While laying down and listening to the chimes and the instructor's teachings of the body's seven main chakras, I could vividly see the colors she described in my mind. Much to my surprise, it brought a sense of calm and peace that had been missing amidst the past year's stresses. Moved by this experience, I stayed afterwards to meet the instructor and learn more. She graciously shared her knowledge and invited me to her nearby studio, where she held weekly sound baths. For the first time in ages, I slept soundly that night.

In the following weeks, life was busy with the usual things. Our cycling team kicked off a new season. I traveled for work, and my friend continued to seek any possible treatment that would kill the cancer cells multiplying in her body. She found a special holistic program and retreat in Jamaica for people with severe health conditions. She didn't leave a stone unturned in her quest to beat cancer. She described the science behind these programs in common language a third grader could understand. Any question I asked, she could answer. She always amazed me with her knowledge. I admired her energy, perseverance, and resourcefulness.

After she returned home from her adventures in Jamaica, she invited us over. She told me and my husband story after story about her life-changing experience in Jamaica. She never seemed happier, healthier, or fuller of life. On the drive home, as we talked about her trip, I was convinced she was beating cancer. I was so convinced I got out of my usual check-in routine with her. I was buried at work as we geared up for our annual conference in July.

Shortly thereafter, I had the rude awakening that cancer doesn't stop. One of my cycling friends, who had battled cancer for more than 20 years, lost her fight. On the way home from the calling hours I thought to myself, I need to see my best friend tomorrow. I haven't seen her in a few weeks and it's going to be a beautiful day. Rather than take the afternoon off to go to this funeral as originally planned, instead, I'll go spend time with my friend. I decided against calling her on my way home to make plans because I knew she would ask me where I was, and I didn't want to tell her another friend had just died of cancer.

The next morning, after some unexpected work calls, I picked up my phone to text my friend about coming over. Instead, I got the news that I had been dreading. My friend's husband texted me that she woke up in the middle of the night in crippling pain. They went to the urgent care and were sent to the ER. She had a perforated bowel, which if not operated on, she would die. However, because of her advanced cancer, they would not operate.

Reminiscent of an afternoon when my stepmom called me to help care for my dad soon after he got home from Oregon, I dropped everything and went straight to the hospital. My friend's parents, brother, sister-in-law, niece, and best friend from childhood and another dear friend from college were all in the waiting room. The moment I walked into that dark cold room, I burst into tears. The unspeakable reality was present and hard to face. We each took turns going into the small ER bay around the corner to sit with her. She was awake and alert most of the time. True to form, she described in detail what the doctors found and tried to direct everything that was going on around her. At one point that afternoon, I sat next to her, telling her I loved her. Through tears running down my face and gasping for air as I sobbed, I shared my hope that when my time comes, I could muster half the bravery and strength she has shown throughout her battle. I told her all the things I admire and love about her. I'm forever grateful for the chance to share these feelings with her. I hated that I cried in front of her. I wanted to be strong like her, but I couldn't stop the tears.

Due to a shortage of hospice rooms, she stayed in the ER overnight. Finally, late the next day, she was moved to a hospice room, which was more comfortable and peaceful. Yet, we all knew it meant the end was looming. Over the next six days we watched her fade away. As we shuffled between her room and the nearby waiting room, her husband and I talked about her wishes. He asked me to plan her celebration of life. I felt incredibly honored to be given such an important job.

We held her celebration on our sixth wedding anniversary. It was perfect because my friend made our wedding cake and drove it from Ohio all the way up a mountain in Virginia. Sharing this special day on the calendar with her celebration of life felt perfect. Her celebration was held at a quaint place called "The Kitchen". Also appropriately chosen, given she was a superb cook and had her own baking business. Throughout that emotional afternoon, I felt the warmth of her smile shining down on us. In my eulogy I shared her desire to dedicate her life to helping others. I challenged everyone to continue her legacy and carry out her wishes to help others and to go out and perform a random act of kindness for a stranger.

With little time to truly grieve the loss of my friend, we were faced with another challenge of caring for my mom. Four days after celebrating my friend's life, my mother had shoulder replacement surgery. A few weeks later, and only the second night she was back in her own home after recovering at our house for weeks, my mom fell down her staircase. She broke her clavicle in two places, fractured several ribs and her vertebrae. She was extremely lucky she didn't die from this fall.

After weeks in the hospital and rehabilitation center, she recuperated in our home for seven months. During this time, we faced hard life decisions. After finding a ranch home located less than a mile from our house, we sold the house she had lived in for the past forty-one years. While still recuperating from the injuries of her fall, we downsized her cherished belongings, renovated the new home's kitchen, main floor laundry, and had the wood floors refinished before moving her into her new neighborhood.

Some nights, the weight of grief of losing my friend and the stress of being a caregiver kept me awake. My mind raced with questions and memories that left me feeling both exhausted and numb. Why are we on this earth? What's our purpose? Will there always be suffering at the end of life?

What legacy do I want to create? Thinking about these questions and recalling my fateful afternoon in the Geode guided me to decide to become a sound bath practitioner. I purchased a set of crystal healing bowls, and soon passed levels I and II certification levels. I became a Master Sound healer at a retreat in Sedona, Arizona this past spring.

The first time I played the crystal bowls, I was entranced by the sounds. I felt my heart begin to calm, as though the vibrations were gently lifting the weight of grief from my chest. The melodies of the sound bowls washed over me, and I experienced a sensation like I'm floating and drifting in the sky. With each session, I've felt a deeper connection to the loved ones I've lost.

I enjoy watching people awaken out of the slumber of a sound bath with a calm, relaxed smile. I feel a deep sense of purpose and gratitude. Being able to help others through the gift of sound is an amazing blessing. I believe my friend would be proud as I honor her memory by sharing the healing power of sound with others.

About Mary Beth Cowardin:

Mary Beth Cowardin, a marketing executive, is passionate about connecting people and helping them find balance. Her journey into sound healing began during a challenging time when she discovered the relaxation of sound baths. Inspired, she became a certified Master Sound Healer through Life Changing Energy and now runs Calming Chimes, her sound practice through which she hopes to positively impact as many people as possible. An avid sports enthusiast, Mary Beth, enjoys tennis, pickleball, hiking and cycling. She co-chairs Girls with Gears, a grassroots peloton that has raised over $2 million for cancer research. A graduate of The Ohio State University with an undergraduate degree in French, and an MBA, Mary Beth lives in Columbus, OH, with husband, Gregg, and dog, Luna. She cherishes time at their Blue Ridge Mountain home. Discover more about her sound bath practice at www.calmingchimes.com and follow Calming Chimes on social media.

Time to Fly
By Gretchen Melo

There is nothing like a good old-fashioned tragedy to get you to scrutinize your life's path.

When my parents divorced, I found myself questioning my entire upbringing. At 33 years old, three years married, and in my first trimester of pregnancy, it was my first, honest-to-goodness, full-blown Dark Night of the Soul. It sent me spiraling into years of social isolation, but on a parallel journey of healing and self-rediscovery.

You see, within minutes of getting the news about my parents, a sudden realization washed over me. Up until that point, I had always been so subservient, so quick to fall in line whenever I sensed that going my own way would disappoint or anger someone. Now, even through my shock and grief, I was overcome with an overwhelming sense of liberation. I would no longer concern myself with the pressure to please other people at the expense of my own well-being, sense of identity, purpose, and happiness.

I began to ask myself questions like, "Who am I, truly? What do I believe? What do I want to accomplish in life?" I had glimmers of answers, but mostly what felt like a big bag of confusing memories and unfulfilled wishes. At the time, I knew what I *didn't* want, and I was able to determine some general ideas about what I *did* want.

I was an airline customer service supervisor at an airport, and while there were many rewarding aspects of that role, I had a general sense of dread at the thought of continuing into my 40s and 50s as an airline employee. I was coming up on 12 years with the airline, and I knew if I didn't get out of that career soon, I would become a "lifer."

Please don't get me wrong! For some people, a lifelong career in that field is an absolutely beautiful thing with many amazing perks included! But for me, staying felt like I would be betraying who I really was. I didn't want to live my entire life that way. It took me a few years of complaining to all my friends and resisting change, but one day, I did it. I ripped off a piece of printer paper, scrawled out a note of resignation, and marched it down to my manager's office.

A couple of weeks later, as I drove home after my last day of work at the airport, REO Speedwagon came on the radio, singing *Time for Me to Fly*. I laughed at the God wink, singing along loudly through tears, a sense of liberation flooding over me.

I'm not suggesting that the way I went about this transition was the best way or that I would recommend ending a career like this. I knew this decision would mean sacrifice and struggle, but something in me felt ready for the challenge. Everything in me told me that this abrupt career decision would force me to open up to other possibilities.

A short year later, I stepped into an entirely different role, literally overnight. I saw an ad for a bilingual classroom teacher. My degree was in Spanish and theatre, and years earlier I had taught ESL while living in Mexico. I felt a strong sense that I should try for the job, despite the hurdles. Before I could psyche myself out and change my mind, I filled out an application and hit "send." The next day, I was interviewed, and the day after that, I was attempting to set up a classroom.

After years of feeling like I was meant to be doing something different, I began doing something I had always known I would do well: teach and make a difference while using my Spanish skills. I felt right at home in the classroom, even though I had a humongous learning curve as someone stepping in with an emergency temporary license and no formal teaching training. I will forever be grateful to the principal who hired me. She told me, "You can't teach passion, but we can help you with the rest," and she set up wonderful mentorships for me.

Living in better alignment with my desires and deeper identity offered me the emotional bandwidth to discover the power of mindfulness and meditation. I began to tune into possibilities and manifest small things, like a used car and several months of free housing when we moved from Minnesota to Texas.

Yes, my intuition was awakened, but it wasn't fully developed, and I was still processing a lot of pain. It wasn't an easy leg of the journey. As I continued my healing journey and began releasing my own pain, I started experiencing some unexpected turbulence, if you will.

I began to notice something strange happening. I would feel other people's physical pains as well as their emotions before we even talked about them having any difficulties. Sometimes I would sense people's pain and later find out they had been experiencing physical discomfort at the same time I was feeling it in my body.

What was going on?

I remember once, on vacation, my husband and I visited the Chimayo Sanctuary in New Mexico. As we entered the church where thousands of people have gone with hopes of experiencing healing, I went from feeling like a relaxed, unattached tourist to suddenly being completely overcome by emotion, dissolving into a heap of tears on one of the pews.

This went on for several years. I can't even tell you how many times I would feel physical pain or anxiety, wonder what was wrong with me, and then find out a nearby acquaintance or a far-off loved one was experiencing an ailment or hardship. The good news is that as soon as I was able to pinpoint whose "baggage" I was carrying, my own symptoms would vanish.

Slowly, I began to realize I was an empath.

While this insight opened me up to exploring what it means to be an empath, I have to admit that, at first, it felt useless to me.

Who wants to have random pains, aches, and anxiety from other people and not be able to do anything about it? Prayer is powerful, but I was bedraggled by all the suffering of others, to the point where I struggled to find my center. What good was this "gift" if I was constantly weighed down by others' burdens and unable to help? I felt like a sponge, absorbing emotions and physical maladies I didn't want, unable to squeeze them out or shield myself.

I started to seek information about how other people coped with being an empath. I began to learn about shielding, but it wasn't always effective. Someone suggested Reiki. I knew Reiki was powerful because I had experienced it once during a massage, but at the time I was grappling with these empath symptoms, I couldn't afford Reiki treatments.

Then came the final straw—another tragedy, though not mine.

One sunny day, I was at a park with my son. Looking around at all the families, I noticed an acquaintance sitting under a tree, her newborn baby lying on a blanket beside her.

At that moment, I was suddenly overcome by a sense of fear and panic. I didn't understand why. I didn't even think it had to do with my empath "curse." I chalked it up to social anxiety. Remember, I was still healing and rather isolated socially, and I was still new at dealing with being an empath.

A week later, her baby died. I was horrified.

Apparently, I was **not** well "shielded" that day at the park. My heart ached for the family who lost their baby. I began to wonder if there was some way to get a handle on how to respond to these moments when the empath "curse" kicked in. What *good* was it to have this sixth sense or empathic ability if I couldn't do anything about it?

Being an empath felt like being aboard a runaway train.

I remembered the suggestion to try Reiki and decided that instead of seeking treatments from others, I should learn to use it on myself. That way, I could have an instant tool to cope whenever I felt distress or physical pain.

I found a teacher and began taking Reiki lessons. My attunement was a very powerful, beautiful experience. Over the course of a few years, I learned about Reiki and experienced its benefits.

Learning Reiki was like finding armor for my soul—a way to hold onto my own peace while helping others. I began to find relief in several areas of my life. I felt stronger protection than ever before when it came to my empathic abilities. Eventually, I earned my Master Reiki certification.

Reiki has helped me tune in and figure out which feelings and sensations are mine and which belong to others. I no longer feel like a victim of outside energies.

Reiki also helped me refine my intuition, which has grown stronger and stronger over recent years. I've found healing in many aspects of my life and reconnected with parts of myself that had been dormant for years: my love of writing, music, helping others with their struggles, and the leadership confidence I had as a child. Reiki opened the doors for me to learn other healing modalities, as well.

My life is not perfect by any means, and there have been other dark times. But with God's help and Reiki, I more easily maintain a sense of peace and confidence, even in very difficult situations and circumstances.

Looking back at my first Dark Night of the Soul, I now understand why it's part of my story and how, in a crazy way, it helped me in the long run.

It was a catalyst for much-needed change in my life. Similarly, my growing pains as an empath were rough and sometimes involved tragedy, but they pointed me toward a journey of deeper healing for myself—and now, for others.

Nowadays, I am fine-tuning what it means to be led by my heart, and so far, my heart has not let me down. It can be scary, but my life so far has been all about transformation, and every journey has brought something worthwhile to the table.

As an example, back in 2022, I took the leap to leave the classroom and focus on my Montessori Spanish curriculum business. Around that time, I started seeing posts from a former Montessori colleague talking about her therapy center, where she combined behavior therapy with the Montessori approach to serve neurodivergent children.

By then, I was just coming back to a place where I wanted to socialize with people and make new friends. But it was still completely out of character for me to take the initiative to plan a get-together. However, I felt a growing nudge inside, telling me I should reach out to her. I couldn't ignore it.

You won't believe what has happened as a result, but before I get to that, I need to share another part of my story.

Over the past couple of years, while working on my Spanish curriculum business, I also felt a growing urge to do something involving sound frequency. I listened to the call and am now certified in several areas, about to include a vocal component—which takes me back to something I've loved since childhood: singing! Including sound healing in both my personal and professional life has helped me embrace parts of myself I had hidden for too long. This type of overlap would never have happened had I not tuned into my heart.

Because I listened to that voice and reached out to my former colleague, I gained a friend. Not only that, but I also earned a staunch supporter of my Montessori-inspired Spanish curriculum and my sound healing work.

In fact, at her facility, I now support neurodivergent children not only in learning Spanish but also through "sound experiences," as I call them. At the time of writing this, there is a strong possibility she will open a school and has invited me to be a founding member—offering me even more support than I've ever had!

You never know what magic can happen when you listen to the voice within—especially during the most difficult times. Looking back now, it seems like every decision I made from the heart was another piece of the puzzle, coming together to reveal a life I truly wanted.

I now realize that my journey wasn't just for me; it's meant to inspire others to listen to their hearts and let their own light guide the way.

Do you ever feel lost? Maybe you're going through a dark time, stuck in a rut, or facing something that makes you feel trapped. My advice, if you're open to it, is to start asking yourself—in quiet stillness—who YOU are.

Knowing you are a child of God may be comforting, but I'm talking about you as a soul inhabiting a human body. Truly ask yourself: Who *are* you? Be willing to sit in discomfort and silence to discover the answers already within you.

One actionable step to help you through a healing process is to start paying attention to your feelings—even your physical ailments, no matter how small. They are often linked to emotions or trauma in some way. Give that part of yourself compassion and love.

We are not guaranteed an easy life. This remains true even after we choose to follow our inner guidance and travel along a healing path. In fact, we will probably face more Dark Nights of the Soul. But as for me, I am now better equipped to face them. I can honestly say I am open to going wherever my heart leads, and I've learned not to get too comfortable. When we follow our guidance, doors open, and sometimes we are practically pushed through. My Reiki teacher warned me about this, and she was not wrong!

Something tells me more change is just around the corner.

Can you feel it, too?

Is it time for *you* to fly?

By Gretchen Melo

Gretchen is a lifelong learner and transformer who has taken an intuitive journey back to wholeness, and has encouraged others to do the same throughout her life. While her master's degree is in curriculum and instruction with a concentration in bilingual education, her certifications include:

- Spanish Teacher
- Master Life Coach
- Reiki Master
- Sound Healer
- Instructional Design

Gretchen is a proud mother and spouse, and values time with her family. She is the founder and creator of El Puente Bilingüe, LLC and PeaceScore.World, and is unleashing from her niche to reconnect with music, writing, healing, peacemaking, and joy.

Lifelong Learning: A Journey from Crisis to Insight
By Ellen Aresty

At 23, I was filled with passion and purpose, pursuing a graduate degree to teach deaf-blind multi-handicapped children. My fascination with sign language had brought me to this field. A summer immersed in classes with deaf adults had cemented my love for the language. The beauty and depth of communicating without spoken words felt both artistic and practical. I was captivated by the idea of using this skill to help children navigate a world that often felt inaccessible to them.

Deaf-blind children, like all others, are curious, playful, and full of potential. But their unique challenges required specialized teaching. It was my role to help them master skills others took for granted—pouring liquids without spilling, navigating spaces through touch, and using their remaining senses to interpret the world. I thrived in this structured, supportive environment, where the focus was on individualized learning and steady progress. I felt calm, capable, and confident. I was certain I was exactly where I was meant to be.

But then came the requirement to student teach in a regular classroom—a world that couldn't have been more different. Gone were the calm, focused spaces I had grown to love. Instead, I was thrown into an open-concept classroom where walls didn't exist, and the noise from four different groups of students blended into a constant roar. I struggled to distinguish my students from others, let alone manage the chaos. The other teachers seemed unfazed, moving through the cacophony with ease. I, on the other hand, felt like I was sinking.

To make matters worse, my supervising teacher constantly compared me to the student teacher she had worked with before me. She spoke often and fondly of him, praising his ability to connect with the boys in the class and his effectiveness as a role model. While I respected her admiration for him, her comparisons left me feeling inadequate. It was clear she didn't see me the same way, and her indifference made an already challenging situation even more isolating.

Then came the day that changed everything. During class, the teacher addressed an emotionally disturbed child, telling him—and the entire class—that if he hit someone, she would let the whole class hit him back. My stomach dropped as I heard her words. Why would she say something so irresponsible? Then, without further explanation, she abruptly left the room, leaving me alone with the students. My chest tightened as I realized the impossible position I was in. My hands grew clammy, and I could feel panic rising.

It didn't take long for her words to ignite chaos. The emotionally disturbed child hit another student. The noise level spiked, and suddenly, the entire class surrounded me, chanting that they should all hit him back because "the teacher said so." The energy in the room shifted, turning from tense to chaotic in an instant. My heart pounded in my ears, and the room seemed to close in around me.

I tried to steady myself, but my mind was racing. I had been taught never to make threats I couldn't follow through on, but what could I do now? The faces of the students blurred together, their voices rising in unison, demanding retribution. I felt paralyzed, my hands trembling as I tried to think of a way to regain control.

The boy who had been struck stood frozen, his face a mix of fear and betrayal. I saw myself mirrored in his wide eyes—both of us helpless, caught in a situation spiraling out of control. I was supposed to be the adult, the one who kept things calm and safe. Instead, I was drowning in the chaos.

Desperation overtook me. In a misguided attempt to defuse the situation, I made the split-second decision to let the child who had been hit strike back. I hoped it would satisfy the others and calm the room. But it didn't. The tension only deepened, and I knew immediately that I had made a terrible mistake. The look on the boy's face as he retaliated hit me like a physical blow. I had failed him, failed myself, and failed the class.

Afterward, I was summoned to a meeting with the teacher and principal. Walking into that room felt like stepping into a courtroom where I was both the defendant and the accused. The teacher sat with her arms crossed, her expression unreadable, while the principal's gaze felt heavy with judgment. I tried to explain how overwhelmed I had been, but my words felt hollow. Their silence was deafening. I left that meeting feeling humiliated, certain I didn't belong in a classroom.

After that meeting, I returned to my student teaching placement in the special needs classroom. The contrast was a relief. The structured, supportive environment allowed me to regain my footing. The next year, I got a job teaching multi-handicapped children, returning to the work I loved and the calm I needed.

Still, the chaos of the open classroom stayed with me. I couldn't forget my supervising teacher's suggestion, after the meeting with the principal, to explore a mind-training program called the Silva Method. I was skeptical as to why she thought I would benefit from this program. How could I take advice from someone who had put me in such a terrible position? Yet, as the days passed, curiosity took hold.

I researched the Silva Method and found it promised tools for active meditation, stress management, and mental clarity. It sounded like something I needed. I decided to give it a try.

The Silva Method began with a unique mental exercise: creating a laboratory in your mind. My laboratory overlooked a beach and the ocean, perched high on a cliff. In it, I imagined a large screen, like a television, where I could visualize or interpret the information I was seeking. There were also files and a computer containing all of humanity's information—resources I could "access" during exercises.

When we began practicing Extra Sensory Perception (ESP), we worked with partners. One of us would enter a meditative state and "go into" our mental laboratory while the other read the name, sex, and location of a person with a health problem from a set of cards. During my first attempt, I visualized the person on my mental screen. His head appeared clearly, but his body kept blinking on and off. My partner asked what that might mean to me, and I hesitated before replying, "Maybe he's paralyzed?"

I was right.

I couldn't believe I had done that. I had to calm myself down to continue the exercise and send him healing energy.

Learning and using the Silva Method in my life helped me realize that I could find calm and clarity within myself, even in the midst of chaos. For the first time in months, I felt empowered to take control of my life.

That moment was my breakthrough. I realized I didn't have to be a victim of external chaos. The Silva Method taught me I could find calm within myself, no matter what was happening around me. It was a powerful realization that changed the way I approached life.

My family embraced these techniques as well. My husband used the Silva Method to manage stress and physical ailments, including clearing up eczema and stomach pains. These changes helped him excel in law school, moving from the top 20% to the top 10% of his class—a remarkable achievement. My children used the techniques for school and health, transforming stressful situations into moments of focus and calm.

One memorable example occurred in Boston. I wanted to take my children to a bookstore on a busy shopping street, but parking was notoriously scarce. Before we arrived, I asked my children to visualize a parking space opening up near the store. As we turned onto the street, three cars pulled out right in front of the bookstore. Moments like these reinforced the power of visualization and belief.

After my training in the Silva Method, I had an experience with a nurse when I gave birth to my second child that may have eventually led me to accept what Reiki could accomplish. I wasn't feeling well the night after I gave birth. Feverish and unsettled, I couldn't sleep. A nurse came into my room and stood quietly beside me, placing her hands gently on different parts of my body. Slowly, I felt my body relax. The feverish feeling subsided, and I drifted into a deep sleep.

That night planted a seed of curiosity about how touch could provide such profound relief. It wasn't until later, when I began exploring other healing techniques, that I understood how intentional energy work could affect the body and mind.

Reiki, another healing modality I explored, led to equally profound experiences. One evening, I was out to dinner with a group of friends when one of them began struggling to swallow his food. Concerned, he excused himself to the restroom, but the problem persisted when he returned. I offered to help, and when he agreed, I used Reiki for a few minutes. The change was almost immediate—he was able to eat normally again. The reactions around the table ranged from excitement to skepticism, but I was just grateful to have been able to help.

On a flight, I once sat near a woman who couldn't stop coughing. Embarrassed, she explained that she wasn't contagious but couldn't control the cough. I offered to help and used Reiki for a few minutes. To her astonishment, the coughing stopped. She looked at me with wide eyes and asked what I had done, saying she would look into Reiki herself.

Another time, I worked weekly with a woman who had chronic back pain. Over the course of our sessions, she began to see her pain lessen. Reiki was working on other issues she had as well, whether a cold or restless leg syndrome. She experienced improvements in many areas of her health. By the time we stopped, she no longer needed pain medication and had returned to work. She described the process as "peeling an onion," with each session revealing deeper layers of healing. Witnessing her progress reinforced my belief in the power of energy work to address both physical and emotional challenges.

I have continued to explore and learn about various energy and healing modalities, including Ho'oponopono, sound baths, and Native American flutes.

Exploring sound healing has reminded me of the power of subtle yet profound vibrations. Much like Reiki or meditation, sound seems to reach deep into the layers of one's being, offering relief and balance. Learning about sound baths and healing vibrations has become the latest step in my journey to discover how energy and intention can improve lives.

It's remarkable to think that a moment of chaos in a noisy classroom—a moment that felt like failure—could ignite such profound transformation. That experience not only shaped my career but also awakened a lifelong pursuit of growth and healing.

Today, I approach challenges with a deep breath and a calm heart. I visualize the outcomes I want but accept life as it is. I've learned to trust that even the most overwhelming situations often carry the seeds of something beautiful. If I could speak to my younger self, I would tell her to breathe, stay calm, and trust that this moment will pass. I would also tell her to listen to advice, even when it feels unwelcome—it might just lead to something life-changing.

This journey has transformed not only my life but also the lives of those around me. It's a testament to the power of growth, even in the face of chaos. For that, I am deeply grateful.

About Ellen Aresty:

Ellen has been married to her supportive husband for 48 years, having met him 52 years ago. She is a mother of three and a grandmother of two, with another grandchild on the way. Ellen is an artist, weaver, enamellist, metal smith, and jeweler who also cuts, shapes, and polishes stones for settings.

Since the mid-1970s, Ellen has been exploring meditation, energy work, and other techniques. She is a practitioner of the Silva Method, Reiki, Ho'oponopono, and sound baths, utilizing singing bowls, gongs, drums, chimes, Native American flutes, and other instruments.

Ellen integrates her art and energy work whenever possible and is currently working on incorporating images of sound vibrations into her enamel pieces and other creations. She enjoys collaborating with friends, family, and others who are interested in promoting relaxation and enhancing life's meaningful moments.

website: ellenarestydesigns.com

email: earesty@hotmail.com

ALL THE PIECES
By LoriAnn Bouchard

I am, what I like to call, a serial entrepreneur. I seem to have a habit of seeing a problem and feeling an urge to find a way to create a business to help solve that problem. This part of my journey really began in earnest in 2016. At the time, I had no idea that the birth of my grandson, followed by tragic losses, a pandemic, and divorce, would result in my becoming a sound healer and a founding member of a non-profit organization whose mission is to support neurodivergent children and their families.

In 2016, while still reeling from the loss of my father-in-law followed right away by the loss of my own father, my beautiful grandson, Ben, was born. He was born drug-addicted. His mother was taken to jail right from the hospital, and she has been allowed no further contact with him. Right away, Ben was faced with something no baby should have to face: addiction to heroin. Watching a newborn baby going through excruciating withdrawal is one of the most heart-wrenching things you can experience. This tiny, beautiful baby boy spent his first two weeks in the NICU on an IV of morphine to help him with the extreme pain of withdrawal. Then, once the heroin was gone from his system, he faced the daunting task of withdrawing from the morphine. This little boy stole our hearts from the very beginning. His strength and ability to smile at us even through all this pain made it impossible not to love him. Because my son and his mother were not married at the time, Ben was placed immediately into the foster care system. It took us a month of fighting the state of Pennsylvania with an expensive attorney to get him back with us. After weeks of fighting the system, living in a hotel far from home, and only being allowed access to Ben one supervised hour a week, my son was finally awarded custody, and we were able to bring him home.

Raising a drug-addicted child is challenging at best and even more difficult for a young single father. He was forced to relocate from Pennsylvania to northern Maine with us so that he would have the support and help he knew he would need to raise a child alone. Ben seemed to be blessed with few side effects at first, and my son settled into his new role as a single father with the support of his family.

Less than a year later, my oldest daughter, Maya, just after her 23rd birthday, was killed in a tragic car accident. This sent the entire family reeling, trying to sort out how to begin living differently without her. The loss of a child is something a parent never recovers from. You do not get to go back to your life the way it was before. One must find a new way. We were grateful that Maya was able to meet and spend some time with Ben before her passing, but we will always be sad that Ben will not remember his aunt. My grandson's presence did give us all a focus and a purpose as he grew and began to talk and walk.

A year after that, I was opening a new bakery in a small town in rural northern Maine. Things went well at first, and Ben spent time helping me and my youngest daughter, Jolie, at the bakery. He would open the door for customers to come in while also smiling cutely with his hand held out, wanting payment for entry. I had to tell customers to please not indulge him and not to give him money (although he did make more than I did on some days).

Just when we had settled in and began to get the bakery business going well, Covid happened. Like many other small businesses, mine did not survive. Even though I was still doing remote accounting work, as I had all along to pay bills, I found myself needing to do something more purposeful. I needed to do something to make a positive impact on more people as well as to help myself and my family. I began to see a problem that needed solving.

I then started my sound healing journey after reconnecting with an online friend that I had known on and off for years. It turns out my friend, Vickie, was the owner of this incredible new business, Life Changing Energy! I quickly began taking sound healer certification classes and building up a collection of tools and instruments. Reconnecting with this friendship also led me to become a Reiki Master, and then later through another venue, I was certified in hypnotherapy. I was "collecting" all these different skills, but I was still very uncertain about what exactly I was going to do with it all. I knew I needed to do SOMETHING! I continued learning as much as I could while always hoping I would "find" my intended path.

During this time, my grandson thrived with only little indication of the troubled start he had in this life. But then… we saw him begin to really struggle. He was eventually diagnosed with Disruptive Mood Dysregulation Disorder (DMDD), Attention Deficit and Hyperactivity Disorder (ADHD), and Autism. We were told this trifecta is the worst-case scenario. My son was soon living a nightmare. We watched this amazingly bright and intelligent child struggle with a lack of impulse control due to the damage from the drugs in utero. He would go from sweet and loving to screaming and threatening in seconds. It is devastating and terrifying to watch, and I can only imagine it is terrifying for Ben to experience. He was put on strong anti-psychotic medication which basically zombified him. Where we live, there are only basic medical resources available. Anything really specialized requires significant travel, which isn't practical, especially for a single parent. There was only one available pediatric psychiatrist in the area, and to say she was ineffective and uncaring is a grave understatement. She routinely ordered mind-numbing drugs that left my grandson a shell of a child and provided minimal oversight. In a system that allows access to only certain doctors, it can be impossible to get help that is needed. We were heartbroken watching Ben suffer while he could not understand what was happening or why he was feeling these emotions. There were times that he was so disrupted and out of control that he had to spend time in-patient at a local crisis center. He would at times be quite sweet and silly, and always extremely intelligent, but then for reasons we don't always understand he would abruptly turn into a violent, angry, uncontrollable, and inconsolable child. He would be playing with his toy cars, and we would ask him to wash up for lunch, which would result in a violent outburst, throwing of toys, etc. He even broke the exterior door to the house in a fit of anger. We all knew that we needed to do something for Ben as well as for my son, but none of us knew WHAT to do.

During this time, my son got married and then a few years later divorced. He worked tirelessly to build his business as he knows that being self-employed is the only way to gain the freedom he needs to manage a child like this. As I watched my son try so hard to do it alone and not always succeed, I knew I needed to use some of my sound healing tools to help him. I began to formulate an idea that I would focus on helping parents of special needs kids. I had been able to utilize my skills to help keep myself sane and emotionally available through this, so why couldn't I do the same for him and other parents with similar stresses? I watched as my son struggled to figure out how to manage his own ADHD, being a single parent, AND trying to manage Ben and all of his issues and not completely fall apart in the process. As hard as it is to watch Ben go through his problems, I also have to witness my son's pain through all of this. Unfortunately, my son inherited his stubbornness from his mother. He was, and sometimes still is, resistant to allowing me to try to help him directly but has always allowed me to do whatever I can to help Ben. I began to allow Ben into my sound room (all the while praying that he does not break anything expensive!). But lo and behold! Ben fell in love with that room. Even when I moved after my divorce, he loves coming to spend time at "Memere's Sound Room." He would ask me, "Can we do tunin' forks, Memere?" Eventually, he not only wanted his own therapy, but he felt a desire to learn about it and how to use it to help others; always wanting to "do tunin' forks" on me after we are finished with him. I was delighted to see the positive impact this new arena of healing was having on him. We even added some things I learned as a hypnotherapist, and now Ben has his very own "happy button" on the top of his head. He most joyfully and very respectfully assists me with online sound baths for other sound healers. He is always wanting to learn and do more! I was finding the perfect application for these beautiful healing methods. I am learning just how magical a hug full of grounding, calming Reiki energy can be for an overwhelmed child. I learned how easy it can be to reach a child through sound, frequency, and curiosity. As I am finishing certification in Sound Healing for Neurodivergent Kids, I know I am adding to my bag of tricks.

Despite the positive steps forward, there are always intense bouts of moving backward. The most we can do is try to arrange our lives to give Ben the most consistency and positive reinforcement that we can and to make the backward moments easier.

As my son finds himself in new relationships, I am ever grateful that Ben is able to have more advocates in his life. This is a difficult situation, and anyone who wants to be a part of my son's life must be quite committed to all of this and strong enough to take all the ups and downs as they come—usually on a daily or even hourly basis. The extra support at home is a blessing for all of us.

Eventually, we were able to take Ben off of all the medications. We cleaned up his diet and began to see him thrive again (in spurts). He is incredibly intelligent but has little impulse control, and the issues that come with autism make it all even more difficult.

Soon, my son started to really experience the problems of living in such a rural place. While Ben is extremely smart and ahead academically, the school day began to be a problem that grew each week. We struggled to communicate effectively with staff and administrators. They didn't really have an understanding of Ben's needs despite an IEP (Individualized Education Program) stating what his needs are. Eventually, my son decided that a move to a different town might be what Ben needs. After some research, we determined that the town I had just moved to, in order to be closer to them, had a school that just might be a saving grace. So, I moved out and let them move into my home.

At first, Ben was doing excellently, and this school was much easier to work with. But soon, the usual problems began again. The constant calls from the school saying they cannot handle him that day caused my son to cancel clients and lose money and business. Settling into a new place and new set of routines for Ben became overwhelming quickly. My son was at the brink of his own meltdown when he called me and announced that "either he needed to become a doctor or start a non-profit or something and fix the issues with this system himself!"

This poked my memory. Within one of the certifications at Life Changing Energy, I had a Zoom meeting with Isabelle Vladoiu, who has a program that will guide you through the process of creating a non-profit! Ding, ding, ding! It suddenly all started to fall together!

This is now culminating in the creation of a new non-profit, All The Pieces Foundation, created by my son and myself to bring resources, education, and awareness for neurodivergent kids and their families with a focus on areas that are underserved. I am now realizing better just HOW I can use all of this to help others. I am able to utilize the skills I have learned in taking the Sound Healing for Neurodivergent Kids certification along with all of my other healing tools, add in some accounting skills, and a personal agenda for my grandson, and the magic is beginning to happen!

About LoriAnn Bouchard:

LoriAnn holds a Bachelor of Science in Accounting degree and was an Enrolled Agent for many years. She is a certified Master Sound Healer from Life Changing Energy. She is a Reiki Master and is currently learning Quantum Reiki methods. She is a certified Hypnotherapist fro MindValley with Paul McKenna.

She is a founding member of All The Pieces Foundation which is a non-profit that promotes awareness, education, and provides resources for neurodivergent kids and their families in areas where access to these things is difficult.

By the time of this publishing, she will be certified in Sound Healing for Neurodivergent Kids from Life Changing Energy, and will be starting her certification in Herbalism from Brighter Healing Foundation.

Believe
By Carolyn Soto Bell

I gripped the phone tightly, my pulse pounding as the last shred of hope seemed to slip away with each fault the realtor listed. This wasn't just a house—it was supposed to be our chance to finally breathe, to close the door on years of heartbreak and start anew.

Fifteen years before, we set out on a course to fulfill the dream of returning to real estate, creating a business of historical renovation and home-flipping. We began the journey by restoring a three-family home at 61 Market St., which we lived in while restoring. It was the start of something promising. In the span of five years, we both left our careers to focus on our family business. Our reputation for high-quality renovations spread, and realtors wanted to sell our properties. Local carpenters began collaborating with us, resulting in several partnerships.

As our reputation grew, so did the number of people eager to join us. This led to a flurry of projects and partners, yet the real estate market began to shift drastically. Real estate prices were inflated regionally, and buyers weren't biting. Our partners started to feel the pinch in their ventures, and the burden of shared expenses grew heavier. Greed and stress crept in as some partners became desperate to maintain their profits. Some fell behind in their financial contributions, while others perceived that we were financially thriving. One filed a lawsuit against us, claiming he was owed hundreds of thousands. Being forced to hire legal counsel to defend ourselves led to a countersuit and crossclaim, which, under General Law Chapter 93A, allows for triple damages in unfair business practices against us. The partners, already struggling financially, retaliated with another claim, demanding millions in damages.

Despite the mountain of evidence showing that we had invested hundreds of thousands in projects while others contributed less than half of that, the legal battle raged on. We initially spent tens of thousands on attorney fees and had to sell properties to avoid further ruin, some for just a dollar, asking for nothing to prevent dragging others into the mess.

We had lost nearly everything—vehicles, savings, and legal representation. In desperation, we filed for Chapter 7 bankruptcy. Even the bankruptcy was a legal fight. I remember schlepping in legal box after legal box. It felt hollow. We kept scraping together money to pay for bankruptcy.

Meanwhile, our personal home was affected, too, and now we were ready to sell. My husband was paying the dues, literally, and I was paying, in pain, the dues emotionally. I walked through daily life in a sort of delirium, losing chunks of time during the day as if in a daydream, going through the motions without conscious control. Tears spilled out of the corners of my eyes randomly, spontaneously, without control. Every day felt like I sank deeper into an abyss. I had no career, my children had distanced themselves, and I had no sense of who I was anymore. It was as if I'd become a ghost in my own life. I walked through life in a trance, the weight of each setback pressing down on my soul, leaving me numb and untethered. I'd lost everything that once defined me, and I wasn't sure I'd ever find myself again.

Above all, there was the daunting decision of where we would go once the house sold. Concurrently, we needed to figure out how to make this work financially. At this juncture, many decisions weren't entirely up to us.

I went to the ocean that morning, a hollow shell of a human, and to my surprise, visualized my wishes. A calmness washed over me as I watched the waves lap the shore. I closed my eyes and saw myself as a whole—strong and resilient, sharing my story with others for the first time in years. At that moment, I knew I wasn't just meant to survive but to help others find their strength. Unexpectedly, I saw myself in my mind's eye; inspiration flowed out of me and into others. In this vision, I was a motivational speaker, addressing an audience riveted to my every word. I saw myself speaking with passion and flawlessly in my delivery. There was laughter—I must have said something funny, and it struck them. They roared with delight.

I felt peace for the first time in what felt like years.

The sun was blazing hot as I sat in my chair. I opened my eyes briefly and watched the waves roll in, lapping the shoreline with the rhythm of *tshhhh, tshhhh, tshhhh,* back and forth. It was magnificent, and I felt I could conquer the day, put myself in a direction, and move toward the dreams and desires I just discovered were valid for my future. The goals to be obtained were right there, within my reach. I came to a core realization at that moment. I am meant to heal, teach, and serve. I'd always known this, but somehow, it had gotten lost—until now.

I got home in time for the technician to evaluate and service our boiler issues.

Then, upstairs in my office, the phone rang. My realtor was on the other end of the line. The sale fell through; there were no buyers. She yammered on and on about believing, having faith, and hope—that it would be all right.

In an exceptionally soft, quiet voice, I said, "OK, very well. Send over the paperwork, and please, please stop talking." She tried to interject something, but I quickly cut her off and said calmly, "No, nope, please, just stop—not another word, no more discussion, nothing, please. We'll revisit this another day, not today, not tomorrow, sometime soon, OK?"

"But, what about the corner—"

"I need to hang up now. I'm going to say goodbye. Goodbye." Click.

As luck would have it, I called my realtor the next day and expressed our interest in buying a multi-family. She exclaimed, "Wow, 61 Market St. is up for sale! What do you think?"

Securing a loan would be an uphill battle. We approached a local bank known for taking tough cases like ours, and our hopes were high. For the next several weeks, I gathered information, scanned it, and got it to the bank. I explained our hardships verbally, backed up by documents. Oh, the reams of paper. I went in and met with the underwriter. We talked for over an hour as she worked hard to wrap her head around the past eight years of our financial life.

Stunned, she said, "I want you to have this loan. I will work tirelessly to gather the information to present to our Loan Committee. This committee approves or denies under unusual circumstances. Once their decision is made, though, it's almost always final. Having said that, would you please write a narrative of why you went bankrupt? Please gather the following information, and let's meet on Monday."

Of course, I went home, gathered those remaining items, and began the narrative.

Several days later, I sat down at my computer, hoping a new task would refresh me, but again, there was news: our loan had been denied.

The fallout on this day created a completely different result.

The emotional snap took away the spontaneous tears, the dissociative state, the deep seething darkness, and the penetrating fear. I was confronted with my inner strength and refused to sink into sadness and victimhood. There was a calling, an intuitive knowing—a message from the Holy Spirit. I knew it was time for me to step into my power.

In the weeks that followed, we shifted our focus. The house sale became less about escaping the past and more about creating space for the future. And I did know. Deep in my heart, I knew that the roar of my soul was only beginning to be heard. I had walked through fire, and now it was time to rise—stronger, louder, and more alive than ever.

I started working on myself, reconnecting with the part that knew I was meant for more. I began to embrace the belief that everything we had gone through wasn't just a series of setbacks—it was preparation. Each failure, heartbreak, and loss shaped me into the person I was becoming—the person who would step onto that stage and share her roar with the world.

The setbacks, delays, and disappointments weren't the end of the story. They were just chapters in a much bigger book. And I wasn't done writing yet.

The carpenter's lawsuit was eventually dismissed; however, the partners suing for triple damages continued their pursuit. The Bankruptcy Trustee threw out their Chapter 93A claim for lack of merit, and when it finally made it to civil court, it fell apart. After five grueling days of testimony and 15 banker's boxes wheeled in with evidence, their claim for triple damages was denied. Greed had driven their actions, and they left with less than they had initially. We walked away, proving we had done nothing wrong. We fought for our integrity and won, though the cost was immense. But it was time to move on.

The day we finally signed the papers to sell the house felt like a quiet victory. It wasn't the triumphant moment I had once imagined, but it didn't need to be. The real triumph was internal—knowing that I had survived the storm, knowing that I had come out on the other side stronger, more resilient, and more aligned with my true self and my husband.

A quiet peace settled within me as we drove away from that old house. I had fought through fire and emerged stronger, ready to embrace the journey ahead. I knew that my past wasn't just a series of hardships; it was the foundation of my purpose.

I took bold steps, settled on a graduate school program, and completed it, earning licensure as a psychotherapist. I finally found my calling—holding space for others as they step out of their darkness. My pain wasn't just a burden; it was a source of wisdom and strength, a guide to helping others find their way back to themselves. I created a niche specializing in trauma and addictions and added retreats. Now, I look forward to the gift of holding space for others, supporting their goals to heal and recover as they emerge from the darkness and step into the power of knowing who they are and what their hearts desire.

As we drove away from that old house for the last time, I reflected on a saying that has resonated with me for decades: "Believe; everything is possible for him who believes." Mark 9:23 had been my North Star all along. Life is a journey with countless unknowns, but if we hold on, we'll find that even our darkest moments are part of something larger, a path guiding us toward who we are meant to be.

About Carolyn Soto Bell:

Carolyn Bell is a Holistic Licensed Mental Health Counselor (LMHC) and Senior Instructor for the School of Psychological Studies with Cambridge College at Bay Path University. She specializes in trauma and addictions, integrating therapeutic interventions, including DBT, Mindfulness-CBT, Hypnotherapy, and EMDR. As the founder of Carolyn Bell Psychotherapy, LLC, and Roar of the Soul Retreats, Carolyn offers therapy and retreats focused on holistic healing and personal transformation.

Her corporate leadership background includes roles in specialty healthcare and strategic consulting. Before transitioning into psychotherapy, Carolyn was a Sales Training specialist and a Managing Partner in Historical Restoration. She holds an M.Ed. in Counseling Psychology, a BS in Psychology, and diplomas in Clinical, Interpersonal, and Transpersonal Hypnotherapy.

A member of the American Counseling Association and recognized in Marquis Who's Who for her professional achievements, Carolyn is dedicated to helping clients explore their true desires and heal from trauma, empowering them to lead more fulfilling lives through self-discovery.

Survive, Thrive, PTSD, and Addiction

By Jennifer Pechumer

I ask myself almost every day, "How did I endure complex PTSD, starting before the age of four, and overcome 20 years of cross-addiction to opiates and cocaine?" Generally, a person can't come back from that. My story is the difference between the addict still sick and suffering, struggling with mental health issues, and the addict who finds true inner peace. In 2017, the overdose rate was 70,237 people. Tragically, one of those people was my mother. How am I a survivor? Join me on the hero's journey of how I found unconventional therapies like Reiki, massage, and sound and vibrational healing seven years ago, and in turn, found myself. Addiction affects 100% of the population in some way, and I hope my story can help at least one person.

Numerous studies have documented an association between substance use and exposure to psychological trauma. I come from a line of veterans, and most times, that comes with alcoholism or other mental health issues like PTSD. My trauma began between ages zero and four. My mother worked evenings as a bartender, so she wasn't around as much as we needed her to be. My dad was physically abusive to my mother, and he frequently hosted parties around us as kids. As a result, my siblings and I was exposed to alcohol, drugs, and sexual abuse at a very young age. Unfortunately, the deeply dysfunctional family dynamics I experienced as a toddler were suppressed, leaving unresolved challenges beneath the surface.

Although my story of trauma isn't necessarily unique, the fact that I overcame addiction to opiates is. Statistics show that 90% of people with opioid use disorder relapse. I was part of that statistic, with countless relapses and several trips to jail, prison, inpatient, and outpatient therapy. None of these institutions fully deterred me from drug use or a life on the streets. So how am I medication-free, mentally thriving, and nearly six years sober when 90% of the population can barely make it to one year?

Unfortunately, many addicts remain dependent on heavy medications like Suboxone or methadone. My sister has been in a methadone clinic for 10 years, is on several medications, and still struggles with her mental health.

My mother's life was cut short, and my sister's life is one of mere survival. Despite all the times I was involved in the criminal justice system, none of the imposed conditions rehabilitated me. The system failed to stop my self-destructive behaviors or prevent me from hurting myself and my loved ones. I was defeated, considering myself a loss to society.

I vividly remember being in a motel room, crying out to the angels, "I can't do this anymore!" Yet, I continued on the same destructive path, wreaking havoc. Nothing could stop me. Sadly, this is the reality for many men and women caught up in the system, addicted to drugs, and suffering from mental health issues. Recidivism rates remain high. Our souls become fractured, and I truly believe that until I was able to heal my spirit, I could never heal my mind or body. Little did I know, the angels were about to answer my call for help in the most unconventional way.

I wasn't officially diagnosed with C-PTSD by a counselor until I was about 34 years old—the same year my mother died of an accidental overdose. I was absolutely defeated, desperately seeking peace from the devastating effects of childhood trauma, addiction, and the unending cycle of relapses and self-destruction. Conventional rehabilitation methods—counseling, jail time, and medication—could not address the spiritual and emotional void that kept pulling me back to substances.

I sought support from family and NA/AA but still struggled to stay sober. I continued to self-medicate, numbing the pain. It felt like looking at a massive puzzle with one crucial piece missing. I reached a point where death felt inevitable, just another statistic like my mom. Yet somehow, my story took a different path—a path of survival and sovereignty.

In losing everything, I felt a faint flicker of resolve—there had to be something beyond this darkness. I was utterly lost until a surprising encounter with Reiki and energy healing began to help me rise from rock bottom.

After losing my mother, a coworker mentioned Reiki, and I immediately felt a strong pull toward it. I scheduled an appointment and soon found myself lying on a Reiki practitioner's table. Within the first five minutes of the session, I began to cry uncontrollably, almost like having a panic attack. I thought to myself, "Why am I crying? What is happening?"

The practitioner's hands hovered above specific areas of my body, occasionally making subtle movements. After the session, I stood up, feeling dizzy, and asked her why. She explained that my crown chakra had been blocked and that universal life force energy was now flowing through me. That initial healing stirred something deep inside me. It wasn't a magical wand that suddenly fixed everything, but it was the beginning of my shadow work.

"My dominoes began to fall," and it was profoundly uncomfortable. That year, I had my first near-death experience by overdosing, went to jail, and conceived my second child. Using drugs was no longer an option. It was as if the angels had a plan, leaving breadcrumbs to guide me in a new direction. I later learned that Reiki helped release deep-seated emotional trauma, allowing for profound healing. Years of abandonment, neglect, and sexual abuse had left my chakras void of crucial life force energy.

The word "chakra" comes from Sanskrit, meaning "spinning wheel." Each chakra is a spinning wheel pulling in a specific color from the light spectrum, with an element, emotion, and organ system attached to that center. For example, the sacral chakra is part of the organ system which controls the reproductive system and is located just below the navel. The sacral chakra is said to govern creativity, sexual energy, pleasure, and intimacy. Experiencing sexual trauma can disrupt the flow of energy in the sacral chakra, often leading to the expression of negative emotions and behaviors. When the orange light in this energy center becomes distorted, it creates an imbalance that leaves us feeling disconnected from our sensuality and emotional selves. Perhaps this explains why, at 19, I felt so confused about my self-worth and allowed my body to be exploited.

I received my second Reiki healing when I was about three months pregnant, living in a trailer with my son's father. By pure chance, my Reiki practitioner was my neighbor—a remarkable coincidence! I found myself casually lying on her couch for a session that brought profound releases, helping me confront deep-seated traumas traditional therapies couldn't touch. This experience strengthened my divine connection to Source and allowed me to access parts of myself buried during my 15+ years entangled in the criminal justice system.

Little did I know how priceless her words during that session would later become. June, my practitioner, prophesied two things that day. She told me I would have a baby girl—which I did—and that I should study at Irene's Myomassology Institute. I asked her, "What is that?" She replied, "A school to learn massage and the sacred healing arts." Instantly, I knew she was right. My inner pilot light was ignited, and I never forgot that moment. A blend of karma and destiny had crossed paths. I walked through destiny's door that day, and karma was waiting to greet me.

The reality was, I was pregnant, addicted to drugs, and had no idea what I was doing. I've had to overcome an enormous amount of shame about my thought process during that time. I used more drugs, thinking a miscarriage would make everything better. You know the old saying, "It's always darkest before dawn?" That was my rock bottom.

I gave birth on December 1, 2018, to a beautiful baby girl. The hospital took her and placed her in the ICU because she had several toxins in her bloodstream. I am not proud of this moment, but she was my saving grace. To this day, I deeply regret that I ever hurt my innocent children, but it shows how easily cycles of trauma and addiction can repeat. Healing is a journey, not a destination, and I will always have more work to do. However, my daughter became the powerful catalyst that pushed me toward sobriety.

After CPS took custody of my children, my inner fire was lit to battle this demon called addiction. I began to recognize my worth and reclaim my sense of self. Mind, body, and spirit were fully committed to the fight, and I am proud to write that my sobriety date is January 8, 2019!

With "God of the Angel Armies by my side," I could focus on two things: regaining custody of my two beautiful children and studying massage and energy medicine at Irene's. Energy medicine is based on the idea that the body is made of vibrating molecules, defined as a collection of practices that balance the body's energy flow. I couldn't believe the science behind the sacred healing arts and their positive effects on trauma and addiction. Where had this been my whole life? I can only imagine the ways I could've benefited from these healing practices as an adolescent.

I immersed myself in learning and, as the law of attraction would have it, on my 36th birthday, I attended my first sound bath. It was in a beautiful wooden cabin and local to my area. The price for the therapeutic sound meditation was surprisingly very affordable as well. I was only four months into sobriety and in the process of weaning off Suboxone. The sound healing experience was transformative and uplifting. Each crystal singing bowl resonated through the room, filling my light body with pure, musical tones. Any area void of crucial life force energy due to trauma or detoxing was being reorganized, energized, and purified.

With each session, layers of hurt and resentment melted away, replaced by a lightness I had never known—a glimpse of a life I thought was lost. I knew I was on the right path.

Then came the milestone: my first day at Irene's Myomassology Institute! If I could make it this far using alternative healing, anyone could. At this point, I was a person in recovery from heroin and crack cocaine for six months. Although I was heavily weighted down by my open cases in the criminal justice system and detoxing horribly from opiates, nothing could stop me from getting my license as a massage therapist! I was so excited to dive into this new reality and easily stayed firm in my commitment to recovery. My daily mantras were "One day at a time" and the Serenity Prayer.

I felt blessed beyond measure to be exposed to such an expansive world of healing arts at my new school. My classes consisted of one hands on massage by a student every week, which felt amazing, healing decades of trauma stored in my tissues. I explored a variety of energy medicine electives, from Reiki and polarity therapy to herbology and one of my favorites: sound and vibrational healing. Each time I trained in one of these modalities or I received the medicine these modalities had to offer, I found that these practices provided me a transformative path to self-acceptance, inner peace, and sovereignty. They brought me freedom from the trauma that had once controlled my life.

During that time, I had my aura photographed and noticed there was no green in my light spectrum. Recognizing this as a sign that I needed more love, compassion, and forgiveness in my life, I decided to purchase an F-note crystal singing bowl, after all I had recently completed a two day elective on sound and vibrational healing. When I played it, the bowl emitted a green from the light spectrum, filling my heart with the frequency of forgiveness. At that point, I was deeply seeking to forgive—both others and myself—in ways too numerous to detail in this chapter.

A year later, I had another aura photo taken, and there it was—green radiating around my head and feet. That moment reflected the devotion to my healing journey, which later led me to become a licensed massage therapist, Reiki master, and certified sound practitioner. Today, I work with a complete set of eight quartz crystal singing bowls, spanning from a low C to a high C, each one harmonizing perfectly to support and balance my entire light body. I've led numerous sound meditations, and while each one is unique, one thing remains constant: people are always amazed by the profound power of the crystal singing bowls.

Today, nearly six years later, I live a life of stability and purpose as a full-time mother of my two beautiful children. I am fully employed, sober, and at peace. Nobody talks about trauma like we do now, and with each client, I share the knowledge that helped me find freedom.

I must advocate for all those voices who never even got a chance to heal or be heard. My story of trauma may not be special but my quest is a testament to the power of alternative healing for emotional and spiritual recovery where conventional methods fell short. It's a hero's journey of survival, resilience, and transformation—one that inspires others to explore the possibilities of a holistic approach, offering a lifeline to those facing addiction and PTSD.

Every time I help someone find their center, I remember my own first steps toward healing. It's a reminder of the beauty of this journey and the strength I found within. I'm honored to give others what I was once given: hope, relief, and a way out of the dark.

The wisdom I offer is this: don't give up! I survived a traumatic childhood, years of substance abuse, and devastating loss. Yet through Reiki, sound therapy, and other energy practices, I am sovereign. These modalities helped me reconnect with myself and led to lasting sobriety and a new purpose as a healer.

You don't need to endure a difficult experience or possess special healing abilities to access the grace these practices offer the soul. As they become increasingly recognized in the mainstream, I truly believe every person on Earth should experience at least one healing attunement. After all, isn't this the return of Christ consciousness? Beginning your journey to wholeness is as simple as reaching out to a certified practitioner. You may begin now.

The holy man is not special; the holy man is simply that—he is whole. May your journey to wholeness be abundant and blessed.

By Jennifer Pechumer:

Jennifer Pechumer, originally from Grand Rapids, Michigan, now resides in Metro Detroit. A devoted mother, she is a licensed massage therapist, Reiki master, and certified sound practitioner passionate about helping others heal and transform. She specializes in chakra alignment and clearing through techniques like voice toning and sound healing meditations with therapeutic instruments.

A graduate of the Irene Myomassology Institute, Jennifer further refined her skills through an apprenticeship and has three years of professional experience. She was nominated for Therapist of the Year in 2022. Once labeled a convicted felon, Jennifer has completely transformed her life, embracing her gift for healing and finding purpose in her work.

Jennifer's dream is to bridge the criminal justice system and mental health, advocating for alternative healing methods to complement counseling and recovery programs.

Facebook: @JenniferpechumerLMT

Email: **Singottattune@gmail.com**

A Walk Through the Trees to the Sea

By Jill Perrin

It's 2019, and I am beginning my 16th year as a music educator. The school year did not start as a normal year, as I had just lost my dad and was planning a funeral. My story begins with a deeply challenging time—the loss of my father while trying to start a new school year as a music educator. Losing my dad felt like losing my anchor, and I was adrift, struggling to ground myself in a job that once brought me joy. He was the one constant in my life I could turn to, the person I could confide in to say all the things I wanted to say in sticky situations and to advocate for myself. At this time, I did not have the confidence to do so without him. I also had to take care of my mother, who was not doing well either after losing her husband. I became the caregiver and counselor for her. I didn't mind, but I put my own grief on the back burner.

Amid my grief, I found solace in a budding relationship with Dan, who brought a sense of peace and comfort, even as I continued to navigate the changing dynamics of teaching in the pandemic era.

Let us jump to the 2020–2021 school year. Teaching music online was interesting. Some families felt that music, art, and PE were not necessary times to be online, so I had some classes where students either weren't there or were present but not paying attention. How was I going to inspire and motivate my students? How was my music training going to help students not only learn but also feel safe in school, however that was going to look? By the end of the year, I could tell my profession was changing, and I did not feel the same as I did at the beginning of my teaching career some 17 years earlier.

As pressures mounted and the educational landscape shifted, I started to question my purpose, feeling disillusioned as budget cuts and undervaluation of the arts affected me profoundly. I feared that what I once thought was a valued subject was becoming dispensable. Believe me, the fight to give more weight to the arts had been ongoing for much longer than this one year, but the direction things were going felt like an uphill battle I was losing. I was getting tired of fighting.

By the 2022–2023 school year, I found myself hating my job. The beginning of the school year was just as difficult as it was in 2019. On the same day that my father passed away, my mom also passed away—four years to the day. She left this world, and I faced yet another emotionally taxing start to the school year. The year was just not joyful to start, and this was another blow to my emotional wellness. The environment I was working in was not healthy for me. I felt defeated daily, exhausted most days, and this was not conducive to accomplishing anything meaningful.

I was tired of defending all that was important to me and of trying to help others feel peaceful and safe by teaching them how music is integral to learning. I was crying daily, and music started to feel like an enemy rather than the healing force it had always been in my life. Each song I taught seemed to drain a little more from me, leaving me hollow and with nothing left for myself. I was holding space for everyone to make myself feel better, when I should have been giving myself grace and permission to listen to what my body and mind needed. I was haunted by the thought that if I didn't meet every expectation, I'd lose the respect and validation I'd spent years building.

At the same time, I was working as a mentor to other educators across the state. This work was rewarding but also draining. I came to the realization that I was not happy. I wasn't sleeping, and it was easier to be angry and isolate myself from my interests, the people I cared for, and most importantly, myself. How does that work, you may ask? To be honest, it was easy. I ignored my needs and happiness, focusing solely on others. I was good at playing the role of problem solver, and no one would have guessed I was exhausted, unhealthy, and unwell.

This had to change. My personal life was filled with amazing things, and home was a comforting place, but I knew I had to return to work the next day, which prevented me from fully enjoying it. When my doctor told me I needed a break, it felt both terrifying and liberating—it was the first time someone gave me permission to put myself first. She made me realize it was OK to step back and take care of myself. Put me first! This was exceedingly difficult to do, but I did it. I promptly took a leave of absence. Eight weeks to focus on me, and focus is exactly what I did. I did not miss what I had been doing up until this much-needed break.

Determined to rediscover joy and purpose, I embarked on a journey of self-care and exploration. Taking a break from teaching allowed me to reconnect with music in a new way, as I began studying sound healing with Life Changing Energy. It allowed me to fall in love with music all over again—not as a duty, but as a tool to fill my own cup first.

The answer became clear: I would take early retirement and become who I was meant to be.

This journey introduced me to the profound effects of sound and energy, helping me find not only self-empowerment but also a new calling in holistic healing. Practicing sound healing and receiving feedback from others, I grew into a healer who understands the value of creating a space for others to heal while nurturing myself. I slept peacefully throughout this break, and the study of sound healing made me feel like myself again. I loved what I was doing, and even my health issues began to lessen. My body and mind were improving—a welcome and long-overdue feeling!

I took this process slowly at first. I wasn't in a hurry because I wanted to feel comfortable and confident in this new work. As I completed modules and earned certifications, I practiced my craft, received feedback from others, and developed my own style. This journey went through several changes, and the people I practiced on were incredibly helpful. I began to understand how my clients were feeling, and I could sense what they needed. It was a great experience to see them relax, focus, and take something positive from the sessions. Mind you, not everyone experiences sound healing in the same way. I had to remind myself not to take it personally if someone didn't have a profound or noticeable experience after a session.

For the first time, I let my intuition lead, discovering my voice not just as a teacher but as a healer. I began sharing this with more people, and it was time to hold space and bring my new business to life. My friend and aesthetician had a yoga studio attached to her skincare business, and she shared many inspiring stories about how she started her business. Encouraged, I asked if I could host a sound bath in her studio. She was incredibly supportive and excited, offering me the space for free for my first session. She wanted me to have an opportunity to share my work with her clients and attract potential clients for myself.

The night of my first session came, and unfortunately, my friend was the only one in attendance. However, I realized this was not unfortunate at all. It gave me the chance to practice in a larger space and experience my own healing. Yes, as a healer, I also need time for my own healing and grounding. Holding a sound bath for myself and the one person in attendance was, quite honestly, perfect.

I continued to host sessions at this wonderful space, and attendance slowly grew. I had many conversations with people about the best times and days for sessions. This feedback was helpful, and I also realized my own energy felt better at certain times. I moved my sessions from a weeknight to Sunday mornings, which turned out to be a great fit for both clients and my energy. My first few months of retirement from teaching were busy but deeply satisfying.

During this time, I also got married and officially launched my new business: **Purple Frog Vibrations and Healing**. The name reflects two things I love—frogs and the color purple. A former student studying graphic design even created my logo, which made it feel even more special. Creating **Purple Frog Vibrations** felt like coming home to myself—finally, a space where my passion, intuition, and love of music could thrive. The connections I was making were authentic, and I knew there were even more waiting to show up. Each session, each sound bath, is an opportunity to remind others that they, too, can find the strength to rewrite their own stories.

By the fall of 2023, I had been working on all aspects of my personal and intuitive journey. I had the honor of reconnecting with a woman I went to college with. She, too, was a former music teacher and now works in her own energetic healing business. I had been following her on Facebook and was intrigued by her offers to help people use their energy to heal themselves and gain empowerment. This was yet another great opportunity for me to grow as an entrepreneur. Working with Brenda Winkle Empowerment has been a big part of my journey, along with Life Changing Energy and Vickie Gould.

I now know that I am strong, talented, and beautiful inside and out. What I do as a healer is so important. My goal is to offer energetic healing to people who are ready to fill their cups to the top with self-love and create abundance and peace in their lives. Through sound healing, Reiki, and my work as an empowered empath entrepreneur, I am confident my clients will leave sessions knowing they are strong, confident, and beautiful. Their walk through the trees to the sea—whatever that represents for them—is real and achievable, just as mine was.

I make it a point to walk on the beach as often as I can. The vibration and energy of the beach and water is my happy place.

Since beginning my healing journey, my business has felt aligned and rewarding. There is growing interest in what I do, and I've had exciting opportunities to collaborate with other healers. Reflecting on this book has opened my eyes to how much I have grown as a healer, friend, wife, and business owner. My husband and I currently have two homes, and I am thrilled to be able to host sound healing sessions in both amazing places.

I want to thank Vickie Gould for her incredible sound healing programs. Life Changing Energy has been a huge part of my transformation. I also want to give a shoutout to Brenda Winkle Empowerment—how wonderful to reconnect with a friend from years ago. My Reiki training and breathwork practice have been integral to my healing and inspiration, guiding me to become who I am meant to be.

The creation of **Purple Frog Vibrations and Healing** represents a shift from a life of service to others to one of mutual healing. I now help clients find peace, balance, and self-love. If you'd like to connect with me, follow **Purple Frog Vibrations and Healing** on Facebook or **purple_frog_vibes** on Instagram.

About Jill Perrin:

Jill Perrin is a certified sound healer and retired music educator with 25 years of experience teaching kindergarten through 5th grade, including 10 years as a modern band instructor. As the owner of Purple Frog Vibrations and Healing, Jill helps clients find relaxation and grounding through the soothing vibrations of sound. Her certifications include Usui Reiki Level 1, Sound Healing Fundamentals, Expert-Level Sound Healing, and Vocal Vibrations. She specializes in crystal bowls, tuning forks, and Tibetan bowls.

Jill facilitates sound healing sessions in Colorado and California, with plans to offer online sessions soon. Through her work, she guides clients toward peace and clarity in their busy lives.

Outside her healing practice, Jill enjoys travel, fiber arts, and music. She lives with her husband and two Boston terriers, Doozer and MJ. Connect with Jill on Facebook at Purple Frog Vibrations and Healing or Instagram @purple_frog_vibes. Email: purplefrogsounds@gmail.com.

From Darkness into Light
By Mary Sue Dale

One afternoon, I was sitting at my desk in my office. I turned around, looking out the window at the sky. It was a beautiful day—the kind with that gorgeous blue sky somewhere between baby blue and ocean blue, scattered with big fluffy clouds you could capture in your mind like photographs. I was so happy. I hadn't felt this happy in a very long time. I was almost giddy.

I quickly spun around in my chair and retrieved some of my mom's stationery from twenty years ago. I smelled the paper—it had that distinct old paper smell. Not musty or moldy, but like a well-loved book. I held it up to the window and noticed it was the same color as the sky outside. Smiling, I began writing letters to each of my children and grandchildren. With every letter I wrote, I became more excited. I told them how much I loved them, how much they had meant to me over the years, and what I wanted each of them to have of mine, explaining why those things were so meaningful to me.

After all these years, I couldn't get over how excited and happy I felt, especially since I had been depressed for most of my life. I knew tonight would be the night I could take my own life—for real this time.

I put each letter in a separate envelope and addressed them to my children and grandchildren. Confident that I had said everything I needed to, I went to the bathroom and looked through the medicine cabinet. I believed that if I combined enough pills—several different kinds, along with a brand-new bottle of aspirin—it would do the trick.

That night, before my husband came to bed, I placed my clothes neatly by my side of the bed and turned off the light. As I waited in the darkness, with a faint stream of light filtering through the edge of the shade, I could feel the weight of a lifetime pressing down on my chest. The pressure from years of despair, loneliness, pain, and anguish was about to end. It was as if the shadows were swallowing me whole, leaving no glimmer of light.

My husband finally came to bed and fell asleep. I knew he wouldn't take long to drift off, but I wanted to be certain he was sound asleep before I made my move. Quietly, I slipped out of bed, went to the bathroom to get dressed, and gathered the pills I had hidden earlier.

With the pills in hand, I went to my office and grabbed my CD player, already loaded with one of my favorite meditation CDs. Then I went downstairs, stopped by the cupboard where I kept my liquor, and poured myself three shots of Crown Royal. The first burned a little and smelled unpleasant, but I managed to down it in two gulps. I was never one for taking shots. The next two went down a bit easier.

I grabbed a bottle of water, went out to the garage, and got into my Chrysler LeBaron. Putting on my headphones, I poured handfuls of pills into my hand, swallowing them one by one with water. Handful after handful, until they were gone. I sat back, covered myself with a blanket, and waited to drift off. In that fleeting sense of calm, I thought my story was ending—but instead, it was about to unfold in ways I couldn't imagine.

The next thing I knew, I was awake and looking around. Oh, hell—why didn't it work? I was so disappointed and once again felt like a failure. My mind was in a strange, fuzzy state, almost like a dream. For a moment, I wondered, *Is this it? Did I succeed?* But as I opened the car door and stood up, everything came pouring out of me—pee, poop, sweat. I couldn't stop it. The sensation was weird, uncomfortable, and overwhelming.

I felt almost drunk, not fully present. Could I have been so close to leaving this world? Did I change my mind, or did someone—or something—intervene, deciding I wasn't done with what I was sent here to do? At that moment, I felt there had to be a reason I was still here.

Somehow, I managed to get back upstairs, rinsed my clothes repeatedly, and tossed them in the laundry basket. I grabbed some sweats and went back downstairs. By then, it was after four in the morning. I lay on the couch, covering myself with a blanket. Sleep wouldn't come. I just lay there, wondering—what went wrong? Or maybe… what went right?

Was I still here because I was meant to be? Was it possible someone else needed me? Could everything I'd been through serve a purpose—to help someone else make it through their own struggles?

Around seven a.m., I turned on the TV but couldn't focus on anything. My body felt like it was spinning one way and then the other. My husband came downstairs and asked what was going on. He mentioned that he'd noticed I wasn't in bed when he got up during the night. I told him I wasn't feeling well, probably coming down with the flu.

I stayed on the couch as long as I could. When he went to take a shower, I crawled upstairs and collapsed into bed. My stomach felt excruciatingly painful. Around eleven, he came in and showed me a pill he'd found lying next to the car door. "What did you do?" he asked.

I dodged his question, asking where he'd found it. He suggested taking me to the hospital, but I convinced him it was too late for that now, saying too much time had passed since I'd taken the pills. That explanation made sense to him, though I wasn't entirely sure it was true. He did insist on scheduling an appointment with my psychiatrist.

The earliest appointment we could get was three days later, which worked out since it took me that long to feel well enough to get out of bed. My husband insisted on coming with me.

By then, I had realized that the strange sensations I'd experienced might have been caused by the new antidepressants I was on. I'd never felt that way with any other medication. When I saw my psychiatrist, he agreed it was likely the new prescription. He decided to switch me to a different antidepressant and recommended that I go to an inpatient facility.

He called several facilities, but none had any available beds. So, we went home, and like so many others, I fell through the cracks.

A few weeks later, I knew I needed to get back to work. I reached out to one of the agencies I typically worked with and found a traveling med tech job in Alaska. I'd always wanted to go there, especially because being near water had always been so healing for me.

I took the job in Sitka and began working at the local hospital. After a week, I called my husband, crying. I told him I couldn't do it—I was scared and lonely. He encouraged me to give it more time, so I did.

I stayed in Sitka for a month before they needed me to work at one of their clinics in Haines. That change turned out to be the best thing for me.

My house overlooked the bay, and my favorite place became the Eagle Preserve, which had a river running through it. It was the most beautiful place I had ever seen. The eagles were majestic—free and resilient. That preserve became my happy place. My best memory there was the day after a snowstorm, with the trees blanketed in white and the river flowing peacefully. Eagles perched on logs, drying their wings or swooping down to fish. I went there almost every weekend during my four-month stay in Alaska.

While in Alaska, I began to feel calmer and more at peace. However, I knew soaking up the wilderness alone wasn't enough to heal completely. I needed to find a deeper, more sustainable path to healing.

After returning home, I realized I had already begun my healing journey. I reached out to a friend and asked if she knew anything about Reiki. I had come across it during my research but wasn't sure what it entailed. To my surprise, she had just become a Reiki Master.

We arranged a time for an attunement, and I received my Reiki Level One certification. While I appreciated the experience, I didn't feel a strong connection with her teaching style. I decided to search for someone else nearby to continue my training.

Through the Reiki International website, I found Jill, who taught Reiki Levels One and Two. She also mentioned animal Reiki, which immediately intrigued me. Unfortunately, Jill wouldn't be teaching it for another six months, and I didn't want to wait that long.

Through the same site, I discovered Kathy in Wisconsin. We connected instantly. I took her online Animal Reiki Levels One and Two courses, and later that summer, she offered an in-person Reiki Master program. I signed up, and the experience was incredible. During that attunement, I felt the energy stronger than ever before.

When I returned home, I began practicing Reiki on my two dogs, and they loved it—especially Sasha, our oldest Shih Tzu. She would come to me when she needed a healing session, and it brought her comfort. My daughter and I were there with her, offering Reiki, when she passed. Ellie, our other dog, also sought out Reiki sessions when she needed them.

We later brought a new puppy into our home and quickly realized she was terrified of loud noises like thunder and fireworks. I used Reiki to calm her, and it worked beautifully. Even my husband noticed how much it helped the dogs and would bring them to me when they seemed distressed. Still, he never believed Reiki was for him.

As I practiced more, I began feeling better myself. A sense of calm washed over me—like releasing a breath I didn't realize I had been holding. It was a quiet reminder that healing was within reach.

I wanted to share the benefits of Reiki with others. To practice, I enlisted my daughter, her girlfriend, and a few close friends. Seeing the relief and calm on their faces after a session filled me with a sense of purpose I had been searching for. It was then I realized that my struggles had led me to a calling: helping others heal.

I began to dream about starting my own Reiki practice. However, my husband wasn't particularly supportive. We didn't communicate much about my aspirations. I tried Reiki on him once, but he said he didn't feel anything and dismissed it. His reaction made me doubt my abilities and whether I was worthy of helping others. Who was I to help someone else heal when I wasn't fully healed myself?

Still, I believed Reiki was helping me. I continued searching for other healing modalities to explore, hoping to find even more ways to grow.

One weekend, a friend invited me to an online workshop to create vision boards. I had made one before, so I thought, *Why not?* They were always helpful. The woman leading the workshop, Mindy, was a life coach. At the time, I didn't know what a life coach did, but we set up a meeting after the workshop, and I joined her Dream Builders group.

Joining that group turned out to be one of the best decisions I ever made. I met amazing people and learned so much about myself. I learned how to forgive—especially myself. I learned how to dream, to envision what I wanted and needed in my life, how I could help others, and, most importantly, how to be happy.

Through this process, I discovered my true desires and how to bring them to life. One of the first dreams I wrote down was to write an award-winning book. I am thrilled to say that dream is on the verge of becoming a reality.

During this time, I also explored other healing classes. Thanks to the internet, I discovered Brett, who taught magical awakening healing methods and psychic Reiki. I also took a course on Ho'oponopono and became certified in all of them.

I love learning, and my journey didn't stop there. I found Vickie online and began studying sound healing under her guidance. She was an incredible teacher, and I soon started integrating sound healing with Reiki. This combination brought tremendous strides in my own healing process.

For me, the synergy of Reiki and sound healing has been transformative. I haven't felt depressed in years. While I still experience sadness sometimes, it's no longer an unbearable heaviness. I finally feel worthy of my place in this life.

One of the most important lessons I've learned is that healing yourself must come first if you want to help others heal. We are all here to heal, learn, and support one another, sharing the wisdom we gain along the way.

My ultimate goals are to finish my book, turn it into an award-winning movie, and use the proceeds to build Holistic Healing Centers and 55+ communities. I also dream of finding a partner who believes in me, shares my passions, and loves spending time with me as much as I do with him.

By achieving these goals, I can help others heal and become the best versions of themselves, just as I continue striving to be the best version of me. We are all here to learn and teach one another. My advice? Learn something new every day.

About Mary Sue Dale:

Mary Sue Dale has embraced many roles throughout her life, but her most cherished is being a mother. Her career began in the 1970s as a waitress at Mister Donut in Burnsville, MN, followed by 13 years in the circuit industry. She later pursued a long-standing career as a Medical Laboratory Technician, which spanned nearly 30 years.

Mary Sue's passion for healing led her to become a Reiki Master Practitioner, Animal Reiki Practitioner, and Sound Healer, alongside exploring various other healing modalities. She is also a writer, with her debut book set to release in early 2025.

Recently certified as a travel agent with Archer Travel and Evolution Travel, she has found a way to weave her love of travel into her journey. Mary Sue continues to grow, learn, and embrace life, dedicated to healing herself and others while cultivating self-love and a zest for life.

Life Changing Transformation
By Kerry Martin

This was the worst time of my life—I was 28. I had a 3-year-old child. I was married for three years to the father of my child. I was an addict and alcoholic—not just your run-of-the-mill excessive drinker. Before and during my marriage, I was using drugs consistently but managed to conceal it from my family (or so I told myself). I had trauma issues and grew up with generational trauma.

After my divorce, a judge ruled that I could not see my child without supervision and that I had to be drug tested. This decision brought me to a very dark place. The darkness consumed me. My soul was drowning. I used hard drugs and drank daily. I was existing, not really living, trapped in a hell of my own making. I didn't care what happened to me—period. Knowing I had let my life spiral to the point where I couldn't see my child broke me. I couldn't see a way back. My use of alcohol and drugs altered my personality and behavior in negative ways.

If you have felt this kind of pain and darkness, you know it's hard to describe. I could not breathe. I didn't dare stop or stay sober enough to think about my beautiful, beloved little girl. If I did, I feared it would destroy me, yet I felt powerless to stop it. So, I kept slowly killing myself, punishing myself day after day.

I had nowhere to live. One of my old coworkers let me stay in their basement. It was dark, musty, and had no real windows. I slept on a small mattress on the floor. I didn't care—I felt this was what I deserved. I worked in a bar that reeked of stale smoke, vomit, and old beer, frequented by local bikers. It was loud, raunchy, and filled with plenty of opportunities to stay drunk and high.

I met other people who were on similar dark paths. I spent meaningless time with these people. It didn't matter who they were or what they did. I didn't want to change what was happening. I couldn't even try. Eventually, I lost my job. I didn't care. I found another job in a darker, more dangerous bar. It was worse than the last place. I continued my downward spiral. Every night was the same: numbing myself with whatever was available. I lost that job too. Whether I left or was fired, it didn't matter. Nothing mattered—my world was gone.

I left my friend's basement and lived in my car. It was an old car but good enough to drive me to a different area of the state to continue on my spiral. I couldn't find a job in my condition. Instead, I hustled on the streets, stealing items from stores and pawning them for money to buy drugs and alcohol. My car was cold at night, and I couldn't keep it running all night. Finding places to park without being bothered by cops or security guards was a constant challenge. I used public restrooms in restaurants or donut shops. I had no contact with my family anymore. My parents didn't even know if I was alive.

Obviously, I wasn't paying taxes or keeping my car registration current, so eventually, my car was towed. I couldn't afford to get it out. I was truly living on the streets now, sleeping wherever I could. Eating whenever I could, mostly snacks from bodegas. Food wasn't a priority. The priority was running from the pain and trying to forget. This went on for months.

One morning, I went to a local grocery store to steal batteries and disposable cameras. This was before everyone had a cell phone with a camera. I had done this before. I felt sick but kept going. I got caught by security. Instead of giving up or going quietly and not getting in too much trouble, I resisted. I strongly resisted. I tried to get away by hitting and kicking. I really fought. I ran. I got caught and arrested.

I was in a local jail. I had no money and couldn't post bond. I called my mother. She was glad to know I was alive but said she couldn't help me with money or a lawyer. I got angry because I feared what would happen next. I hung up on her.

After about 24 hours, I was transferred to the state's only large women's prison. It was shocking and scary. I had experience with the streets and other addicts, but I had never been to prison. The drugs and alcohol were wearing off, and I was terrified to deal with reality. My heart was racing, and so was my mind. I was placed in a plexiglass holding cell with six other women. They all looked like they hadn't taken care of themselves in a while. I'm sure I looked the same. Some paced and shouted for the corrections officers (COs), but the officers didn't respond. We waited to be processed.

Processing was as unpleasant as it looks in the movies. Everything I had was taken from me. I had to take a cold shower. The water felt like razor blades on my skin. Female COs ensured I wasn't carrying any substances on or in my body. I was given an inmate number and a prison-gray sweatsuit. I quickly learned to never forget that number. It became my identity.

I spent more than a couple of weeks detoxing from substances. It was awful. I felt like I was dying. I couldn't get out of bed. My bed was a used twin mattress on the floor of a gym with at least 100 other women. The prison was overcrowded, and we were called "overflow." I could barely think, much less hold a conversation. My body rebelled after years of abuse. No one wanted to be near me because of all the vomiting and other unpleasant side effects. It was a slow, painful process.

Eventually, I was transferred to a shared cell—a room with bunk beds, a metal toilet, sink, and desk. It was New Year's Eve, 2000—Y2K. Gossip circulated that at midnight, all the computers would malfunction, and the cell doors would open. It never happened. At midnight, the women simply shouted. I spent that night in disbelief, thinking about how far I'd fallen. I had once imagined celebrating the year 2000 in a much different way. Now I was locked in a cell, forced to confront the full weight of my poor choices. The walls mirrored the mental prison I had built for myself, reinforced by denial and self-loathing.

A few months went by. I started to think clearly. I remembered my life before substances. I was a smart student. I loved to read. I liked to write. So, I got a job in prison—the best job you could get there. I landed it because I could type. Since these jobs were highly coveted, they were usually reserved for lifers—the women serving long or life sentences. We received separate lunches and a few other privileges. I was trained by a convicted murderer serving 45 years. I was intimidated but refused to show fear.

Because of this job, I was housed with women serving the longest sentences. We lived in a section called Zero Building. It was nerve-wracking. I kept to myself and avoided the drama. I read constantly, walked around the prison yard, and began taking care of myself as best I could. I started reading about mindfulness, meditation, and yoga.

At one point, I had dreamed of a future filled with purpose, but as I sat alone in my cell, that vision felt like a distant, painful memory. This was the darkest of dark places, yet it was also where a flicker of hope began to stir. For the first time, I faced the uncomfortable truth: I had created this reality. And if I created it, maybe I could uncreate it too.

This was a new concept to me. I started to think differently.

It was life-changing.

I realized I had brought myself to this point. No matter how dysfunctional my family or upbringing was, I had made the bad choices that led me here. This was my karma. I began to meditate and get quiet. I learned to be present in the moment. I thought about my life up until that point, realizing that it had been on a downward spiral since I started drinking in junior high. I wondered if I could truly change that negative trajectory. I still couldn't think about my daughter. The fear of what those thoughts might do to me kept her out of my mind. Yet, as I watched women around me stuck in similar cycles, I began to ask myself: Could I be different? Could I escape the life I had created?

This became a pivotal moment in my journey. I am sharing it because I want others to know that anything is possible. You can be at the lowest point in your life and still find your way back to your true self and your family. Every mindful breath, every moment of stillness in prison, became a promise to myself. I would create a life worth living—a life my daughter could be proud of.

I finished my prison sentence and was released to a halfway house. I found a job doing makeup at the mall. The halfway house wasn't much better than prison. Almost everyone there was trying to get drugs or meet up with their boyfriends or girlfriends, falling right back into old patterns. Those things hadn't worked before, so why would they work now? I left the halfway house.

I moved into a tiny, rundown apartment near downtown. I relied on public transportation and kept to myself, avoiding unhealthy relationships and old habits. Still, I avoided thinking about my daughter. I was terrified of facing my family and the pain I had caused them. But I also knew I couldn't keep running from the sadness and brokenness. I had to confront what I had left behind. If I didn't, it would destroy me. The years ahead were some of the hardest of my life.

During those years, I continued to struggle. I worked in the restaurant industry, which may not have been the best environment for me, but it was what was available. I moved between different restaurant jobs and fell into a few relationships I had no business being in—more distractions from the work I needed to do. Still, I tried to hold on to the lessons I had learned in prison. Meditation and mindfulness became my lifeline.

Eventually, I grew tired of struggling. I began reading more books on mindfulness, yoga, and meditation. I started practicing daily, even if only for short periods. This became my way of adapting—my way of facing life and slowing down. Gradually, I began to think about my daughter. It was painful, but I knew it was necessary. I was moving forward in positive ways, taking on more responsibilities, and building a better life.

Here is how I did it: **I forgave myself.** Forgiving myself was the most challenging—and most crucial—step of all. Without it, I would have remained chained to my past. This didn't mean ignoring the damage I had caused. On the contrary, I made amends wherever and whenever I could. Over time, I reconnected with my daughter. Seeing her regularly became the most rewarding part of my life. Slowly, we built a relationship we are both proud of. Being part of her life is the most remarkable thing I've ever done.

While I was healing, I used the following tools to create the life I live today. These tools helped me earn an official pardon, go back to school, become a Registered Nurse, and work as a Certified Health Coach specializing in helping women:

- Slowing down and getting quiet.
- Journaling regularly.
- Making conscious decisions.
- Meditating and practicing breathwork.
- Chanting and incorporating mindfulness into daily routines.
- Doing something creative every day.
- Setting small, achievable goals and reviewing them weekly.
- Practicing self-care: not working when sick, avoiding overscheduling, and maintaining healthy boundaries.
- Eating balanced, nutritious meals.
- Exercising three times a week but forgiving myself if I missed days.
- Listening to calming music or meditation chants.

- Prioritizing 7–9 hours of sleep each night.

- Creating a dedicated space (no matter how small) for prayer, meditation, and sound therapy.

- Spending time in nature every day.

- Incorporating the elements—fire, water, earth, and air—into my practices.

- Helping others regularly.

I continue these practices even when traveling, especially then. This is not selfish. On the contrary, I am the best mother, grandmother, and partner I can be because of these practices—not in spite of them. I take responsibility for my actions. I strive to be kind to people, animals, and the environment. I'm not perfect; I make mistakes. But I live with gratitude and mindfulness, which often means unlearning what we were taught growing up.

Without the distressing experiences I endured, I'm not sure I would have healed or become a healer. Each woman I help, each story I witness, reminds me of the power we all have to rebuild—one conscious breath at a time. Everyone faces hardships. It doesn't matter what they are; what matters is how we respond. Do we continue down the same path, or do we find better systems to live our best lives? My Wellness Balance System has helped countless women, and it would be my pleasure to help anyone ready to move forward in a positive direction.

Love and light to you!

About Kerry Martin:

Kerry Martin, RN, is a Registered Nurse, Certified Health Coach, and founder of Wise Concierge Wellness LLC, established in 2023. Motivated by the gaps in modern healthcare—particularly the lack of kindness and true self-care—Kerry created a practice centered on holistic well-being and personalized support.

Her Wellness Balance Process integrates evidence-based clinical practices with mindfulness to meet each client's unique needs. Specializing in life transitions, breaking unhelpful patterns, and fostering self-awareness, Kerry empowers clients with tools and strategies for lasting change. She emphasizes the connection between mind, body, and spirit, guiding individuals to embrace conscious self-care practices that fit seamlessly into daily life.

Through her compassionate approach, clients uncover barriers, explore their inner selves, and find paths that align with their heart, achieving balanced and authentic lives.

Kerry lives in Connecticut with her partner of 16 years and their three dogs. Learn more at wiseconciergewellness.com.

Sharing the Light
By Vicki Wissig

Where do I begin? October 31, 1990, when my mom died suddenly at the age of 57. I felt lost and devastated. This couldn't be true. How could I go on without my mom? I was heartbroken and angry at the world. I was having a hard time talking to people—those who offered condolences made me cry and relive it all over again, but if someone didn't say anything, it made me angry, as if they didn't care. My emotions were all over the place. Then, in 1991, I met my wife, who helped me through the healing and grieving process. We married in April 1993 and rented an apartment in her former boss's house. He meditated daily, and you could see the peace radiating from him just by looking at him. When he spoke, you immediately felt calm and serene. He shared his meditation practice with me, including the music he listened to each morning. At first, I wasn't sure if this was something for me. Could sitting still with music really help me cope with my pain? But something about his peaceful demeanor made me want to give it a try.

After our landlord shared the tapes he used for meditation, I went out and bought one for myself. It was filled with crystal sounds, and I just loved it—it took me to a peaceful state I hadn't experienced in a long time. This was the start of my journey into wellness, and what a journey it has been. It continues to this day. I began meditating daily for ten to twenty minutes, and it made an incredible difference. I felt a sense of peace and calmness wash over me. My whole day seemed to flow more smoothly, and I felt more focused and grounded. My wife would wake up, look at me, and say, "I'm so glad you got to meditate today." I asked her how she could tell, and she said it was written all over my face—she could see the peace radiating from me. Feeling so great, I wanted to tell everyone about it so they could feel as good as I did. My only frustration was with guided meditation—I wanted to go deeper, but I could never see the staircase, the beach, or the forest that they described. It was so frustrating to me.

Then I heard about a doctor's office that hosted different events every Tuesday night, introducing topics like numerology, laughter meditation, aura readings, and meditation. I attended the meditation event to find out why I couldn't visualize what guided meditations described. When I explained my struggles, the instructor reassured me that it was perfectly okay—not everyone sees objects during meditation. I told her that instead of staircases or beaches, I mostly saw colors like purple, green, and red. She said that seeing colors was even more difficult than visualizing objects and that I should embrace this gift. She explained that I was likely trying too hard and blocking myself from going deeper. Her advice—"go with the flow and enjoy the journey"—stayed with me. Once I stopped trying so hard to see specific images, I was finally able to go deeper into my meditations, and it was absolutely amazing.

She eventually offered a series of classes, and I eagerly signed up. I was so happy I did. We learned about energy and how everything in the world has it. She introduced us to crystals and taught us about their properties and uses. During one exercise, we were asked to exchange an object with a partner to pick up its energy. I gave my watch, and my partner gave me his ring. We then described what we felt from the other person's object. It was an amazing and eye-opening experience.

Another night at the doctor's office was focused on aura readings. They had a machine that captured your aura and displayed the seven main chakras. I decided to have my aura photographed. Afterward, I committed to meditating every day for at least 15 minutes. A month later, I had my aura photographed again. The difference was unbelievable—my chakras were now perfectly round and balanced, and my aura expanded across the entire image. Seeing such a dramatic transformation confirmed for me that meditation truly works. It opened my mind to endless possibilities.

On my 40th birthday, I received my first crystal bowl in the note of "C" as a gift. I loved playing it and feeling my stress melt away. Over time, I added a few copper bowls to my collection and found myself playing them whenever I felt overwhelmed. Stress was a constant in my life. I was running a busy orthopedic surgeon's office, and my wife was diagnosed with Stage 4 cirrhosis of the liver caused by a fatty liver. During one of her specialist appointments, I received the devastating news that my father had two malignant, inoperable brain masses. He passed away just five weeks later, leaving me to manage his estate. My siblings and I decided to update his house and clean out over forty years of belongings while working full-time jobs. The process lasted almost eight months and was emotionally and physically draining. One night, after hours of sorting through my father's belongings, I felt an unbearable weight. I realized I wasn't just losing another loved one—I was losing myself. I was completely drained—physically, emotionally, mentally, and spiritually—and I wasn't sure how I would get through it.

Finally, we finished the house, and it sold quickly. I knew I needed to recharge, but I didn't know how. I decided to visit Sedona, a place I had always heard about for its powerful energy. It didn't disappoint.

While in Sedona, I visited the vortexes and felt the incredible energy. One day, I was meditating at a vortex with an amethyst stone in my hand when I suddenly felt someone grab my hand. I opened my eyes, but no one was there. Later, a friend who is gifted told me it was my mother. She explained that my mom was protecting me because I was too close to the cliff and also wanted to let me know that everything would be okay—that I was on the right path. That experience reaffirmed my belief in the journey I was on. I also had a channeling session while in Sedona. The channeler told me I was a healer. Back in 1993, after my mom passed away, I visited a medium who told me I had "two health hats"—one in the health field and one in healing. It made sense to me because I have always felt drawn to helping others. My mom often told me to focus on helping one person at a time because I couldn't help everyone at once.

Around this time, I discovered Reiki, a Japanese hands-on healing practice. I started searching for classes and found one nearby. I completed Reiki I and II, followed by Reiki ART (the third level). A couple of years later, I decided to earn my Reiki Master certification. At my first Master class, I reconnected with a young woman I had met at a Reiki healing circle hosted by my teacher. She told me that a conversation we had at one of those circles inspired her to pursue Reiki and that she was now working toward her Master certification. I couldn't remember exactly what I had said to her, but hearing that was incredibly humbling and heartwarming. She had brought her boyfriend to the circles in the past, and I asked if they were still together. She laughed and said no, adding that her current partner was a "keeper" and was also a sound medium. I later attended one of his sound baths, held inside a salt cave. He used copper bowls, gongs, and rattles, and the experience transported me to another place. I knew then that I needed to learn more.

I began teaching Reiki and working with clients, incorporating meditation into sessions or at least encouraging them to try it for themselves. The meditation album my former landlord had shared with me remained one of my favorites, and I often played it during Reiki sessions. Clients found it deeply relaxing and would ask me about it afterward. Over the years, I've helped many people with physical and emotional issues through Reiki. It has been so fulfilling to see others find relief and healing.

I noticed that many clients struggled with emotional pain—phobias, past traumas, and deep fears. Reiki helped immensely, but it also brought me back to the time I was grieving my mother's death. During that time, I read several books on past lives and how they can affect us in the present. One of the wellness centers I attended offered a course on past life regression. Intrigued, I signed up and became certified in past life regression. Learning this new modality added another way to help my clients, as well as my family and friends.

Meanwhile, my wife's health challenges worsened. She had three major back surgeries within two years, with complications after the last one. It was terrifying to see how quickly things could change. While she made some progress over time, her recovery was never complete. Due to the surgeries and other medical conditions, she began falling frequently and has been wheelchair-bound for several years now. Wanting to help her even more, I started taking formal classes in sound healing. She always loved sound baths in the salt cave and enjoyed the bowls I played for her at home. This inspired me to deepen my practice. Over time, I expanded my sound healing toolkit to include crystal bowls, copper bowls, tuning forks, gongs, rattles, drums, and chimes. Performing sound baths has been an incredible experience, with reactions that never cease to amaze me. One man, who had been colorblind his entire life, told me he saw colors for the first time during a session. We were both blown away.

In the past year, my wife received a new diagnosis that has completely changed our lives. Recently, she was hospitalized twice in one week and the third time within the month. The first and last time because she couldn't breathe. The second time was even worse. While in the hospital, she went into respiratory distress, and a code rescue was called. A team of 12 to 15 people worked urgently to save her life. It was one of the scariest moments of my life. In those moments of fear, I turned to the very practices that have supported me through so much—Reiki, sound healing, prayers, and meditation. These tools not only calmed me but also gave me the strength to support her during these crises. I cannot imagine my life without these healing modalities. They keep me calm, grounded, and strong, while allowing me to help others on their journeys as well.

Now, I work with many people through Reiki, sound baths, chakra work, meditation, and sacred ceremonies. My personal journey and the experiences of my clients have made this path truly rewarding. My advice is to go with the flow and enjoy your journey. Whether you're seeking peace, clarity, or purpose, the tools are out there, waiting for you to discover them. Take the first step—you won't regret it.

About Vicki Wissig:

My name is Vicki Wissig and I am a Reiki Master, certified in Sound Healing and Crystals and Chakras. I am in the process of studying and being certified in Sacred Ceremonies, Neurodivergent Sound Healing for kids, Astrology, Ear Seeding and Herbal Essentials.

I also have a full time job in Healthcare for over 30 years, from working in doctor's office to managing every aspect of an orthopedic surgeon's office and now working for hospital doing accounts receivable for physician billing. I am have my CPC, certified professional coder.

My goal is to help and teach as many people as possible with their health with any or many modalities. Would love to help you on your journey to wellness with my teachings and gifts.

516-987-4618 allenergyhealingllc@gmail.com

www.allenergyhealingllc.com

Join my FB group All Energy Healing, LLC

Follow me on FB and Instagram

Breaking Generational Cycles: Reclaiming My Emotional Expression and My Identity

By Ashley Cantor-Birnbaum

To begin, I want to ensure we are all on the same page and provide some definitions you may find as eye-opening as I did. I went through life hearing about emotions, feelings, and words related to them, but I never realized how much value I would find seeing them in black and white. Being able to refer to them during times when I needed to regulate my emotions and reflect was life-altering.

Emotions: "... originate as sensations in the body, are intense feelings (exhilaration, terror, despair) that last only seconds to minutes. They are controlled by chemicals our brains release in response to a trigger or event." -Spencer, M. (2022)

"Emotions are active mental processes that can be managed, so long as individuals develop the knowledge and skills to do so."- Brackett, M., Delaney, S., & Salovey, P. (2024)

Feelings: "While emotions start as sensations in the body, feelings are generated from our thoughts about those emotions. Feelings are how we interpret emotions and let them sink in….they can be diluted or distorted by the stories we've unconsciously created based on past events or experiences."- Spencer, M. (2022)

Emotional Intelligence: "..the capacity for recognizing our own feelings and those of others, for motivating ourselves, and for managing emotions well in ourselves and in our relationships"- Goleman, D. (1995). The five components are self-awareness, self-regulation, motivation, empathy, and social skills.

Emotional Competence: "... the skillful application of emotional intelligence in daily life"-Goleman, D. (1995)

Emotional Self-Efficacy: "... is the belief in one's ability to successfully manage emotional experiences influencing how individuals cope with challenges and stress" (Schroeder et al., 2010; Pfitzner-Eden, 2016).

Emotional Resilience: "...the process and outcome of successfully adapting to difficult or challenging life experiences, especially through mental, emotional, and behavioral flexibility and adjustment to external and internal demands.- American Psychological Association

"Emotional resilience is not about winning the battle. It is the strength to power through the storm and still keep the sail steady."- Chowdhury, M. R. (2021)

Emotional Regulation: The ability of an individual to modulate an emotion or set of emotions. -American Psychiatric Association.

"Emotion regulation effectiveness depends on the ability to flexibly choose strategies, such as cognitive reappraisal or emotional acceptance, to match the situational demands" (Gross, 2015; Webb et al., 2012)

Emotional Dysregulation-"... occurs when individuals struggle to manage or adjust their emotions appropriately, often resulting in intense emotional reactions that are out of proportion to the situation" (Gross, 2015; D'Agostino et al., 2016).

Emotional Expression: "Our ability to know and acknowledge how we feel and understand that expressing it is crucial to relate to others." -Novick, A., & Fiore, T. (2005). *Anger management for the twenty-first century.*

Emotional Inheritance: "One generation lives inside the other, and they share an unconscious, they communicate with each other." (Atlas, 2022). The transmission of emotional patterns, behaviors, and coping mechanisms across generations

Emotional Resemblance: A process "where individuals unconsciously mirror the emotional expressions and responses of others, often through mechanisms like mirror neurons, which create emotional connections, especially in family dynamics, particularly parents and children" (Mayseless et al., 2023; Rizzolatti & Arbib, 1998)

****

It was July 2021, and the world seemed to be taking its first breaths of freedom after a long period of restriction. Although I would still have to wear a mask at the hospital, other mandates were lifted. And I felt a sense of relief knowing my husband could be by my side when I welcomed our daughter into the world. Hallie's arrival, a week early, with her unexpected red hair, was the most beautiful moment of my life, but with it came an unexpected silence—one that left me face-to-face with myself.

The silence of the daytime, late nights, and early mornings was jarring. Grappling with the silent spaces of motherhood, I realized I didn't have the tools to navigate my emotions, guilt, or the self-compassion needed to soothe the inner critic that grew louder with every unkind thought. The joy of having a newborn was accompanied by this undeniable pressure to ensure that I taught Hallie the things I was unfamiliar with—things I didn't yet know how to do for myself.

Before Hallie was born, I had been working with children in some capacity for 20 years. Most recently, I was all-in as a teacher. My days were spent advocating for my students with severe disabilities, creating programs, and leading projects. It wasn't just a job—it was who I was. My identity was deeply tied to my work as an educator and the connections I could make for students with severe disabilities. But now, I was at home, far from the work that had defined me. Guilt seeped in like an unwelcome visitor; I felt ashamed for enjoying my time with my daughter and guilty for not being there for my students. For so long, the achievements and validation from my professional life had masked a lack of personal emotional resilience, leaving me feeling lost and asking myself, 'Who am I now that I am not in the classroom? Who am I without my job? Do I still matter?'

The accolades and acknowledgments that once reassured me now felt distant, and the confidence they had once given me crumbled without the foundation of my professional life. Realizing that my self-worth had been tethered to my accomplishments left me feeling hollow as if I had built my identity on sand.

I was struggling but determined to teach myself the positive patterns, habits, and behaviors associated with the situations we encounter in life. Whether positive or negative, I reflected on my emotional expression. I began to develop the ability to see how my body responded to different emotions and whether my expression matched what I was feeling and trying to communicate. Consistently checking in with myself allowed me the time to identify where/when my patterns and processes began and the role that emotional inheritance, emotional resemblance, and mirror neurons played in my development and responses. I used it as fuel to create new connections and pathways for healthier responses for my daughter and me, and I was excited to feel good about them.

This awareness was empowering, but I felt overwhelmed. Still, I asked myself another question: What are the next steps I need to take to learn the tools to help myself so I can teach them to my daughter?

> February 2022: Six Months Later

When my friend suggested seeing a therapist—any therapist—I hesitated. Not because I opposed the idea but because I had always chosen female counselors, someone I felt I could trust more easily. Looking for a male therapist was typically out of the question, but desperation pushed me beyond my comfort zone. I scheduled an appointment with a male therapist. I wasn't sure what to expect, but I knew I needed help navigating the overwhelming uncertainty and emotions. I needed the loud ticking clock, reminding me how vital the first three to five years are in a child's brain development, to finally quiet down.

As I sat looking into my screen at this man I did not know, I asked him my first question: How am I supposed to teach this sweet little girl how to navigate life's curveballs when I don't know how to navigate them myself when life hits me with them?

My second question: How do I develop self-regulation?

This marked the beginning of my journey to understanding my needs and boundaries, as well as improving my emotional regulation and resilience through the development of self-compassion. Therapy, coupled with art experiences and my reconnection to the healing power of sound, became central to my transformation.

After building trust, I could look deeper at how I responded to different situations. How my therapist held space for me provided a new perspective on emotional safety and how trust felt. It allowed me the chance to practice and reflect on new coping mechanisms for my "emotional toolbox" and to begin building my new foundation for emotional competence.

Only in the face of motherhood, when I was stripped of the safety net of my job, could I stop being avoidant and begin untangling my profession and identity. I learned to identify the various first signs my body would give me to indicate that it was having a response to an emotion (spoiler alert: it was way before I initially thought). This helpful piece of knowledge allowed me the time to practice accessing and implementing healthy coping skills before the emotion felt unmanageable and my expression was reactive. I recognized myself having an easier time identifying my feelings, staying present, and getting to know them. Becoming more acquainted with this side of the human experience felt invaluable.

Initially, it was challenging to identify these indicators and feelings and find better ways to respond because I lived in a world of reaction instead of being proactive. To help move me between these two worlds, my therapist and I explored topics of self-care and stability. He started small and posed the question: what makes you feel calm?

Immediately, I identified art. It was instinctual. Creating art and providing experiences for others to connect with themselves creatively always brought me a sense of stability.

Then we repeated the exercise: what makes me feel calm? At this moment, he pushed me outside my norm of relying on art, and a figurative light turned on. I realized sound and its profound effect on me. Sound allowed me to take control of my emotions and redefine what loud sounds felt like. As I reflected on my life, I noticed that every time I reclaimed loud sounds, I didn't do it through silence but through the expression of music. Music always made sense to me. I used to think that only singing loudly brought me comfort in music. But when I walked into a Tibetan art shop in 2016, my world cracked open.

Standing in a 20-inch singing bowl, I experienced love at first strike. The sound felt like my mind was at rest, and my soul was illuminating.

As the bowl's resonance faded, my thoughts shifted to how I could bring its sound into my classroom to benefit my students. I didn't think about how to incorporate this sound into my personal routine for peace of mind. Instead, I purchased the bowl because I thought of my students' needs, not my own.

The excitement in the room when I introduced the Green Tara singing bowl, was palpable, and its effects on the class community were enough to make me forget about its personal benefits for me. Even while I taught virtually during the pandemic, students would ask me to play it. It became a symbol of the start of class and the expectations we needed to uphold. The bowl became part of our class community. Its effects resonated far longer than the ear could hear, and that was enough for me for a long time.

In the midst of discovering the different layers of myself, I kept finding myself being drawn to my Green Tara Tibetan singing bowl. It had lived in a corner of my home that I curated just for it during the pandemic. This bowl always felt sacred. Its resonance had brought comfort to my students and me during my teaching days, and now, as I sat in the meditation space I had created for it, I struck the bowl and let its sound wash over me. It was as if I was finally giving myself permission to feel its benefits for myself.

Since the day I gave myself permission to play my Green Tara bowl for my benefit, it has become a reminder of my personal peace. It symbolizes how much work I've done—and continue to do—on what personal peace means and how it evolves as I evolve. Changing my internal dialogue about how I use the singing bowl was my first experience of being gentle with myself and trusting myself with this tool to feel better.

Through therapy and my deepening relationship with sound, I learned to identify and regulate my emotions, leading to newfound trust in myself. The more I accessed sound as a coping mechanism, the more I realized it was more than a tool for calm—it was a way to connect with the deepest parts of myself. It felt good knowing that I was modeling and introducing my daughter to this tool at such a young age, and it felt even better to watch her explore it independently since she was a couple of months old. After seeing firsthand how sound benefited my student's interpersonal relationships with their peers and their families, my toddler's development, and how it has continued to reshape me throughout my life, I knew in my heart I was being called to share the power of sound with others. I needed to create more access to these instruments for the community so more people could benefit; I just didn't know how or where to start.

With my background in education, I wanted to ensure I was knowledgeable and educated on best practices before facilitating sound to others. It was almost as if the universe was waiting for me to ask because, almost immediately after, someone I admired began offering a Vibrational Sound Practitioner training course. It was taking place on the weekend, and I WAS ABLE TO ATTEND.

The day I stepped into the Vibrational Sound Practitioner training, I felt a spark reignite within me—a sense that I was beginning to "get my pink back," as Lindsey Gurk would say. I saw sound as a way to heal myself and extend that healing to others.

For the first time, I was learning to embrace uncertainty. I no longer needed the validation of professional success to feel worthy. I wrote down my new purpose:

"I am a Sound Practitioner for children," "I am a Sound Practitioner for those with disabilities." "I provide the community access to explore instruments and their sounds for self-regulation and connection."

Each day, as I continued my training and began sharing sound's benefits with others, I felt myself coming back to life—stronger and more grounded than before. I have allowed myself to evolve and see that connecting others to sound doesn't have to be just one way.

Now, I trust myself not only to navigate my emotions but also to create resources for others and guide my daughter in developing the emotional skills I once lacked. I've learned that being gentle with myself allows me to show up more fully—not just for Hallie but for everyone I help.

This journey has shown me that healing is not a linear path but a continuous process of growth. As I continue to learn and teach sound healing, I see it not only as a practice for others but as a daily reminder for myself—of resilience, self-compassion, and the power of finding peace within.

About Ashley Cantor-Birnbaum:

Ashley Cantor-Birnbaum is a Special Education Teacher and Vibrational Sound Practitioner with expertise in Art Education, Sound, Psychology, History, and Social Emotional Learning. She holds an advanced certificate in School Building leadership and School District leadership. Passionate about fostering connection and growth, Ashley uses art and sound to build community and support individuals in finding their most centered selves.

Through her personal journey with ADHD, Ashley developed a deep appreciation for creating tools to stay organized, motivated, and engaged. This inspired her to design accessible resources for educators, practitioners, and individuals of all skill levels. Her creations include the *OVERJOYED! Teacher Planner*, Vibrational Sound Instrument Stickers, Affirmation Cards, the SCANA Skills Program for individuals with disabilities, and resources for social-emotional development.

As the founder of Centered Wellness NY and The Sound Sanctuary, Ashley integrates her talents to empower professionals, children, and families with tools for holistic well-being and personal growth.

Follow @ _centeredwellness_

Learn more: www.centeredwellnessny.com

A Healer's Journey
By Susan Bloom

What brought me to a place of calm and improved health? I never thought I would ever be asked that question.

I invite you to come on a journey—a healer's journey—that transformed me into the person I am today: a less stressed, more confident, and empowered individual experiencing better health and a renewed passion for life. This journey has had many ups and downs, ebbs and flows.

It began on a day that seemed like any other, meaning I was suffering from one of my many migraines. My husband and I had been invited to a party, but I couldn't get out of bed. I felt a strong, unsettling sensation that scared me deeply. Not only did I have a migraine, but I also felt completely overwhelmed—paralyzed, in a sense. My body refused to cooperate. I couldn't get out of bed and push through the day as I had managed in the past. My heart was racing, my breath was short, and my stress level was through the roof. The double vision came back too. It frightened both of us. We wondered if I had taken too much Tylenol for the pain or if something worse was going on with my body.

A few hours later, things improved. Whew. I hoped that would never happen again.

This couldn't be happening, especially not now. My mom had recently passed away, and we had been helping my uncle and aunt move out of their assisted living facility into a hotel. We were getting them acclimated and visiting regularly. This was a time when I needed to be strong, healthy, and reliable. I felt like I was failing my family.

I had spent practically every weekend driving 300 miles round trip to help my mom help them. I noticed how my health was deteriorating, and the double vision was making the drive miserable—and terrifying. But I powered through to help in any way I could. They didn't know how bad my health had become.

Driving with double vision is a nightmare, especially on a four-lane highway. A single vehicle in the other lane would split into two: one phantom vehicle appeared in my lane while the real one stayed in its place.

Which one was real? I had to blink several times before the false vehicle would disappear. I started driving with one eye closed to manage the hallucination, but my chest would feel tight, and my breath would shorten. I was sure it would trigger another migraine, as it often had in the past.

I decided to avoid highways altogether, hoping for better results. While the double vision persisted on smaller roads, it happened less frequently. This adjustment helped, but it wasn't a solution.

Once my uncle and aunt were settled, I finally took some time to focus on myself. But things didn't go as planned. I went from one general doctor to several specialists, some a couple of hours away. Each ordered tests for specific symptoms and prescribed one or more medications, all with a host of side effects. Many of these side effects included headaches and nausea, which required yet another medication to address. I was growing increasingly discouraged and stressed. There didn't seem to be any lasting relief or hope for a normal life. The lack of energy was taking a toll. I felt helpless, as though even the experts didn't know how to help me. How much longer could this go on? I was at my wits' end. I couldn't bear to hear another specialist tell me they had no idea what was wrong or that the prescribed medication "should have worked."

I desperately needed answers. I needed to regain control over the stress and anxiety that were dictating my life. I needed help.

Years of bouncing between doctors and specialists took a toll on me. I lost all hope. I was tired of puzzling everyone who tried to help me. Test after test, medication after medication—many with side effects that made other symptoms worse. I was trapped on the "doctor appointment rollercoaster," trying the lesser of two evils approach to find relief. So much money and time had been spent with little to no improvement. Meanwhile, I wondered how many more surgeries, pills, or treatments I would have to endure only to face disappointment. How many specialists would it take to achieve minimal progress before another symptom demanded attention? Some even told me, "This might be something you'll have to learn to live with."

I remember standing in a doctor's office in tears after hearing that. For a few moments, I let the despair wash over me. Then I thought: Do I really have to accept this as my fate? My reality? No. I had to find another way forward.

It wasn't always like this. When I was younger, I had energy, passions, and interests. I woke up every morning ready to create meaningful experiences and grow as an individual. I believed I would make my mark on the world.

Now, instead of chasing dreams, I was visiting specialists with no notable improvement. I felt like modern Western healthcare had failed me.

I needed answers, and I needed them NOW.

That's when my journey went into overdrive. I began piecing together how I got to this point of dis-ease.

I discovered that stress was the common denominator in all my conditions. It was a big "A-ha" moment. But where did I go from here? I decided to go as far back as I could remember to gather information that might help.

I revisited my childhood and examined the physical, emotional, and spiritual influences in my life. What ideas and philosophies had shaped my stress levels? I had been a sickly child. I thought I suffered from sinus headaches, but they might have been migraines. Stomach issues had plagued me too, though my mom said they weren't as frequent or intense back then. These issues had been with me for so long that I began to think they were normal, which is why I hadn't addressed them sooner.

In my 20s, I developed a big interest in "all things healthy." It was the 1990s, and information about health and wellness was becoming more widely available in books, on television, and in schools. I began studying various exercise routines and philosophies. There were so many approaches to choose from, all claiming to be the best. Each style came with its own set of guidelines: how often to exercise, for how long, and what methods to use. The sheer variety left me confused. I wanted to feel better, but I didn't want to overdo it and make things worse.

Dietary studies were just as confusing. Many diets were overly strict, and some made my headaches worse. They left me feeling out of balance. I couldn't find one that helped me feel healthy, less stressed, and more energetic. So, my search continued.

The next area I explored was "alternative medicine," which at the time was dismissed by much of the medical community. Doctors would say, "You can try it, but don't expect any results." Still, I decided to research and experience some of these age-old practices that had been largely ignored in the West. I read about and tried yoga, guided meditation, massage therapy, sound therapy, and spiritual approaches to life's deeper questions.

At that time, I mostly gathered information and experimented. When I started noticing improvements in my health, I didn't give much thought to what was working. I set the information aside when life became busy. For over two decades, I neglected those practices, letting my ego and stubbornness take over. Unsurprisingly, my symptoms returned with a vengeance.

Fast forward to almost five years ago. I had had enough of my poor health. It was time to take charge. I thought back to a time in my life when I felt balanced, complete, and pain-free. I revisited the notes I had taken so many years ago and found the answer staring back at me. I decided to look at myself not as a fragmented person but as a whole being. I remembered my earlier realization that stress was a major contributor to many diseases. This time, I put it all together and began working on a plan to reduce stress in my life.

Reducing stress is achievable, and the results are measurable when the process is consistently practiced. Today, I want to share a part of that plan with you: Susan's Five Steps to Reduce Stress.

1. Avoid social media and all forms of news one hour before bed.

2. Write down three things you are grateful for in a journal.

3. Write down anything you need to remember to finish the day so it's off your mind.

4. Establish an evening routine to signal your body that it's time to unwind. This could include decaffeinated tea, a relaxing bath or shower, or soothing sounds.

5. In the morning, wait at least 30 minutes before checking your phone for messages, emails, or social media.

By integrating these steps into my daily routine, I finally found a level of balance and calm I never thought possible. I now face each day with confidence, gratitude, and peace. You, too, can achieve daily stress relief. Improved health is just one of the many benefits you will experience.

Thank you for joining me on this journey. Enjoy your new sense of calm.

About Susan Bloom:

Susan Bloom is a holistic coach and the owner of Holisticoach113East.LLC. At 59 years old, she decided that she would like to step out of her comfort zone. She has been studying many aspects and modalities of alternative therapy for over 30 years. With this knowledge, she has shared with many others in navigating the journey of life. She has discovered that a "one size fits all" approach does not work. She uses many modalities that are available to empower her clients. When she is not working, she is enjoying life in a small town with her husband, two dogs and a cat.

Email: Susan.hc113east@gmail com

IF YOU CAN'T SEE THE LIGHT AT THE END OF THE TUNNEL... MAYBE YOU ARE THE LIGHT

By Teresa Kamiya

Overall, I am a private individual when it comes to my personal life. Even with my friends, it has never been easy to open up. I kept what was happening inside the doors to myself.

Writing my story is a big step in my life, and it makes me feel completely exposed—like a fish in a desert.

I do not have experience writing. I have never even consistently kept a journal. But at this point in time, I believe it is long overdue to open a window into my life because something in me knows it's time to share my truth.

So…thank you for reading…me. This is not just a story. This is me. My life.

I was born in Peru. My parents, who are now in a better place, were Japanese descendants. They upheld a very traditional lifestyle passed down from their ancestors. Although we followed some Buddhist traditions at home, my parents embraced Catholicism, and my siblings and I were raised as Catholics. This blend of cultures and beliefs played an important role in shaping me into the person I am now. I am not necessarily religious but spiritual, embracing and respecting a blend of different philosophies and beliefs.

As a young adult, I immigrated to the United States all by myself with a suitcase full of dreams, leaving my family and loved ones miles away.

Coming to this land, I felt both intimidated and excited. Full of hope, I saw the future as bright as the sun. I wanted to start a brand-new life.

With years of hard work, I achieved the milestones of getting a steady job, buying my first car, getting married, owning a house, and being blessed with a beautiful son.

I had established a family and settled into my life.

This sounds like my dream came true, right?

Behind closed doors, the relationship was turbulent. My partner struggled with alcohol habits. Under the influence, he became someone else—angry, belligerent, and violent. It didn't matter where we were—at home, on family trips, at reunions with friends, or even at weddings—arguments and fights would break out. Sometimes, they were between us; other times, they involved family or other guests.

We learned to stay quiet to avoid making things worse or causing a public scene. We hoped no one we knew was around to witness what was happening or to pity us. Looking at pictures from past events, I see us all smiling. But behind my smile were tears I hid to appear composed. Those pictures are still hard for me to look at.

At the beginning of our life together, these situations didn't happen often. But as time passed, they escalated to nearly daily occurrences.

I remember, in the early years of our marriage, before I had my son, receiving threatening calls from my partner when he was intoxicated. Before he came home, I would hide in closets to feel some semblance of safety, but I was always found.

Constantly hearing denigrating words, I eventually lost my self-confidence and had zero self-esteem. I began to question myself: Was it my fault? What can I do? Should I change? I felt I wasn't good enough for anyone to care about me. Somehow, I believed I deserved what I was going through.

I felt small and insignificant. I started to believe the words I constantly heard.

So, I became quiet and passive. As I mentioned before, I am private, but I turned into someone who wouldn't speak her mind. Looking back, I realize I lost the integrity between who I truly was and how I presented myself to others. I was living a double life. At work, and in front of my son and friends, I was this carefree, happy person, always smiling and joking around, as if I had no problems at all. Every phone call to my parents and brothers in Peru was filled with stories of accomplishments and happy updates. I pretended everything was perfectly fine.

I started having recurring dreams of being trapped in a dark, intricate maze—scared and desperately searching for a way out. These dreams haunted me for years.

I felt like I had nowhere to go, and I was completely alone. Slowly, the real me faded away, quietly lost beneath the mask of pretending.

At this point in the story, you may be wondering: Why? Why did I stay? Why didn't I leave? Why didn't I ask for help?

Well, after every stormy fight, the next day brought a different person—full of heartfelt remorse, sincerely repentant, and promising change. For a short time, things would improve, and I believed things could get better. But soon, everything returned to ground zero.

Wishful thinking is powerful. Love is powerful. Yes, I loved the person he was when he was sober. I wanted so badly for things to improve and for us to keep the family together.

On the other hand, my son's smile gave me strength. Seeing him hug me, sleep peacefully, and grow—his first words, his first steps, his first day at school—brought me moments of joy that made me focus on the positives.

Living in the middle of this life, I learned to adapt as best as I could. I convinced myself that this was just a challenging phase and that one day, the broken pieces would come together.

I even considered attending Al-Anon meetings but never followed through.

I thought about returning to Peru with my son to live with my parents, but I didn't want to burden them with my problems.

Eventually, to cope with everything, I started embracing destructive habits: not eating well, barely sleeping, becoming a workaholic, and drinking. Dark thoughts crept into my mind, and I became cynical and numb. My mantra became: "This is my life…accept it…ride it."

My health started deteriorating, and I got sick easily.

THE TURNING POINT

One morning, as we were getting ready for work and school, my husband looked at me and said, "You look bad…your posture…your face," shaking his head in disapproval. I thought angrily, *"Good morning to you too!"* But his words lingered.

I went to the bathroom to look at myself in the full-length mirror.

I stood there for a long time, staring.

Who are you? I asked myself. It was as if I were looking *through* myself. I wasn't even aware of whether my clothes matched. What I saw wasn't me. I was shocked.

There stood an underweight person, less than 90 pounds, weak, and looking much older than her age. She was pale, with lifeless eyes, dark circles that makeup couldn't hide, and a somber expression. Her shoulders were rounded, her back curved.

She looked exhausted. She looked sad.

My first thought was: *Here is an ugly, angry, dumb, and very sad woman.*

I didn't like that person.

I realized that while I hadn't spoken about my private life to anyone, my entire being—body, mind, and spirit—was screaming it out loud for me. I was a walking reflection of my pain and despair. I was looking at the image of my soul, and it was crying for help. That moment was a wake-up call with a slap in the face.

My son's voice pulled me out of the moment. He had finished breakfast and was ready to ride with me to school.

I left the bathroom, disturbed, and went to meet my son. There he was—his big smile, radiant face, bright eyes, and boundless energy staring straight at me.

Looking into his eyes, I felt his love. And in that instant, I felt my unconditional love for him. I felt deeply connected. It moved me to my core.

It was as though some benevolent force was trying to wake me up using tough love. It felt like another slap in the face right after the first one. All the emotions I had buried for years suddenly surfaced. My heart raced, and I struggled to hold back tears.

I dropped my son off at school and continued driving to work.

During that hour-long drive, I couldn't stop thinking about my son. I wanted to see him grow up healthy and strong. I wanted to be by his side for life's roller coaster moments, celebrating his accomplishments and comforting him when he felt down. I wanted to *be there* for him.

And I realized this might not happen if I continued walking the path I was on.

A mix of thoughts, emotions, anger, and guilt consumed me. I blamed myself, calling myself selfish and useless—not a good mother.

Then, I stopped the mental chaos. I started asking myself: *Why are you doing this to yourself? Why are you punishing yourself? What happened to the real Teresa? The one who once left her home with the courage to create a new life far from loved ones?*

Teresa was gone. I had lost myself. I couldn't even leave an unhealthy relationship.

THE ACKNOWLEDGEMENT

That's when I realized the most toxic relationship in my life was the one I had with myself. I needed to respect myself and create boundaries. Words of denigration meant nothing if I didn't believe them.

At that moment, I didn't know exactly what to do, but one thing was clear: *I needed to change. I needed to empower myself and take action to reclaim my life.*

Making a sudden decision to leave wasn't realistic at that moment. Leaving meant dragging my son into uncertainty, with no specific safe place to go. I had no family or close relatives nearby.

I realized I needed a logical plan. I started setting small, attainable goals, one step at a time, leading to my ultimate goal. I began creating structure in my personal life.

THE ACTIONS

I decided to start by changing my lifestyle. I needed to adopt healthier habits and take care of my physical and mental well-being. I began exercising at a local gym after work. At first, it was just once or twice a week, but soon I was going at least five days a week.

Next, I turned back to spiritual practices that had always fascinated me since childhood.

With my Japanese background, I had grown up familiar with the healing benefits of Reiki. So, I signed up to become a Reiki practitioner. Reiki helped alleviate joint problems, especially in my knees, and brought me a sense of mental calm.

Soon after, I discovered the benefits of Yoga and fell in love with the practice and its philosophy. Yoga taught me to accept my past without judgment and to build a new life with compassion—for myself, for others, and even for those who had hurt me.

I began to see life in a much more optimistic way.

I became more disciplined with my meals, eating healthier and at regular times, and I started sleeping better. Each positive change built upon the last. My health improved, and I began regaining my self-confidence. Slowly but surely, I felt more centered and balanced.

My relationship began to grow apart, but this time it was for the better. I established boundaries and started reclaiming my life.

Believing Yoga had saved me, I felt called to share its benefits with others who might be facing their own challenges in life.

One day, I made a bold decision: I packed a backpack and traveled solo to India to train as a Yoga teacher. I spent two months in that beautiful country, immersing myself in its culture.

It wasn't an easy trip, but it was a meaningful learning experience that catapulted my life forward. I came back feeling like I could do anything and everything. With each step I took, an old, familiar spark rekindled within me. It reminded me of the woman I once was—and could be again.

Teresa was back. Ready to discover new adventures, to learn, to start a new life. Fear was fading away.

THE OUTCOME

Alongside my corporate job, I began actively teaching Yoga and offering Reiki.

I advanced my education as a Yoga instructor becoming a certified Continuing Education Provider and started getting involved in training new Yoga teachers. Also, I became certified as a Usui Reiki Master Teacher and began to train Reiki practitioners.

As a lifelong student, I continued learning new alternative healing practices. Using the ancient art of Qi Gong, which prescribes movements as part of Traditional Chinese Medicine. I became certified as a Yoga-QiGong instructor. I also became certified as a Sound healing facilitator, using crystal singing bowls, tuning forks, and other tools..

By combining these methods with Yoga and Reiki, I created a unique fusion that optimizes the self-healing power within us.

I strongly believe in the mind-body-soul benefits of these ancient practices. I also believe that by making them accessible to everyone, we can help create a healthier, more balanced, and centered community. These tools can guide people through life's difficulties in a proactive way.

I am deeply grateful for how my life has turned around. My son, now an adult, has grown into a kind-hearted, independent person. My ex-husband has cleaned up his lifestyle and rediscovered the good person he always was.

Life presents us with many challenges, but ultimately, the decision to change is ours. Sometimes, the hardest step is the first one.

But I want you to know: no matter where you are, you are never alone on this journey. Let's walk this path together toward health, light and joy.

If you can't see the light at the end of the tunnel…

Maybe *you* are the light.

About Teresa Kamiya:

Teresa Kamiya is a 500 hours Yoga Instructor, trained in India and San Diego, a Reiki Master teacher, Sound Healing Specialist and Certified Yoga-QiGong teacher, using Traditional Chinese Medicine as part of her practice.

She believes the mind, body and soul are interconnected affecting each other and they need to be properly cleansed, nurture and balanced.

Whether the concern is physical, about the lack of range of movement, joints, pain or not physical like lack of sleep, mood changes, to name some. Teresa will incorporate different methods of alternative medicine to create a unique holistic fusion that will address the body, mind and inner energy toward self-healing. All customized to each individual needs. Her non-judgmental practice had successfully helped clients to reduce level of stress, depression, addictions and suicidal tendencies as well as improving physical health.

For further information contact:

Email: **Tekyoga24@gmail.com**

Instagram @tekyoga

Facebook: Teresa Kamiya

From Grief to Peace: A Journey of Healing and Transformation Through Holistic Practices

By Rashida Sheffield

Grief is more than sorrow. It is the surface and suppressed emotions you feel for your loss. When dealing with severe grief, you can experience a magnitude of emotions simultaneously. These emotions sometimes cannot be named, and you cannot stop them from surfacing. It is like trying to dry up the ocean. The motion of these emotions is like tides and waves—they come and go. This chapter will show how I overcame severe grief and learned to embrace it. I must apologize ahead of time if this chapter triggers you.

When I was growing up, the most I knew about grief was that it meant losing a loved one and that they were in a better place, in heaven. On May 7, 2018, my life changed forever. On my way to work, I had a nagging feeling to call my father, but it was 5 a.m. in his time zone. He was in Arizona, and I was in Georgia. During the two-hour drive to work, I fought my intuition. I finally decided to call him after work because I didn't want to disrespect his household and disturb my stepmother.

The last time I spoke with my father, he was proud of his health and boasted about how much healthier he had become. You can imagine my shock when I got a call after lunch saying my father had died. It felt like time stopped, and an overwhelming sense of paralysis took over. I thought to myself, "This must be some sick joke my cousins are playing on me." My cousin from my father's side of the family said she would have felt bad if my brother and I had found out about my father's death on social media. My cousin from my mother's side put us on a three-way call. The little girl in me took the news the hardest. When I told my manager and asked if I could go home, she said no and threatened me with a write-up. Stress began to boil in my body. I needed my job to pay my bills, but my emotions were running rampant because this news couldn't be true. It felt like a horrible dream. She changed her mind two hours later, at 3:00 p.m., just before my shift was supposed to end at 5:00 p.m. All I could think about was how appalling it is for someone to receive heartbreaking news, only to be met with complete insensitivity and a lack of empathy from their manager.

On my way home, I tried to rationalize what had happened. Could I have saved my father? Was I supposed to hear his last words? Could I have kept him alive? I had so many questions and no answers. All I knew was that my father was gone, and nobody knew what had happened. I wondered if my family knew the truth about his death, would they tell me? I was the oldest of two and my father's only daughter. My brother, who lived in Texas, always longed for our father's love. His dream was to go hunting with him. We both craved more time with our father. Monday became a day where I felt as though I was drowning in an ocean of emotions.

My job gave me five days off for bereavement. During that time, all I could do was cry. My boyfriend encouraged me to find out what happened to my father since everyone around me claimed they didn't know. He said it was my duty as a daughter to uncover the truth. It wasn't my family or his wife who gave me the details of his death, but the detective assigned to the case. When I called the detective, he said the scene was a picture of hell. I felt like I was falling into the abyss. He told me my father had committed suicide and had three wounds—one on his forearm, one on his chest, and one on his sternum. Before I could stop myself, I told the detective that my father would never have committed suicide; he had to have been murdered. I said I heard him, but everything he described sounded like foul play to me. So, I agreed to disagree. Having watched plenty of cold case shows, I knew the person closest to the victim was often the perpetrator. I told him to follow the money. My mind couldn't accept the idea that my father had taken his own life.

My father had been living his best life before his death. He had been married to my stepmother, the woman of his dreams, for 15 years. He had divorced my mother after 25 years of marriage. A rush of memories flooded my mind. I vividly recalled a time when my father and I were driving around town, and he told me, "I never loved your mother." So much anger rose within me when he said that. I asked him why he married her. He explained that his siblings had told him to marry into the Holmes family because my grandfather, a peanut farmer, was doing well for himself. My grandfather had 11 children—four boys and seven girls—and he often helped my father and his siblings because their parents had passed away by the time my father was five years old. My father complied with his siblings' wishes, but it was evident that he was deeply unhappy and had been living a life that didn't align with his true self. His unhappiness, combined with the tragic circumstances of his death, made me realize the profound consequences of life choices—not just for oneself, but for those left behind to deal with the aftermath.

After his passing, I learned how crucial it is to choose the right life partner, as the wrong choice can have devastating effects. This loss taught me many things. I learned that my stepmother, as his wife, had control over all my father's affairs. Despite being an heir, I couldn't get a copy of the autopsy report and had to accept what I was told: suicide was the cause of death. I looked to my intuition for guidance, but it was as confused as I was. I left the funeral with a clearer understanding of my family. The only sense of unity I discovered was in the deceit and the harsh truth of my family's genuine feelings toward me. I wasn't allowed to view my father's body with the family. My brother and I had to wait for the public viewing. During the wake, I saw my uncle ask my father's step-grandson about some paperwork. I assumed they were looking for insurance policies. The step-grandson replied that he couldn't locate them. It was a sight to see, and I couldn't wait to get back home. I told my mother how grateful I was that it had always been just the three of us—my mother, my brother, and me—supporting one another. Her support gave me solace.

I cried the entire nine-and-a-half-hour drive back home. Once there, all I did was sleep. When I was awake, I felt waves of uncontrollable emotions crashing over me. I kept my room pitch black, with the curtains drawn. I only got out of bed to shower, eat, or use the restroom before retreating again. Alone in my room, the despair was suffocating. Memories—both good and bad—kept surfacing. Two memories kept resurfacing: one was when my father taught me how to cook steak and make a good drink, saying those were two things a man wanted to come home to. The other was when he slapped me across the bed at my cousin's house for coming home late from a party when I was 16. When I told a family member, she didn't believe me until my cousin confirmed it. These memories haunted me, and I avoided talking to anyone. When someone called, I would let them speak without responding. I felt like I was losing my mind. Nobody had ever told me that grief could feel this way.

In 2017, I had journaled my thoughts about my father, meditating on the relationship I wished to rebuild with him. I longed for the father-daughter time we never had—the chance to create happy memories together. My father often promised me quality time, but it never happened because he prioritized others over me. Growing up, this made me feel unlovable, as my love language is quality time.

I loved my father, but I needed to find a way to forgive him and release the anger and disappointment I held. I did deep soul-searching through shadow, where I realized I had become a workaholic to escape the toxic household I grew up in, where my parents frequently fought. Feeling like I was losing my sanity, I took a certified grief specialist course to understand more about grief and a five-week course on Radical Forgiveness. These courses jump-started my forgiveness process. I wanted something to shift my energy, release the pain, and heal my broken heart.

I turned to holistic energy healing and learned about Reiki and Sound Energy Healing. My first Reiki session was transformative. As I lay on the table, it felt like someone was painting colors on my eyelids every time the practitioner played her crystal singing bowl. Each sound evoked a new color. While scanning my body, I saw her hands glowing with sparkles, even with my eyes closed. I kept questioning what I was experiencing until the session ended. During one session, as the sound of the crystal bowl reverberated, I felt a release—a softening of the grief I carried. It was as though my soul whispered, "You're not alone in this." Intrigued, I began attending more Reiki sessions and sound bath ceremonies. Each session felt like I was shedding a layer of stagnant energy, and the waves of emotions began to calm.

Though I couldn't have known it at the time, this loss became the catalyst for my journey toward healing and transformation. Holistic energy healing shifted my energy profoundly. I found peace with my family and the way they treated me during my father's funeral. I learned valuable soul lessons from the experience, including the importance of self-love and grace. I came to understand that I couldn't change what had happened to my father. Even if I knew every detail, it wouldn't bring him back. I chose to put my energy into myself because grief is not one-size-fits-all. I tried everything—traditional counseling, grief share groups—but found the most healing through holistic practices.

As I navigated my grief, I realized not everyone knows how to support someone during such a painful time. Grief revealed the true character of those around me. It showed me that people are who they are, and they may never change. I'll never forget when a family member told me it wasn't their place to share the details of my father's death with me. That comment hit me like a dropkick in a wrestling ring, leaving me stunned and hurt. In that moment, I realized the importance of focusing on self-love, forgiveness, and building a new support system with people who genuinely uplift and care for me. Grief reshaped my life, teaching me that sometimes we have to let go of old connections to make room for meaningful bonds.

Grief is a profound teacher, unveiling truths about ourselves and others while reshaping our understanding of life. It forces us to confront pain and vulnerability, leaving us feeling isolated yet teaching us the importance of time, support, and self-compassion. I never want anyone to endure the pain and isolation I experienced, but through my journey, I discovered the transformative power of Reiki and sound healing. These practices became my lifeline, helping me reconnect with myself and find peace amidst the chaos of grief. Determined to turn my pain into purpose, I began sharing what I had learned with anyone willing to listen. Whether it was a close friend, a curious stranger, or someone silently struggling, I felt compelled to offer them the hope and healing that Reiki and sound healing had brought me.

That is why I founded Reiki Recharge (**www.reikirecharge.com**). I believe healing should be accessible to everyone. My mission is to help individuals release emotional blocks and reclaim vibrant, empowered lives. During each session, my goal is to help clients let go of emotional burdens, restore balance, and step into their fullest potential. I'll never forget one participant who, with tears in her eyes, thanked me after a session. She said, "I didn't think I could feel peace again after my loss, but today, I felt a glimmer of hope." Her words reminded me of why I chose this path.

Grief is a complex and transformative experience. It reshapes not only how we view loss but also how we approach life, relationships, and healing. It teaches us that pain and vulnerability, while unavoidable, can become powerful catalysts for growth and self-discovery. My journey through grief led me to embrace holistic healing practices like Reiki and sound healing, which became essential tools in reclaiming my peace and emotional balance. These experiences inspired me to open Reiki Recharge, a space dedicated to helping others navigate their own healing journeys.

About Rashida Sheffield:

Rashida Sheffield is the founder of Reiki Recharge, a holistic wellness practice dedicated to helping individuals heal emotionally and spiritually. Her journey into Reiki and sound healing began over six years ago after the heartbreaking loss of her father to suicide. Struggling with grief and questioning her mental well-being, Rashida sought a natural, holistic path to healing. Through self-forgiveness and a deep dive into holistic practices, she transformed her energy from grief to peace.

As an expert in Reiki, yoga, sound healing, life coaching, breathwork, and meditation, Rashida combines traditional healing methods with modern techniques to offer personalized, intuitive healing sessions. Each session is tailored to meet the unique needs of her clients, empowering them to heal at their own pace.

Rashida believes that healing should be accessible to everyone. Her mission is to help individuals release emotional blocks and reclaim their most vibrant, empowered Lives.

Find out more at www.reikirecharge.com

Out of the Shadow
By Jennifer Penick

I had a migraine for a few days. Not necessarily my "norm," but migraines were not a stranger to me. I had had a migraine or two a month since my teens. This one was a bit different. I didn't know it at the time, though.

I had worked hard. I was healthy, running almost every day, lifting weights, and enjoying a vibrant yoga practice. I had a goal and had reached it. I wanted to "extend" my life—my active, vibrant life—so that I could run across the field at the kids' school with them. I was going to chase them, play with them, and compete with them to see who could hold their handstand the longest! I have five children. In February 2014, they were 15, 13, 11, 9, and 6 years old. I was 44 years old. My husband, an active, handsome, involved, beautiful man and father, was by my side as we moved through our days with five active kids and our busy lives.

My migraine had lasted a couple of days. I had gone to a workout and developed a slight headache—kind of like a "shadow." A day later, I had enjoyed an intense yoga practice with inversions. I was tackling my fear and stepping into courage through my practice of difficult arm balances. I wanted to call up courage on my mat and then take that embodiment off my mat and into my world as I faced my father's recent cancer diagnosis and prognosis.

The next day, my subtle shadow of a headache still lingered. However, now it was accompanied by a strange visual "phenomenon." One of my eyes was not seeing clearly. It was evident when I covered one eye, and the other saw words as if through cracked glass. I thought perhaps I was experiencing my first ocular migraine.

I remember lying down for bed with my right ear on my pillow, hearing the strangest sound. It was a whooshing sound. It sounded like a fetal ultrasound!

It was the evening of February 10, 2014, when I had an emotional call with my cousin. We were talking about my dad. I was sharing how I wanted to find ways to support him and my mom through his chemo and radiation treatments. I was crying. My dad was my warm hug, my cheerleader, and my steadfast supporter. My fear and panic were getting the better of me, and my tears intensified. It was after the call and through the intensity of the emotion and stress that I experienced what felt like a bullet to the right side of my head, somewhere behind or underneath my ear. The pain was hot and sharp. It shot through my right ear, radiating outward into my temple, jaw, neck, and the back of my skull.

I lay on the couch with ice on my head, in tears, with my husband by my side. It was 9:30 p.m. or so. We needed to wait for our oldest son to return from a show rehearsal before we could leave to go to the ER, so the kids would all be together while we were gone. The thought was that we would go, and I would receive the "migraine cocktail" I had received a few times before, rest for a couple of hours, and then come home.

The ER was busy that night. As I described the days leading up to the migraine assault, the interest in my vision issues became a focus of concern. I was taken back for an MRI, and my husband went home to be with the kids. It would be a while. We also anticipated a release after receiving my "migraine cocktail infusion." I lay on the bed in the ER, blanket pulled up, curled on my side, trying to block out the beeping sounds. I rocked myself gently in an effort to soothe myself: slow breath in, slow breath out. "Soften around the pain" in my head. "Soften everything."

The doctor entered and sat down beside the bed. I remember his voice and his words suspended in the air like they were bubbles floating off a kid's bubble wand. The words he spoke: "Jennifer, your MRI has shown what looks like an internal carotid artery dissection." My thoughts followed by words: "Dissection? What? Carotid artery? What? Wait. Dissection means to take apart?" It was as if time just stopped. My world was turned upside down. One moment, I was a mom doing handstands with my kids, pushing my limits in yoga; the next, lying in the ER unable to grasp the words "carotid artery dissection"—words that threatened the life I'd worked so hard to build.

I spent a week in the hospital. Blood thinners, morphine, a femoral angiogram. A tear so significant inside the carotid artery that it was too risky to surgically implant a stent to open the artery. I learned about my Circle of Willis. I learned that I have excellent collateral blood flow. I learned that morphine and I are not friends. I learned that you can "pop the plug" out of your femoral angiogram site, and that it causes significant pain. I learned about self-advocating while under care in a hospital. I learned that fear can become an absolute monster. I learned that not all doctors have good "people skills." I learned that I was desperate to stay alive and steady for my husband and for my kids. I also learned that I was a miracle to not have suffered a massive stroke or worse. This was a very rare and life-threatening condition.

Our kids went to bed one night and awoke the next morning to the news that I would not be coming home for at least a week or so. They could only call me. It was flu season, and they were under 18 years old and considered too high risk to bring in germs. It was a very long week for me, for them, and for my husband.

I returned home with a walker to ensure that I did not fall as I recovered and healed from the angiogram. My artery would be watched through CT and MRI scans. I lived each day feeling guilty for not being able to "be there" for my dad or mom in the way I had hoped to and planned to. I felt guilty for "putting our kids and my husband through" this scary and uncertain situation. I felt terrified to move too fast, lift too much, or do too much. The active life I'd fought to build for my children, for my husband, and for myself—it suddenly felt as fragile as a candle in the wind.

I lived with 20 or more days each and every month with a migraine. For years, I have continued treatments every 12 weeks in an effort to diffuse, minimize, and lessen my migraines.

My dad passed away on July 8, 2014. My migraines continued to challenge me almost daily. My mom needed my support. I was committed to living for them. For my husband. For my kids. For my mom. My sister. My friends.

I did. I healed. My artery healed and opened to a level that allowed me to be "released" from my neurologist's care and into the care of my migraine specialist. My migraines have subsided in intensity and frequency.

I have survived. For everyone. And in the process, my spirit shrank and withered. I had lost touch with myself in an effort to live for everyone else. I had so many days wondering how I was going to go on. How was I going to live my life like this?! How was it worth it to live if I was in so much pain so much of the time?! Multiple preventative medications were tried and not tolerated. Traditional migraine medications were not approved for me. Pain management referrals came when I uttered these thoughts to my doctor. This led me to practices like breath work, relaxation, and meditation. No one seemed to understand how it was within *my* world. Within *my* head. Migraines brought slightly slurred speech and "sloggy" thinking. Word finding was difficult, and my train of thought was "glitchy." I lived my life feeling like I had a backpack on that was filled with rocks. Each migraine felt like another reminder of what I had lost—

the running, the yoga, the life I had built for myself. I was physically present but felt like a ghost in my own life.

I became more and more isolated as I backed out of gatherings and coffee dates with friends. The invitations slowed and eventually became a rarity. I didn't think I could do these things if I was in pain, so I chose not to. My inner world was angry, grieving, bitter, scared, frustrated, and lonely. The world saw a functioning mother, wife, and friend. But inside, I was carrying the weight of unseen battles, an exhausting struggle just to make it through each day.

With each passing year and scan, my artery and pseudo-aneurysm were stable. I was told I could feel more confident that this was behind me. Genetic testing to see if there was a *reason* for this injury to "just happen" to me uncovered that all was well. I was told it was just a "freak thing" and that the chances of it happening again were slim.

I had given 10 years of my life to trying to find a *why*, feeling angry, bitter, sad, frustrated, and fearful that it could happen again. I was so tired of the narrative. I felt that I had stepped so far from myself, and I began to feel a desperation to come "home." I knew that I could not do it alone. I had been so removed for so long.

I was called to reach out and share my story with a dear friend and yoga teacher. She and I had been friends for many years, far before my dissection had happened. I invited her to my home, and we spent hours together. I cried. I shared. I allowed myself to be open, raw, and vulnerable. I allowed myself to be seen. She offered me the tool of sound and song—chanting. We sang together. I have been singing and performing on stage since early childhood. It is part of who I am. That day, our time together, opened me up and showed me a path home.

I began searching for how I could utilize sound, song, and chanting to integrate and call together the "parts" of me that felt scattered about. With each vibration, each note, it was as if I was piecing back parts of myself I had lost along the way.

I then reached out to another yoga teacher and studio owner, and we spoke at length about my experience. She heard me, reflected back, and gave guidance. Each time I opened up, I felt a weight lift, as if sharing my pain with someone else allowed me to shed its burden, piece by piece.

Through giving voice to my experience, through sharing with people I trusted, I began to heal. The physical healing had already happened. It was the emotional, energetic, and spiritual healing that needed to happen. I began to call women's circles together again. Slowly, I began to return to myself and my calling.

There isn't a day that goes by that doesn't feel touched by this injury. I had worked to be healthy. I had worked so hard to be strong, resilient, and courageous. In doing so, a "perfect storm" happened that threatened all of that.

I am triggered. I am triggered emotionally, psychologically, and physically. Now, when this happens, I meet it with a practice of tenderness, kindness, acceptance, and integration. I have learned to share my experience and be unapologetically authentic with myself and others. I honor myself. I come back to "ease and grace" daily with myself, with others, with my schedule, and with my "to-do" list. I schedule dates, gatherings, and coffee dates. I no longer hide. In embracing my "mess" and showing up just as I am, I found not only strength but freedom—a deep peace I can finally call my own.

Today, I have my voice. I speak my truth. I sing my truth. I have an outward expression of the "current" within. I have the gift of sound, resonance, and vibration. I have discovered crystal singing bowls as well! This has become the most profound and potent healing vibration I have found for myself. Since the dissection, yoga, running, and active exercise can trigger migraines for me. It has been incredibly difficult to cope with that loss. The crystal singing bowls have gifted me with a sound meditation that allows me to "suspend time" and really, everything. Playing my bowls, allowing my voice to float and intertwine with the vibration and sound of the bowls, is deeply healing for me—spiritually and energetically. It is as if it is the path laid out before me to follow along, leading me each and every time to a deeper sense of peace within myself. It brings integration of the "scattered pieces" of myself; it brings me home.

I meet myself with grace, tenderness, and love. I reflect back and carry forward with me my strength, courage, fortitude, commitment, and deep love and drive to survive, thrive, and find my way "home" to myself once again. This is the most beautiful and exquisite example of the "ripple effect" of inner healing, heart healing, and spiritual healing.

These tools, discoveries, and gifts have been powerful and life-changing. They are tools that I will continue to use and explore. They are tools that will support me as I journey onward in this life. They are tools that I will bring forth and share with others on their path to healing and wellness. By sharing the tools that saved me, I am able to show others that healing is possible, even when life feels unbearably heavy.

This experience, although much of it painful and rugged, has brought so much personal and inner growth, love, and acceptance. Healing isn't always a straight path. It is a journey of small steps, finding tools that resonate, and embracing ourselves just as we are, even amidst the pain. It takes courage to keep moving forward and trust in the power of sound and connection to lead us back to our true selves.

About Jennifer Penick:

Jennifer is married and is the mother of 5 children. She enjoys crochet, singing, yoga, time in nature, writing, creating and spending time with family and friends.

She is a Master Certified Women's Circle Facilitator and has Certifications in Yoga, Pre/Post Natal Yoga and Sound Healing. She is a creative with various mediums and a visionary feminine leader and Community builder.

She has been creating and providing safe space for women to gather together and share their lives, their stories, music, laughter and tears for over 20 years.

Her passion and commitment is for building community, and supporting women as they discover, experience and embody their feminine power, ultimately TRANSFORMING their lives.

@Jennifer-penick-inner-reflection

jennifer@inner-reflection.com

From Broken to Fueled
By Theresa DeLorenzo

My sister and I ate, breathed, and lived gymnastics. We had a beam in our living room *and* in the backyard. We had a bar that hung in the doorway to my room and another one in the backyard. I started when I was six; my sister was two. It was our life. Gymnastics camp lasted all day during the summer.

As we finished up our time on the beam—my least favorite event due to its narrow physique and frightening height—we packed up and got ready to move to the uneven parallel bars. Coach Bobby was leading bars that day. I chalked my hands and stepped up to the bars to practice my release from the high bar to the low bar. I had worked on this particular sequence for weeks and struggled to perfect it.

As I re-chalked between skills, Coach Bobby looked at me and informed me that he struggled to spot me effectively because I had gotten "so big." I stepped away, stunned. The memory of that moment remains crystal clear despite the decades that have passed. All the other gymnasts swung from bar to bar with ease. Was I really that much bigger than them? I stumbled to the bathroom, utterly confused and hurt. How could I have let this happen?

I stared at myself in the mirror and thought, "He's right! I'm not scrawny anymore!" I had boobs. No one else had boobs! I pulled at my thighs, making desperate attempts to slim them in my reflection.

When I walked back into the gym, I felt dizzy. I couldn't believe I had let this happen. Devastated, I approached the bars where everyone was removing their grips and wrapping their ankles for vault. As I did the same, Bobby admonished me again, stating that spotting me on this event would also be difficult at the weight I'd "let myself grow to."

When I got home that evening, I nervously stepped on the scale, dying to know what it read but terrified to look. How big was I? 100 lbs. 100 lbs! I had hit the number I feared. Stunned and ashamed, I stepped off the scale, shaking. Why me!? Panic flooded me.

I looked in the mirror, and all I could see were thick layers of fat covering my body. My head swirled with emotion. I would be a better gymnast if I lost weight. People would like me if I lost weight. Coach Bobby could spot me if I lost weight. Something had to change. I had to fix this, and fast. The sport I had loved my whole life had just gotten a lot more complicated.

I was determined and saw the perfect opportunity to undo what had happened. Just days after the infamous comments, my coaches, who were married at the time, left for vacation. They returned to find the "too heavy" gymnast they could barely spot in a much-altered state. I had succeeded in decreasing my frame from 100 to 87 pounds in two weeks. The startled look on their faces was confirmation that I had done what I was supposed to do. I felt proud. They looked terrified.

Anorexia can be inexorable. You do not see what others see when they look at you. I still wasn't happy with how I looked. I felt there was more work to be done. In fact, it was never enough. People in this situation are never satisfied. They always want to be thinner, no matter how much weight they lose.

When I returned to school that fall in eighth grade, I wore a different body than when I had left for the summer. People stared at me. Many whispered. I heard someone say to a friend, "How can your waist be that small?" I had fixed the problem I set out to fix—but other issues quickly arose. The situation became perilous rather quickly.

As a child, one of my favorite foods was mashed potatoes. Before the issue at hand, I would eat several servings. Eating more than one serving was naturally not feasible anymore. "I feel like Theresa doesn't love mashed potatoes anymore," my sister announced in the middle of dinner as I picked at the minuscule portion I allowed myself. Oh no! They're noticing! I was terrified.

By the beginning of eighth grade, several weeks into restricting as much as I could, I had devised a meal plan to maintain my unhealthily low weight.

All carbohydrate-based foods were worked out into "piece of bread equivalents" so I could keep my intake consistent. Lunch and dinner both consisted of two "piece of bread equivalents," a protein, and a fruit or vegetable. After school, I had a snack, which was one "piece of bread equivalent."

I lay in bed hungry each night, sleepless. I imagined the restaurants we visited and calculated how to fit my favorite foods into my regimen. I calculated how many of my favorite foods equaled a piece of bread: sixteen grapes (four equaled a quarter of a piece of bread), sixty-four Cheerios, eight crackers, thirty-two strands of spaghetti. Numbers needed to be even. Odd numbers left me feeling off balance.

Back at gymnastics, months into my quest for thinness and greatness, my plan came to a screeching halt. Exhausted from the three-hour practice and not taking in enough calories for several years at this point, I wrapped my grips on my hands, chalked up, and began my routine. My lack of energy was paramount as I swung from the low bar to the high bar and back again. My limbs felt heavy as I prepared for my dismount—a giant into what was supposed to be a piked-position flip. Completely out of energy, I bent my knees and crumbled to the ground, my ankle crushing underneath me.

The more I tried to fix my situation, the more broken I felt.

My tendon turned black and blue and swelled severely. The diagnosis was a bad sprain. I spent months in the gym while it healed, doing whatever exercises I could, but nothing that required putting weight on my foot. I lifted weights to maintain my upper body strength, sat in splits on each side for ten minutes at a time to maintain flexibility, and did hundreds and hundreds of crunches to keep my physique under control.

Six months later, finally cleared to return to all activity, I injured myself again. I jumped to catch the bar and jammed the fingers on my right hand, breaking all the bones across that hand. After a year of under-fueling, my bone density had diminished significantly. I realized gymnastics might no longer be realistic. I kept getting hurt and needed something safer for my frail body. I chose diving—similar movements but a softer landing.

Because I wasn't consuming enough calories, I craved sugar, usually in the form of chocolate. During a holiday party at gymnastics, I planned to eat brownies and only brownies. I loved brownies and missed them terribly. I figured out how many brownies I could eat for a meal equivalent. I skipped lunch and counted the brownies as my meal—one for each bread equivalent and one for the "inside of the sandwich."

My friend Erin noticed my odd behavior and commented that she had never seen me eat so much before. I explained that I hadn't eaten anything else. In my mind, it made perfect sense. I'm not sure she agreed. I also felt guilty about consuming so much sugar during this brownie-deprived binge.

Historically, my food rules caused me to put certain foods in "off-limits" boxes. Human nature leads us to want these foods even more. We feel restricted, and when we do break down and let ourselves have those foods, it's hard to stop. The fact that I was low on energy intake overall only added to this problem. Eating something calorically dense after such a long period of inadequate intake is so satisfying. But when we feel deprived, it's hard to stop, and then we feel guilty, which leads to more restriction. It's a never-ending cycle.

I was babysitting in junior high. The mom left out chocolate chip cookies for me and the child to have as a snack. I decided to have one. I couldn't stop. I ate cookie after cookie, the chocolate chips like little nuggets of magic on my tongue. Later, I skipped dinner. My mom was making chicken, mashed potatoes, and broccoli—one of my favorites. Longing to eat the meal and be free of my suffocating rules, I told my parents that I had eaten dinner with the child I was babysitting. Technically, I had eaten.

I couldn't bring myself to eat more after all the cookies. **If I had been well-nourished, I would have been able to stop.** Even though I had eaten all those cookies, I should have had a healthy dinner. I wasn't logical at that time in my life. I have been there! Binging is a result of filling our body with something that's missing. Under-fueling leads to overindulgence. You can employ all the willpower in the world, but until you are properly nourished, your body will win.

During the autumn of my junior year, diving season, I gradually reintroduced a few of my forbidden foods back into my diet. Tired of not allowing myself some of my favorite foods, I decided to try being a normal teenager. Potato chips—or really any kind of chips—had been off-limits for years. Naturally, as with any restrictive diet, when I reintroduced the salty deliciousness back into my diet, I went overboard. I couldn't stop.

When I reached my hand into a bag of Doritos, the crunchy, salty bursts of flavor were impossible to resist. During this liminal phase, Doritos became my favorite snack. The swimming and diving team would all go to Bruegger's Bagels after school before practice. I always ordered a salt bagel, plain.

Toward the end of the diving season, my teammates and I were watching videos from the beginning of the season to see how far we had come on our dives. As we watched my inward dive, one of my teammates commented on how obvious it was that I had put on a lot of weight during the season. Chips were once again removed from my diet. I was up to 93 lbs. **Nooooo!** I was horrified.

At the time, I wasn't sure what they meant by the comment. Were they implying I looked better or worse because I had gained weight? I had no idea, but despite wanting to be more normal and less isolated, I couldn't handle the ramifications.

I decided diving alone wasn't cutting it. I needed more exercise. Restricting my food alone had grown too difficult. I joined the track team. Diving season was in the fall, and during the winter, my teammates and I trained with a nearby college diving coach. I decided I needed a spring sport as well, so I joined track.

I ran a few weeks of the season as a sophomore in high school. At the start of the season, the other track members and I ran through the school's halls because, living in upstate New York, the ground remained snow-covered. Eventually, we went outside, and I began to find a rhythm with a small group of girls.

Finding running more arduous than I had predicted, I trailed behind my teammates. My legs felt like they weighed a thousand pounds each. Getting through the workouts seemed almost impossible. I ran the 800-meter race and struggled to finish. Not only was I undereating, but I also had mononucleosis—most likely caused by my weakened immune system from years of under-fueling.

The illness took me out of track for a month. I felt so weak that my dad had to read my homework assignments to me. After three weeks, I went back to school and resumed running track—but not for long. Too anxious to refrain from exercising, I ended up with walking pneumonia.

"It seems as though it's time to hang up the shoes for the season," my coach said when I informed her. Round one of running for me came to a close.

As an adult, I have learned, through studying dietetics and experiencing multiple injuries, that training for and completing nine marathons required learning how to properly fuel my body. This understanding was something I didn't appreciate years earlier, when just catching the uneven bars on a mount led to breaking all the bones in my right hand. Proper fueling was not only crucial for training but also for recovery and simply living.

I often find with my clients who restrict their eating that when they are injured or recovering from an ultra or a marathon, they restrict even more, making recovery even harder. Healing requires fuel. Recovery requires fuel. But we also need calories outside of running or exercising.

I work diligently with my clients on not labeling foods as "good" or "bad." It only backfires. I recently told one of my clients that she was putting certain foods on a pedestal, and a light bulb went off for her. "OMG, you're right!" she exclaimed.

As soon as she was able to put all foods on a level playing field, she stopped binging. "You mean I can eat cheese, and it's ok!?" she asked incredulously. She went from eating an entire block of cheese at a time because it was "forbidden" to enjoying just a few slices when she wanted, without guilt. It was a game changer. She thought I was crazy at first—rightfully so—but soon realized I was right.

Although I hated my first yoga class, claiming it wasn't enough exercise, I now practice daily. I use yoga therapy in my **Coalescence Method** to help clients reconnect their mind and body, guiding them to break free of rigid rules. Instead, I help them identify what their body is craving, recognize when they are hungry or full, and learn how to honor all of that without guilt.

Through nutrition counseling, yoga therapy, journaling, and food therapy, I guide my clients to nourish their bodies rather than starve or punish them.

About Theresa DeLorenzo:

Dr. DeLorenzo, a Registered Dietitian (RD) since 2001, is dedicated to helping athletes optimize their performance and well-being. She earned her Bachelor of Science in Food Science and Dietetics from the University of Rhode Island and her Master of Science and Doctorate of Clinical Nutrition from the University of Medicine and Dentistry of New Jersey.

As the founder of *Nutrition for Optimal Performance*, Dr. DeLorenzo specializes in tailoring macronutrient and micronutrient plans, developing race-day nutrition and hydration strategies, improving gastrointestinal health, and fostering a positive body image for athletes. Her holistic approach empowers clients to achieve their best performance while enhancing overall health.

In addition to her nutrition practice, Dr. DeLorenzo is a 200-hour trained yoga teacher with a certification in yoga therapy focused on body image improvement. She integrates yoga therapy for clients with anxiety, body dysmorphia, and pain, and teaches aerial yoga in her home studio.

To learn more about the **Coalescence Method**, check out Dr. DeLorenzo's website here: **https://nutrition-4-op.com/coalescence-method**

A More Complete Sense of Self
By Carrie Van Acker

"What makes you happy?" My therapist of decades had asked this question on more than one occasion, and here she was proposing it yet again.

"Taking care of my son and husband," I replied automatically.

"Yes, I know. But there will come a time when he is all grown up, and it will be important for you to do things that fulfill you outside of being a mother and a wife."

Ugh. I hated this question—not because she was out of line or wrong, but because she was spot on, and I didn't have an answer. Before becoming a wife and later a stay-at-home mom, I conducted psychotherapy. Creating a safe space for people to embark on their own healing journeys fulfilled me. Validating people when they had not felt heard or seen before felt like my purpose in life. Becoming a wife and a mother was yet another part of being the caretaker I had always been. That was—and is—who I am.

But, again, she was right. Conducting psychotherapy provided a professional identity and gave me fulfillment outside of "wife" and "mom." People don't really tell you that if you are blessed to have the desire and financial means to be a stay-at-home mom, there is an unspoken cultural opinion that you as a person, separate from that role, cease to exist. People never asked me questions about my education, professional life, or really anything of much depth.

Life, as it pertained to me as a separate entity, was put on hold. And I was all right with that. Providing for the needs of my son and husband was fulfilling to me. But sometimes, the universe asks more of us and, perhaps, wants more for us.

One morning, after returning from fishing (a frequent family outing), I did not feel well. Unable to stop shaking and without any desire to eat, something felt wrong. Normally, I would push through, but something felt different. I needed help. Through tears, I told my husband I needed to go to the ER. I had only been to the ER once in my life. This was a huge deal for me to actually utter the words, "I need help. Something is wrong."

Hours later, the doctor returned with the blood results. Surely they would be unremarkable. Most likely, I was having a panic attack and would be sent on my way after a brief look-over. Anxiety and I had coexisted from a young age, and I was well aware that it could come flooding in at times when I wasn't examining all of my emotions adequately. Given my professional background, I tended to assume most symptoms were psychological, not physical. (Opposite of many folks, I guess, whose psychological symptoms became psychosomatic.)

"I'm extremely concerned about your iron levels. You have severe anemia, and if not addressed in the next few days, you will need a blood transfusion."

Technically, I heard his words, but the seriousness of the situation remained outside of my understanding. Denial and dissociation—two useful coping mechanisms at times—were working overtime.

After returning home, my "old friend" anxiety came flooding in. A side effect of being a caretaker is neglecting oneself. In my case, I was terrible at addressing physical symptoms. I despised medical doctor appointments. In many ways, this felt minor. But in the larger scheme of things, this was a hit upside the head. I needed to make some changes. The status quo wasn't going to cut it anymore. I needed to take care of me (even if the original motivation was so I could be a better caregiver for my family).

After meeting with my general practitioner, we developed a plan to improve my physical health. I began taking a multitude of vitamins, focusing on increasing iron. I decided that drinking alcohol no longer served me and quit it altogether. I was never good at the whole "you need to put on your oxygen mask first before helping others" thing, but I was going to try. I needed to be healthy so I could be a better caretaker. Focusing on my physical health seemed straightforward and doable. After a few months, I felt clearer and healthier. But I was still avoiding the "What makes you happy?" question and "Who was Carrie as a separate human?" How does one even go about answering that? Up until this point in my life, I only knew how to function as someone who takes care of others and enjoys assisting in their happiness.

To some, perhaps this seems simple. Did other people know what they enjoyed doing outside of work and family? My husband's passion was fishing and golfing. I fished with him all the time. Did I really like fishing? I thought so. But would I pick fishing to do if given the chance to pick an activity just for myself? Probably not. What did I like doing? Truthfully, I was going to have to start from scratch.

Why was this so difficult? I felt immense guilt if I even suggested an activity that wasn't something I thought my son or husband would enjoy. The simple act of stating, "I booked this activity that I thought might be fun," felt wrong. Let me be clear: this had nothing to do with them. They would support me if given the chance. This was a deep-rooted issue I had and needed to work through.

I continued my one-on-one therapy sessions, and with a clearer head and a new mission, I began a journey to discover—or rediscover—who Carrie was now. I began searching for activities or experiences that appeared interesting to me. I decided that I was going to book these experiences and invite my son and husband to join me but commit to attending regardless of whether they came. I still craved permission and really wanted them to join, but I needed to almost force myself to follow through. Another important facet was that I was going to attend without any real expectations. Either way, the process would provide me with information about what was now fulfilling to me—or not.

My son and I attended the first booked experience in downtown Los Angeles. It sold itself as an art and light exhibit. Honestly, I had no idea what to expect and dreaded driving into the city. The "show" began as a little too artsy and alternative, but we embraced the process. We entered different rooms and experiences. The ones that stood out to me included a mini sound bath and later an aura reading. I could feel a small spark being ignited.

Luckily, the holidays were upon us, and we attended numerous light shows and cheery, themed events. These made the "do again" list, along with zoo and farm visits. One definitely made the "no thank you" list: an event involving downloading an app and following instructions from my phone for a local scavenger hunt. Nope. Technology and an impersonal experience filled me with frustration and anxiety.

Mother's Day led me to search out a new experience that I would enjoy without thought of whether my family would as well. (Okay, I tried not to think about whether they would enjoy it or not—a work in progress.) A salt cave? This sounded amazing. Meditation music was pumped into the private Himalayan salt cave while visitors were encouraged to lie on the salt floor and breathe in the healing air. Although we went for me, we all felt lighter after spending 45 minutes in this tranquil environment. As we exited, I grabbed a flier advertising a sound bath in the salt cave in the near future. Sounded interesting, but yet again, I really had no idea what this entailed.

Following my new mantra—*I have no expectations except to have an experience*—I secured our spot at the upcoming sound bath. My husband was unable to attend, but my son joined me. As we settled ourselves onto the salt floor, the practitioner began the sound bath experience. What was I hearing? I couldn't put words to the journey my body was embarking on. I felt myself become lost in the process. Relaxed, invigorated, falling into a deeper level of consciousness—I allowed my mind and body to flow wherever they were supposed to go. For lack of a better word, it felt magical.

As the sound bath wrapped up, the practitioner mentioned she was certified. This was a thing? My academic side was activated, and I had to know more. How does one become certified in sound healing? I hadn't felt this motivated to learn about a new area in years. Not really knowing why I had this deep desire to explore further, I began a deep dive into sound healing certification. I quickly learned this was more common than I had imagined. My brain began racing.

What if I became certified? Not for a business, but just so I could learn more about the healing benefits of sound healing for myself and my family? "This is ridiculous," my mind commented. "If you're going to invest your time outside of being a caretaker, you need to go back to being a psychotherapist. That's your true passion." But what if I could have more than one passion?

Excitedly, I ran to my son's room and expressed my crazy idea to become a certified sound healer. His initial reaction was one of surprise and confusion. Just recently, I had been discussing my desire to return to conducting psychotherapy. I'm sure he thought this was coming out of left field.

And it was. What would make me think I could be a sound healer? But I couldn't shake it. When faced with an emotional and intellectual disconnect, I turned to intellectualization. More research was needed. Now, I'm not sure if it was a coincidence or the universe intervening, but I found Life Changing Energy. There was something different about this program. The certification and accreditation looked legitimate. But most importantly, Vickie, the owner and teacher, led with genuineness and an academic background. Okay, now I was truly invested. The nerd in me was fascinated to learn more about the research and science supporting the benefits of the numerous instruments used in a sound bath.

"I have no expectation other than to have an experience." I decided I would verbalize my intent to dedicate some time to this sound healing realm.

Although my husband (who had not attended the sound bath) had no idea what I was talking about, he wholeheartedly encouraged me to become certified. What did I have to lose? He was right—nothing. My son, after initially being unsure of what my intentions were, supported me as well. As I noted earlier, they have always wanted nothing but the best for me. I was holding myself back.

With their support, I excitedly began my courses. Quickly, I went down the rabbit hole and found myself wanting to learn as much as possible. Over time, I began accumulating numerous instruments as well as many certifications. I was fascinated and becoming more and more fulfilled by my new journey. However, I hadn't shared this new part of myself and identity with anyone outside of my immediate family. Why?

Did I still question whether I was a healer or not? Did sound healing stray too far outside traditional academia? Was I concerned about what others would think, or did I still hold reservations and stereotypes about this genre? I obviously needed to dig deeper to figure out what repressed feelings I was harboring.

Part of me feared that others would not understand my passion for sound healing, and their lack of understanding or support could tarnish my newfound happiness. I had worked too hard to discover this new area of interest. Reluctantly, I had to admit that I was battling my own internal judgments. Had I fully embraced the ideas behind sound healing? Was I afraid I had strayed too far outside of what I had envisioned for myself and the path I had paved many years ago? Was conducting sound baths in contrast to practicing psychotherapy?

The word "healer" means something profoundly different to everyone. As a psychotherapist, we don't profess ourselves to be healers or that we provide a "cure" for psychological ailments. But we do create a safe space for healing to occur. Was that so different from what ideally happens during a sound bath? The practitioner creates a safe space for participants to embark on a healing journey. Whether the "healing" is simply a more relaxed state of being, a momentary experience of complete presence, or a cathartic release of buried feelings, the goal is the same. My inner self inherently knew that this was what I was meant to do.

"Well, I have found a new passion that fuels me. I can't believe I'm saying this out loud, but I'm going to start an LLC and see where sound healing takes me." Hearing the words as I spoke them to my therapist immediately filled me with anxiety. But this time, the anxiety wasn't rooted in fear. It was an excited, hopeful anxiety. This time, the fear was about something getting in the way of this new journey. Was I really going to do something just for me and my evolving sense of self? I wanted this. That day in the salt cave, listening to the melodic tones of those beautiful instruments, had awakened a part of me that had been dormant for decades. I was ready for this new path.

I now knew who Carrie was: a mother, wife, caretaker, and someone passionate about providing a safe space for people to "heal," whatever that may mean to them.

About Carrie Van Acker:

Carrie earned her Ph.D. in Clinical Psychology in 2004 from California School of Professional Psychology at Alliant International University. Her main areas of interest included trauma with a specialty in the area of violence. Carrie has recently earned numerous certifications for Sound Healing including: Expert Sound Healer. She is in the process of establishing an LLC in which she intends to conduct private group sound healing experiences. Carrie currently resides in Southern California with her husband of 24 years, and her 17 year old son.

Transforming My Veterinary Practice – A Journey to Holistic Healing Through Island Life, Music, Medicine, Yoga, Animals, & Self Love

By Eve Harrison

Sometimes, I feel my professional journey started as a loss of self. The story of losing myself as a veterinarian isn't something that developed over time. In actuality, this incredibly meaningful path of working with animals has been intertwined with self-betrayal from day one.

Starting in veterinary school, I remember feeling struck by the tone of it all; I instantaneously felt like a cog in a machine. I felt the weight of conformity, of black-and-white thinking: "right or wrong," the unbearable importance of being a "good vet," and the devastation of what it would mean to be a "bad vet." All of that seeped, insidiously, into my bones. The objectification of animals within the paradigm I was learning left me feeling empty. The new medical jargon we were learning (& the pride surrounding its use!) felt pretentious to me.

In that paradigm, I lost track of myself, especially in the psychological aspects of becoming a doctor — the emotional impact of starting to take full responsibility for another living (or dying) being, especially one that cannot speak for its own needs.

I was supposed to love all of this. And yet, the ground fell out from under me as I attempted to shift into this new identity. All I could see was a future where my personality—my beingness—had to conform into something it wasn't, & a lifestyle where I had no time or energy left for anything else I cared about.

During year one, I considered quitting vet school. However, after spending three months as a volunteer vet student on a tropical South Pacific island called Rarotonga in the Cook Islands, I was able to find my center again, remembering why I'd wanted to be a veterinarian in the first place.

While there, I fell in love with the island animals. I also fell in love with the experience, which became a portal into a future vision of how I could do this work well, be myself again, & live my life to the fullest. I experienced fulfillment & meaning here in a deeply integrated way.

Life on Rarotonga was all about working hard for the animals under our care, often performing surgery & wound care with very few supplies.

But it was *also* about letting loose with the island life after hours!

After a day providing life-saving care for dogs, cats, chickens, pigs, & goats, our team might find ourselves bathing in a pale blue lagoon, forest bathing, sipping melon liqueur, or dancing at a tiki bar with new local friends. I remember that as one of the most meaningful & fulfilling times of my life.

Rarotonga reawakened the spark of inspiration—my love for animals & the work of providing care, especially surgery for them—that I had previously tried to force into the "good veterinarian" white-coat persona from vet school (which felt more like a straitjacket to me).

That glimpse into the felt experience of a well integrated life, that spark, got me through the remaining three years of vet school, my internship year, & a successful application to veterinary surgical residency.

Though I continued to teeter on the edge of burnout, impostor syndrome, & a nagging feeling that I was suppressing a part of myself, I'd mostly regained my commitment & functionality within the system—until I started surgery residency.

Needless to say, participating in a surgical residency program at a large corporate urban practice was a far cry from the island life, the aspirational vision I had imprinted onto my heart for how life as a veterinarian *could feel*.

I've never been the typical "surgeon type." I'm empathetic. I cry easily. I'm not afraid to ask for help or admit mistakes. I didn't realize how much these qualities would feel so out of place in this environment. The combination of a cold clinical atmosphere, the extreme objectification of animals, & the strong personalities of surgeons, sent me into a downward spiral. I was supposed to be detached—but how could I detach from these animals in front of me or their concerned caregivers? The pressure to "toughen up" made me feel even more out of place.

The culture shock from my supportive internship the year prior to a multi-year surgery residency was severe. I went from feeling safe & supported in my new responsibilities as a doctor to feeling constantly embarrassed & ashamed of who I was. Each 2 a.m. on-call & every harsh public criticism of my work added another pound of weight to my body—literally & figuratively.

After two years, I found myself clinically depressed, 30 pounds heavier, & on medication for the first time in my life. I questioned whether my mental health warranted hospitalization. Ultimately, I didn't admit myself, but I continued to spiral until I hit rock bottom. Eventually, the whole endeavor fell apart; I left my residency feeling utterly humiliated & like a failure.

The next few years, I wandered through different jobs & positions—general veterinary care, emergency care, shelter work—trying to find a path that felt like my own.

None of it felt right. I always felt I was trying to be good enough to keep a boss happy, part of a machine, doing what I was told rather than providing care from a heart-based place. I felt unable to offer high level care with the full integrity I knew I had within me. I didn't feel good about my work as a veterinarian; I was merely tolerating my career. Eventually, I found myself tolerating my whole life rather than living it.

Only a few years into my career, I became painfully aware of how much I had sacrificed & how much more it would cost me if I continued this way. I needed to find another path to give my patients, their caregivers, & — honestly—myself the level of care we all deserved.

My memories of Rarotonga reminded me (frequently) that it was indeed possible to do this meaningful work with animals & be happy at the same time. To be a veterinarian—a good one— & still continue to be myself. The problem wasn't the act of being a veterinarian or caring for animals; it was the system within which I was being asked to perform.

Knowing something had to shift, I decided to partially put my veterinary career on hold & reconnect with my body to rediscover what my own desires even were at that point. I decided to explore becoming a yoga teacher & to return to my roots as a musician. I even started teaching music again, as I had before becoming a veterinarian.

As a music major in college, I had studied flute, piccolo, Irish whistle, & other world instruments. I felt a strong call to return to that part of myself. This decision was as much about healing my own mind & body as it was about teaching music. I lived humbly during this period, doing light part-time moonlighting work as a veterinarian to support myself while I taught yoga & rekindled my musical path.

Every restorative yoga flow I taught, & every time I picked up my flute, was a form of therapy—a way to breathe life back into myself after years of depletion.

The turning point came when my dear friend, Dr. Marcia Medrano, asked me to do some moonlighting work (veterinarians call it relief work) for her house call practice in San Francisco while she was out of town. She was one of only two people I knew who were practicing in such an unusual way. But I decided to give it a try & help out my friend!

It turns out that first house call was pivotal. *I knew I was meant to be a house call vet.*

In the home, I could work in flow state, in what I call "dog & cat time" with each animal, connecting deeply with their humans, customizing thoughtful, attuned treatment plans. It was like coming home to myself. All of the work I had done in yoga & music by then, while taking a break from the standard veterinary path—it had done something for me. It had healed my nervous system enough that, once it arrived in my life, I had the capacity to recognize the calling.

In early 2016, I decided to take a huge risk & do something completely outside the box for me at the time: I opened my own integrative concierge house call practice in Los Angeles.

Although I knew for sure that I was finally on the right path, having regained agency in my professional journey, I still struggled for several years to maintain boundaries with clients, manage my workload, & keep my practice financially viable.

My full-spectrum transformation truly landed after I decided to make major investments in myself specifically *as a small business owner* with a unique offering. Knowing I was finally *the one* in charge of myself as a veterinarian, I committed to regular therapy, leaned even deeper into my yoga practice (& its philosophy as self-care), & invested in business training, coaching, & ceremonial work.

I took courses in business, marketing, & holistic paradigms of veterinary medicine. I studied acupuncture & herbalism at the Chi Institute of Traditional Chinese Veterinary Medicine. I worked with spiritual coaches & mentors. I also began to lean seriously back into my music, investing in additional training & dedicating time to practicing, playing in orchestras, weddings, performing with my Celtic band *Mayde In Ireland*, sharing folk music at festivals. All of these investments into myself allowed me to nourish my soul & be my whole self AS I poured into my house call practice.

After years of working on myself, inspired in part by a desire to get my business & livelihood feeling good, my practice & life finally became sustainable & truly my own again. I was able to practice from a place of emotional health & well-being in a way that fed directly into the health of my business. I could give my time & energy generously to my patients, clients, & myself—without resentment—providing (& receiving!) the level of care we all deserved.

Once I stepped fully into my life as a solo mobile vet, something else transformed too: I stopped seeing the world through a warped, clinicalized lens where those "above me" determined what health & clinical "correctness" were. And I stopped seeing others as "below me" as well.

I started to recognize that the old way I had been thinking—that black-and-white paradigm that alienates everyone outside of that system, would ultimately burn out those living within it worst of all.

As veterinary professionals, we are trained to exist within a medical hierarchy where clinical opinion rules. In turn, we start to see ourselves through that same lens.

The matrix started to crack when I became a house call vet. It finally shattered when I became a *balanced*, healthy, fully embodied house call vet—someone who felt comfortable in her own skin again. The clinical posturing & rigid thinking, the seeing myself as a cog in the machine, to be validated by other cogs in the machine, to be criticized & judged by those same cogs, to *be* a criticizing judge myself towards other cogs – it all dissolved.

Finally, I started to regain connection to the full range of engaging in the world that had been deeply suppressed by my training. I learned that not everything is a clinical situation to be fixed or to determine how to do "right" or "wrong," with implications for the verdict on my entire existence being worthy or not.

I finally understood that we can get stuck in this black-and-white veterinary or medical orthodoxy, or we can break out of the box & do it our own way—no middleman, no toxic clinic or corporate culture. No hierarchy, including no one above you looking over your shoulder, telling you if you're a "good" or "bad" vet, if you're meeting quotas, or if you've spent too much time with a client.

Instead, it's just you, looking into your own heart, knowing you're doing the right thing on a cosmic level, beyond the limitations of professional systems & hierarchies.

For nearly a decade now, I've practiced veterinary medicine *on my terms* through my own practice. I have amazing clients & patients who I truly *love*, with whom I have authentic, heartfelt connections, & who respect my time & boundaries.

I offer acupuncture, herbal therapy, massage, laser therapy, movement therapy, Eastern & Western pain management techniques, ozone therapy, sound healing, home-cooked recipes, nutritional support, blood work, lab testing, in addition to most other forms of traditional veterinary care for dogs, cats, goats, & other animals. My patients are living their best (& healthiest!) lives. And I love it.

Best of all, I still get to be me.

My journey has taught me that you don't have to sacrifice your quality of life, the quality of care for your patients, or your vision to have a thriving, successful practice & keep your career in medicine or healing work alive. You also don't have to follow methods, systems, or paradigms that don't feel aligned or possible for you.

Learning to respect boundaries around who I am at my core, I found a way to keep giving in a prolific & inspired way—all without losing myself. I finally understood that my own health, well-being, & wholeness were the cornerstones of my career.

Eventually, I realized that my path felt *so good* in my soul that I could support other veterinarians as well. I knew I wasn't the only veterinarian who had struggled intensely with this same flavor of self-betrayal. I knew others could benefit from the path I had taken to return home to myself.

In late 2020, I opened The House Call Vet Academy, where I support other veterinary professionals in building or revamping their mobile practices in a way that feels aligned with their unique vision. Through a trauma-informed veterinary education platform, coaching, & community, I aim to help them create practices that are truly holistic—not only for the animals but for the veterinarians themselves.

My students transform their own unique house call practices in a way that honors their boundaries, their visions for animal well-being, & the wholeness of who they are as human beings, rather than as cogs in the machine of our profession.

To date, I have supported nearly 300 veterinarians & guided them to find their own authentic paths as animal doctors. That may be one of the greatest accomplishments of my life.

Through my veterinary practice (Marigold Veterinary), my educational program (The House Call Vet Academy), my yoga, my music, & now this book, I am committed not only to my own path but to helping others find their own paths in the healing arts (& sciences!) as well. I strongly believe in having a deeply nourished life outside of my work, paired with claiming agency in my life as a veterinarian through entrepreneurship— & I am passionate about helping others achieve this balance too.

I'd like to close by saying that your own healing journey *as a healer* is incredibly important. By self-actualizing & taking back our agency to live as our most balanced, supported, nourished, & whole selves, we become better equipped to serve others in a deeply satisfying & sustainable way. In doing so, we can create potent, meaningful impact in our communities, extending far beyond ourselves—for humans & animals alike.

About Eve Harrison:

Dr. Eve Harrison is an integrative concierge house call veterinarian in Los Angeles. She is a speaker, writer, content creator, & founder of the online CE course: **The House Call Vet Academy**. She offers training, coaching, & consulting to help independent veterinarians nourish not only their patients, but themselves, by helping them to cultivate profitable & sustainable mobile practices of their own. She also is the founder of the annual House Call & Mobile Vet Virtual Conference, & host of The House Call Vet Cafe Podcast.Dr. Eve's passions include stress free animal handling, herbal medicine, music for animals, Traditional Chinese Veterinary Medicine, pain management, creative entrepreneurship, sustainability for veterinarians, boundaries, authentic communication, & releasing people (& systems) who are not a good match for our lives. Outside of her work with animals & their humans, Eve is passionate about music & nature! She is a yogi, mushroom forager, and semi-professional flutist.

LINKS:

Marigold Veterinary: **www.marigoldveterinary.com**

More about Dr. Eve Harrison: **www.dreveharrison.com**

The House Call Vet Academy: **www.thehousecallvetacademy.com**

House Call Vet Cafe Podcast: **https://pod.link/1604252727**

Instagram: The_House_Call_Vet_Academy

Facebook: The House Call Vet Academy

Harmonize Your Heart and Heal Your Soul

By Kimberly Lim

My journey unfolded with what appeared to be a routine pregnancy, but it quickly took an unexpected turn. During my first pregnancy, I was diagnosed with Meralgia Paresthetica, a rare and often misunderstood condition that would dramatically shift the course of my life. What started as a minor inconvenience soon spiraled into years of relentless pain, triggered by a pregnancy-related anomaly, ultimately leaving me with permanent impairment of a nerve in my left leg.

The pain was more than physical; it became a constant companion, radiating from my hip joint down my leg and leaving me with an unsettling sensation of numbness and tingling. Countless trips to the emergency room became routine as I desperately sought relief. I turned to every possible treatment—physical therapy, chiropractic care, acupuncture—each offering a fleeting glimpse of hope, only to fall back into the same frustrating cycle. Despite the absence of lasting results, surgery remained an option, but it came with the heavy weight of risk and uncertainty.

Night after night, I lay awake in agony, haunted by the thought that my body was betraying me. My pain loomed like a shadow, clouding my life, stealing my rest, my serenity, and occasionally my spirit. Yet even in those darkest moments, I refused to give up. Each day brought its own set of obstacles, as the debilitating discomfort forced me to navigate the world in ways I never imagined. Amidst the pain, I discovered a resilience I never knew I had and a deeper connection to my own body and mind. Through it all, I clung to a belief that healing was within reach and that solutions might lie beyond the conventional path. What began as a struggle for relief became a journey of hope and determination, a quest to find something that could finally bring peace to both my body and my soul.

As a homeopathic Registered Nurse for nearly fifteen years and with a lifelong belief in natural remedies, I have discovered that sound healing offers transformative benefits, alleviating pain and enhancing my spiritual awareness. This awakening inspired me to dedicate myself more deeply to my practice and explore a diverse range of sound healing methods, which in turn enriched my understanding and appreciation for both music and the healing power of sound. Since childhood, my passion for music and dance has been rooted in the rhythms and vibrations that have always grounded my movements. This deep connection has naturally guided me toward a broader exploration of sound and its transformative possibilities.

As I delved into these practices, my path led me to intertwine meditation, breathwork, Reiki, yoga, and sound healing, emphasizing how sound can transform our everyday lives. My immersion into meditation ultimately led me to become certified as a Meditation Teacher, a practice that brought a new dimension to my understanding of self-awareness, mindfulness, and presence. Meditation has always served as a sanctuary, a place where I can escape from the chaos of daily life and reconnect with my inner self.

Throughout the years, I began integrating meditation and breathwork into my practice during my yoga teacher training, which brought me a deep sense of tranquility and wellness. The gentle flow of poses, paired with conscious breathing, created a beautiful rhythm that connected with me. I learned that yoga transcended beyond physical exercise; it evolved into a holistic practice that integrated mind, body, and spirit. The principles of yoga resonated with me, merging physical movement with breath and meditation. This experience significantly enhanced my connection with yoga, leading me to become a Certified Yoga Instructor and a Certified Instructor of Kundalini Yoga. The integration of meditation and yoga practices illuminated my path to sound healing, where I achieved certification as an Expert Sound Healer Practitioner. This experience has ignited a deep passion within me to share these healing benefits with others and guide them on their paths to wellness. Through my facilitation of sound healing, meditation, breathwork, and yoga sessions for groups, corporations, and private clients, I strive to cultivate a nurturing environment where others can experience the transformative power of sound, just as I have. Sharing this journey is not only fulfilling for me, but it also ignites a ripple effect of healing and growth within the communities I support.

My first experience with sound healing and meditation took place at Manhattan Beach in Half Moon Bay, California, a place that has always deepened my connection with nature. After strolling along the sandy shore, I decided to collect some seawater to place in my sound healing bowl, which would allow the vibrations to resonate through the water. Many practitioners of sound healing believe that structuring water can amplify its energy and offer various other benefits for physical, emotional, and spiritual health. The connection between sound and water is a fascinating area I wanted to explore, as the concept of structuring water using sound has gained remarkable attention within the realms of holistic health and sound healing.

While lying in front of the tranquil ocean waves at sunset, I concentrated on the sensation of my breath flowing in and out through my nose. Holding my 528-hertz frequency crystal quartz sound healing bowl filled with seawater above my chest, I felt the vibrations deeply resonate within me. These powerful vibrations reached my core, unlocking emotions I had not acknowledged. The gentle sensations at the tip of my nose and in my chest were genuinely transformative. I was astonished that such a simple practice could result in such significant insights. A deep wave of calmness washed over me as if I were gently being swept away from the ocean floor. After this transformative experience, I emerged with a sense of lightness and a heightened spiritual awareness, along with a noticeable release of tension in my left hip and lower back. In this first session, the sound vibrations seemed to wrap around my pain, softening it, and for the first time in years, I felt a glimmer of hope. It was a soothing sensation unlike any I had known, one that moved me to share this gift with my community by offering my time to friends, family, and their cherished pets.

Sound healing awareness has been a continuous journey for me and has opened opportunities to offer my support and experience to others, including a close, loving friend, Kerri, from Lake County, California. She has been courageously dealing with a brain lesion and swelling in her frontal lobe. Kerri endured two strokes and was diagnosed with a traumatic brain injury as a result of a catastrophic car accident twenty-three years ago, which continues to impact her daily life and mobility. During the Spring of 2024, she was hospitalized, and I had the privilege of offering her bedside sound healing and rehabilitation therapy. During one memorable sound healing session, she expressed how the throbbing pain in her arm from a kinked IV site vanished within minutes after listening to my sound healing. At that moment, she awakened and realized the powerful healing benefits of sound.

As a Registered Nurse, my commitment to Kerri's well-being extended beyond the sound healing sessions. I took an active role in coordinating her care, working closely with her neurologist and nursing staff to develop a comprehensive treatment plan tailored to her needs. Initially, she was confined to her bed, progressed to a wheelchair, then to a walker, and finally regained her ability to walk independently. I stayed devoted to providing my sound healing services, determined to help her regain her mobility and thrive. Her commitment mirrored mine; as she embraced the sound healing frequencies I provided throughout her hospital stay and continues to integrate my soothing music into her nightly routine.

I am incredibly grateful for my ability to help her heal through sound. Being involved in her journey is a beautiful gift; she now sees me as her

Earth Angel and passionately promotes my sound healing services all around town! Her relentless support inspires me to continue my work with even greater passion, knowing that I am making a difference in the lives of others. The joy of being her Earth Angel, guiding her on her path, is a reward in itself, and I am grateful for the opportunity to share this sound healing experience with her.

One of the most heartfelt stories I cherish is about a remarkable man, known as Mr. Lakeport, who left a lasting impression in our community. He passed away on February 29, 2024, after a brave battle with a terminal illness in Lake County, California. Mr. Lakeport was a beloved figure known for his infectious charisma and unwavering commitment to uplifting those around him. During his final days, I had the privilege of providing sound healing therapy to him both at his home and in the hospital. Through calming vibrations and melodic frequencies, I fostered a safe space where he could release stress, find tranquility, and tap into his inner strength.

Each session emerged as a ray of hope, illuminating his journey toward inner peace and emotional stability. He would frequently drift off to the soothing sound healing, glancing around the room to ask, "Where is Nurse Kimmie?" He would then request, "Please continue!" It truly touched my heart and soul knowing my presence and sound therapy offered him comfort during his final days. My time with Mr. Lakeport at his bedside will stay with me forever, as I brought him peace and comfort through sound healing. He will always hold a special place in my heart, as his legacy continues to inspire us all.

Every session with Kerri and Mr. Lakeport served as a reminder of the profound nature of this journey—not only to heal myself but to help others experience the peace I have found. My passion lies in sharing my abilities through a diverse collection of healing instruments, such as quartz crystal singing bowls, Tibetan singing bowls, a variety of drums and chimes, gongs, rain sticks, Native American flutes, tuning forks, and many more. These instruments have unique and specific frequencies, which foster healing for various health conditions, enriching one's meditative and introspective experiences in the natural vibrations of life. From the enchanting tones of crystal bowls to the soothing sounds of a flute and the invigorating beats of a drum, the vibrations can have a profound effect on your mind, body, and soul. Immersing yourself in these sounds can help release tension, diminish stress, and cultivate a harmonious state of being.

In my community, I am fondly referred to as Nurse Angel or Earth Angel, a testament to my unwavering dedication and compassion. Over the years,

I have devoted countless hours offering my support and care to those in need, whether in hospitals, with individuals, with pets, or in group settings. I have applied a range of healing practices, such as meditation, breathwork, spiritual coaching, Reiki, yoga, and facilitating sound healing sessions to promote well-being. With every interaction, my presence brings comfort, hope, and healing by touching the lives of everyone I meet.

While my professional skills in nursing provide a solid foundation for my work, it is my genuine compassion and empathy that truly define my approach. I believe a holistic approach is needed in the true healing of a person, which includes physical, emotional, and spiritual support. In my practice, I see each person as a unique individual, and I understand that healing is not just a matter of treating symptoms. True healing involves recognizing the emotional and spiritual aspects that are often intertwined with physical health. I strive to create a space where individuals feel heard, understood, and valued, offering support that goes beyond the clinical setting. I recognize that emotional pain, past trauma, or spiritual unrest can all manifest in physical symptoms, and it is this interconnectedness that guides my approach to care.

Reflecting on a pivotal moment in my life, I remember a spiritual healer who was a close friend of my mother's. Years ago, she shared a remarkable insight—that her daughter, Kimberly, was gifted with natural intuition and other spiritual abilities. As a young girl, I was both fascinated and intrigued by this revelation. It set me on a path of self-discovery that would go on to deeply shape who I am today.

I am grateful for the ability to connect with individuals on a deeper level, sensing their needs, revealing emotional blockages, and offering comfort in times of distress. This connection became a powerful tool for healing, as I realized I could use my intuition to guide and support those who crossed my path. Reflecting on my mother's words, I felt a deep sense of gratitude for the gifts I had been given. These intuitive abilities are not just a part of who I am, but they also empower me to serve others with compassion and understanding. Every interaction is an opportunity for connection and healing, and I am honored to be a part of this journey.

This holistic approach to healing has also extended to animals, including my beloved dog, Salsa, whom I recently helped through sound healing techniques to accelerate recovery and provide comfort. When I adopted her in June 2024, she had already been injured after being struck by a car. Still bearing stitches down her leg, I welcomed her into my home. I could sense the pain and distress reflected in her eyes. Determined to support her recovery, I provided sound healing for her day and night, creating a soothing environment that would aid her in her healing process.

The soft, resonant tones of the crystal quartz bowls created a peaceful, comforting presence around her. She responded positively to the frequencies, often settling into a relaxed state as she listened calmly. One of Salsa's favorites was my crystal quartz singing bowl tuned to 528 hertz. Known for its healing properties, this frequency seemed to resonate deeply within her, as evidenced by her eyes closing and body gradually relaxing. Over time, I observed a significant improvement in her demeanor and physical condition. Her playful spirit began to reemerge. The array of techniques used to aid Salsa's recovery not only solidified my belief in the universal nature of healing vibrations but also strengthened our bond. This journey showed me how the transformative power of sound can provide comfort and healing to all beings.

"Harmonize Your Heart and Heal Your Soul" is an inspiring story of discovering the profound, life-changing healing power of sound. I am passionate about inspiring others, as they take empowered steps toward healing and achieving personal growth. With the endearing titles of Nurse Angel and Earth Angel, I guide individuals on their journey, helping them spread their wings and reach their fullest potential. True healing is a holistic process—one that nurtures not just the mind and body, but also the heart and soul. Through **Heart N Soul Sound Healing**, I am committed to offering sound as a pathway to healing, transformation, and cultivating a life of greater harmony, peace, and joy.

About Kimberly Lim:

Kimberly Lim is a Registered Nurse, Public Health Nurse, Certified Expert Sound Healer Practitioner, Reiki Master/Teacher, Certified Yoga & Kundalini Instructor, Certified Massage Therapist, Certified Meditation Teacher, Spiritual Coach, Herbalist, Biomagnetic Therapy Nurse Healthcare Practitioner, and a Nurse Healthcare Practitioner with Ulta Labs, Premier Research Lab, and Pure Encapsulations. She specializes in sound healing, offering private sound baths, float sound baths, small and large group sound baths, gong baths, and sound healing for animals.

Kimberly offers a wide range of holistic services, including nurse advocacy, massage therapy, Reiki, spiritual coaching, energy healing, meditation, herbalism, biomagnetic therapy, and yoga. She provides mobile services throughout the San Francisco Bay Area, Santa Cruz, Half Moon Bay, Napa, and Lake County, California.

Kimberly A. Lim, RN, BSN, PHN, NCMA, NCEPT, CIMT, CPMT, NCS, CMT, KYT, RYT

Heart N Soul Sound Healing

"Harmonize Your Heart & Heal Your Soul"

www.heartnsoulsoundhealing.com

Email:heartnsoulsoundhealing@gmail.com

The Search for Meaning: My Journey from Law Enforcement to Spiritual Coaching

By Valerie Holden

It was the fifth year of my police career when my life took an unexpected turn. I was invited to attend a seminar on color therapy and Reiki. At the time, I had no idea what Reiki was, but I didn't care—I was excited about color therapy. I imagined it would be something like learning how to paint your walls in colors that evoke different emotions.

When I arrived, I quickly realized I had it all wrong. Color therapy wasn't about home décor; it was about chakras, the energy centers in the body. I was intrigued but still a bit skeptical. Then came the Reiki presentation, and the facilitator asked for a volunteer. My neck had been aching for days, so I thought, *"Why not?"* I sat in her massage chair, and as she placed her hands on my neck, something remarkable happened: the pain melted away. I could move my neck with more ease than I had in weeks. In that instant, a warmth spread through me, and I thought, *"Wow! What just happened?"*

That single moment changed everything for me. It wasn't just about relief from physical pain; it was the realization that something deeper was at play, something I couldn't explain. I was hooked.

From that point, I dove headfirst into alternative healing. I became a Reiki Master and started helping friends and clients. But it didn't stop there. I took course after course, certification after certification, learning every healing method I could get my hands on. What I didn't realize at the time was that I wasn't just collecting certifications for the sake of it—I was trying to fill a void inside me, a deep emptiness I couldn't quite put into words.

I loved my job as a police officer. Where else could you drive around, talk to people, and make a difference in their lives every day? Yet, despite this love for my work, something was missing. There was a piece of me I couldn't quite find, a piece that felt vital to my sense of purpose.

I continued my quest for answers and found myself at a weekend workshop on personal development. There, I encountered yet another alternative healing method: hypnosis. Naturally, I became certified in that, too. I became a hypnotherapist, helping others tap into their subconscious minds. But still, that nagging feeling persisted. The emptiness remained.

What was ironic was that all the inner work I was doing actually made me a better police officer. My coworkers would tell me that when I showed up on a scene, everything seemed to calm down. I even used Reiki once to help a distressed woman relax before the ambulance arrived. But no matter how much I helped others, I couldn't seem to help myself.

Ten years passed—ten years of learning, growing, and yet still feeling lost. The emptiness lingered, gnawing at me like a constant reminder that I wasn't on the path I was meant to be. Some nights, I'd sit alone, certifications in hand, wondering if I was just fooling myself, if I'd ever find what I was truly searching for. And then, one day, I heard about a training program that promised to help you discover your passion and purpose. It hit me like a punch to the gut. That was exactly what I needed.

I remember sitting down with my husband, trying to explain why I had to attend this training. Tears streamed down my face as I told him how important it was for me to figure out my purpose. I sobbed into his chest, feeling as though my entire life had been leading to this moment of clarity. He held me and reassured me that I should go. He could see how much this meant to me.

Those three days of training were transformative. I met incredible people, went through exercises that helped me peel back the layers of confusion, and by the end, I felt like I had finally found my calling. I became certified to help others find their purpose, and for a moment, I thought I had found mine too.

But life has a funny way of testing you. I helped a few people, but soon enough, I found myself falling back into old habits—taking more courses, earning more certifications, still searching for something I couldn't name. People began to ask, *"What are you doing now?"* But their tone wasn't one of curiosity; it was as if they knew I was just going through the motions, seeking something I hadn't yet found.

Then, I had an Akashic record reading—a spiritual reading that taps into your soul's history. The reader told me that I already had everything I needed to help others, that I didn't need any more certifications. But despite this revelation, I couldn't shake the feeling that I wasn't good enough, that I didn't know enough. And so, I kept searching because trusting myself—trusting that I had everything I needed—felt unnatural, like a foreign language.

But with each message, I began to see the world with new clarity. I started recognizing when I was receiving messages from the Divine, guiding me in the direction I was meant to go.

When I finally retired from the police department, I opened a hypnosis practice. I helped clients connect with their higher selves, channeling wisdom and insight that often led to profound breakthroughs. But during one particular session, something extraordinary happened. While connecting with my client's Higher Self, the answer that came had nothing to do with the question I had asked. I asked my client to repeat the answer, and it was the same. It was then I realized the message wasn't for him—it was for me.

The Higher Self was speaking directly to me about something that had happened in my life that very morning, something my client couldn't possibly have known about. I asked, *"Is this message for me?"* and the answer was a resounding *"Yes."* In that moment, everything shifted. I realized I was connected to something much greater than myself—something divine.

At one point during my journey, I volunteered to be a practice client for someone learning the type of hypnosis I was doing.

She needed the practice, and I was happy to help. But something strange happened during that session—I felt the need to stop it early. For years, I believed I ended the session because I was afraid of what I might learn about a personal situation. It nagged at me, this unresolved feeling that perhaps I was running from the truth.

Then, during a later opportunity to speak with the Higher Self, I received a revelation that shook me to my core. The Higher Self told me that my intuition had been more developed than I realized at the time. I hadn't stopped the session out of fear—I had stopped it because I sensed something wasn't right. My intuition had warned me, and without fully understanding why, I had removed myself from a situation that could have turned out very badly.

The fact that I had trusted my intuition in that moment, even unconsciously, kept me safe. That revelation was a profound confirmation that I wasn't just connected to something greater—I was being guided, watched over, and protected in ways I couldn't yet comprehend. This deepened my trust in myself and in the spiritual forces that had been guiding me all along.

From that point on, I began to tap into my spirituality in a deeper way. I connected with the Universe, with Spirit, with the Divine, with God—whatever you call the Higher Being. And as I did, things began to change. My clients started coming to me, not just for healing or hypnosis, but because they wanted to find their purpose. They wanted to know if they were on the right path.

The more I worked with them, the more I realized that helping people uncover their purpose wasn't enough.

They needed guidance—someone to walk with them as they stepped into their power, giving them the tools to live their ultimate life. That's when I knew: I had found my purpose. All the training, the certifications, the years of searching had led me here. I was meant to be a coach—to use every modality I had learned to help others live the life they were meant to live.

One of the most important things I share with my clients is the need to connect with their intuition. I've seen firsthand how powerful finely tuned intuition can be—not just in keeping us safe but in guiding us toward our true purpose and helping us make decisions that align with our highest selves. As part of my coaching, I help others strengthen and trust their intuition. I believe that developing this inner guidance system is a vital part of living a life of purpose and clarity.

Through my program, I empower my clients to not only connect with the Universe but also to listen to the deep wisdom that already resides within them.

In addition, I guide clients through a process of self-discovery and transformation.

Through my Bossy Woo™ coaching program, I help them clarify what they want in life, and more importantly, they gain the confidence and courage to go after it. I combine the practical tools of coaching with the spiritual tools I've gathered over the years—hypnosis, meditation, chakra work, sound healing—to help them connect not only with the Universe but also with their deepest selves.

My client Sarah, like so many others, came to me feeling completely overwhelmed and unsure of what to do next. She was exhausted by the demands of her job, but the frustration didn't end at work. It spilled over into her personal life too. Her relationships with friends and family felt strained, and her health had taken a back seat. Even activities she once enjoyed seemed like chores.

Through our work together, Sarah gained clarity on what truly matters to her, both personally and professionally. As she trusted the process, her confidence and courage grew. Each step she took, no matter how small, brought her closer to living the life she truly wanted.

She now makes intentional choices that bring more purpose into her career while reconnecting herself with the things that bring her joy outside of work. She no longer feels stuck or overwhelmed, and she's embracing her journey with a sense of empowerment and trust in herself.

Another client, Robert, used to juggle three jobs he didn't love just to pay the bills, leaving little time for his family. His relationship with his wife was strained, and he barely had time to spend with his three kids. After working together, Robert gained the confidence and courage to make big changes in his life. He found his dream career, achieved financial stability, and repaired his relationships with his wife and children by making them a priority and spending meaningful time with them.

Those are just two of the clients I've had the pleasure of working with.

Where did Bossy Woo™ come from?

Originally, the term Bossy Woo™ was going to describe the way I worked with my clients as a mentor. After 20 years as a police officer, telling people what to do came naturally. So, Bossy Woo™ was a blend of "bossy"—telling clients the practical steps they needed to take—and "woo"—helping them connect with their spiritual side.

But as I worked with clients, I realized that Bossy Woo™ was not just about telling clients what to do, nor was it just the name of my program. Bossy Woo™ became an attitude, a mindset that my clients began to embrace. It's the attitude of clarity—knowing what they want in their lives. It's the confidence to achieve it, and the courage to go out and make that life a reality.

Bossy Woo™ is the spirit of empowerment that helps my clients design and live their ultimate life. And as you can see from Sarah's and Robert's results, Bossy Woo™ works.

Now, looking back, I realize that everything happened exactly as it was meant to.

It took years of searching, of feeling lost, of thinking I wasn't good enough, to get to this point. But that's the beauty of the journey. Sometimes, we're not ready for our purpose until we've lived through the struggle. It's in the searching that we become who we are meant to be.

Now, I am finally at peace with my purpose.

If you feel lost, remember that every step is part of your path. Embrace the search, and trust that you'll arrive exactly where you're meant to be.

About Valerie Holden:

Valerie Holden is the founder of St. George Hypnosis Center and the visionary behind Bossy Woo™. With over 20 years of experience as a police officer, Valerie blends practical, no-nonsense strategies with deeply intuitive insights to guide her clients through powerful transformations.

Through the Bossy Woo™ program, she empowers women to gain clarity, build confidence, and ignite the courage needed to live the life they've always dreamed of. Valerie is certified in multiple holistic modalities and tailors each client's journey to their unique needs.

Valerie specializes in coaching and mentoring, Oracle card readings, hypnosis, chakra balancing, and sound healing,

Valerie has been a speaker for various community organizations and government agencies.

Visit **www.valerieholden.com** to request your complimentary Life Direction Session.

Facebook: **https://www.facebook.com/ValerieHoldenYourMentor/**

LinkedIn: **https://www.linkedin.com/in/valerie-holden-your-mentor/**

Waking up to Ancient Frequencies
By Mayuri Radha Das

It was one of the days in 2022 when I was randomly scrolling Facebook, frustrated to the point that I was excessively rolling the screen up without reading anything on it. All of a sudden, there was a sound behind me. I locked the phone gently with the right press button and turned around. My angel wooden plaque, for the first time in nine years, was moving as if there were a breeze around it. None of the doors, windows, or fans were on. I was creeped out. Since the phone was still in my hand, I accidentally clicked on it, and the time was 11:11. I usually offer my gratitude and acknowledgment to the divine whenever I see this number, and I did that. I knew there was a message for today. I turned on the phone, and there was an ad for Life Changing Energy's Singing Bowl Certification. Bingo! That was it. Little did I know this sign was the universe's way of guiding me toward a purpose that would redefine not only my career but also my soul.

I have double master's degrees—one in Urban Planning and another in Geography—so it seems unbelievable to me to be doing the things I am doing now. By pursuing sound healing, I have never been this happy in life. It did come with a cost, as I went through a painful phase of understanding how my higher self works with frequency and vibrations at a cellular level. Pain and suffering are inevitable. A baby starts crying to convey its message when it tries to communicate or when it falls while taking its first steps. Does it make the parents or caretakers look bad if the baby is crying? No. The baby was going to cry irrespective of who was around because it was experiencing an internal change of growth. The sooner we stop blaming external conditions and seek tranquility within ourselves, the quicker we grow in life.

In 2021, I had two rough months. One day in June, I was surrounded by excruciating pain and was unable to move, sit, stand, or lift my hand. This was unusual, as I have an active life. In spite of going to urgent care and chugging painkillers, I barely survived a week with this pain. My brain was functioning at its utmost level, but my body had failed. My feet and ankles could not take the weight of my 150-pound body. Struggling to perform simple tasks and relying on my children for care, I faced isolation and uncertainty. After 10 days of calling doctors, I managed to get an appointment with an orthopedic surgeon at the medical hospital close to home. I went to his office with a walking stick, taking one step every 30 seconds. I felt like I had the body impulses of a 90-year-old woman. His team made a couple of X-rays and helped me in and out of the chair. After a while, the doctor came rushing in, saying all my leg bones were fine.

However, I was rushed to the hospital emergency room. They ran a bunch of tests, which revealed that my inflammation was off the charts for my entire body. They put me on a high level of steroids and prescribed autoimmune tests. However, I would have to wait a month to take the tests, as the steroids needed to be tapered down to null before the tests could be accurate.

As an active person with a successful career, the sudden physical limitations were alarming, bringing my life to a standstill. The only two assets I had during this time were my super-functioning brain and the movement of my eyeballs. I diligently meditated and used the Tibetan bowls. I was not an LCE-certified singing bowl healer then. I used to play for myself because I was drawn to the bowls. However, during the inflammation period, I didn't even have the capacity to make a circle around a singing bowl. Each movement felt like a blaze of fire, leaving me unable to lift my own hand. I felt trapped within a body that no longer obeyed me—a prisoner of my own pain.

As days went by, I started to feel better. I never gave up on playing the singing bowls. Within a week, I was able to stand on my own and walk slowly around to get a glass of water. I was hopeful that I was making progress as the steroids were tapered down every week. I continued my meditation practices of listening to instrumental music, fading away, and playing the singing bowls. A month later, when there were no traces of steroids left in my body, I underwent about 12 major tests ranging from autoimmune to cancer diagnostics. The doctors were shocked by the results—there were no traces of any serious diseases. They retested me, and again, there were no signs of inflammation. It was an unbelievable story. To this day, I look back and think it was meditation and the bowls that saved me. After experiencing this health miracle, I wanted to share it with the world. Little did I know that the universe would send me Vickie Gould's course.

I became a Reiki Master, fascinated by how ether, prana, and chi work. I also earned a certification in Ho'oponopono (Hawaiian Prayer of Forgiveness), which validates the existence of the soul through time and space and demonstrates the power of healing. I obtained a mindfulness certification and explored QHHT material by Dolores Cannon, whose work on multidimensional beings intrigued me. Finally, the Sound Healing

Certification came as a delicate thread tying together all my spiritual studies.

In 2022, I eagerly absorbed every aspect of sound healing content from Vickie Gould's Life Changing Energy Certification program. It was a remarkable course. My understanding of frequency had already been imprinted on me, thanks to divine assistance from Goddess Hathor of Egypt, Maa Tara from Buddhism, Maa Durga Shakti from Hindu mythology, Mother Mary from Christianity, and the Archangels. These divine beings helped me grasp how sound creates energy within the cosmos and how the same energy resides within our bodies.

After bathing in this divine knowledge of how frequency creates worlds, I began to see suffering not as something to avoid but as something to embrace, knowing that growth spurts awaited me. If I failed to learn a lesson, it would reappear until my soul understood it. I realized that no external factor could teach me the lessons I came to Earth for—it was internal acceptance and forgiveness that allowed my soul to ascend to higher states of consciousness.

I initially tried speaking at meetings and schools about the advantages of sound and frequency, but my efforts were unsuccessful. Frustrated, I decided to offer free sessions at the local library. Shifting my focus to service strengthened my confidence and my ability to connect with others. This was a pivotal moment; the energy within me shifted, and I became more assured as I began reaching a broader audience.

Engulfed in the world of sound healing, I consistently asked attendees for feedback to refine my approach. The responses were extraordinary. Many felt deeply relaxed because the sessions were held in a comforting, familiar setting like the library. On several occasions, I witnessed attendees shedding tears while in deep sleep. I knew they were releasing old energy, with the cells in those areas vibrating at a higher frequency. I also volunteered to assist women dealing with depression, counseling them through sound healing sessions. Many experienced significant changes, such as promotions or newfound mental clarity, as their energetic blocks cleared.

The first time I played the bowls for a group, I felt a wave of calm wash over me—a sensation beyond words. It was as if the vibrations whispered that I was finally on the right path. Some attendees described extraordinary experiences, such as:

- Out-of-body sensations

- Feeling close to God
- Seeing temples or religious locations
- Witnessing geometric figures, like triangles or circles, and feeling submerged in them
- Visualizing colors like purple and blue
- Entering deep sleep and seeing spirit guides
- Encountering fading faces of loved ones who had passed away
- Feeling as though they were levitating or becoming lighter
- Noticing pulsating activity in specific chakras
- Experiencing fleeting visions, some from their childhood

Before each session, we sit in a circle, and I explain the science and metaphysics of how vibration interacts with the body. I briefly touch on the significance of chakras. Seated at the center, I align the yoga mats in a radiating pattern so everyone can clearly access the vibrations of the bowls. I begin with a loud prayer, inviting ancestors, gods, angels, gurus, and the deceased loved ones of the attendees to guide and protect us on our shared healing journey. During the session, I metaphorically carry attendees through different planes of existence, using high-frequency sounds to transport them, as though on a chariot or spacecraft, while keeping a close watch on them. Walking around, I bow at each person's feet, honoring their soul as a divine being and cleansing their aura through sound vibrations. Each attendee experiences something unique, shaped by their own energetic imprints.

As part of my practice, I experimented with playing certain bowls more often to observe their effects. My favorites are those tuned to the root chakra, heart chakra, and third eye. I adapt the music to match the energy of the crowd, frequently checking on the sleeping attendees. Occasionally, I sense stuck energy hovering around certain individuals, prompting me to use a gong or Tibetan metal bowl to dissipate it. Each participant receives a thorough energy cleanse from their crown chakra to their earth chakra, located at the soles of their feet. Sometimes, attendees exhibit bodily twitches as they process their experiences, and I send Reiki energy to help smooth this transformation.

I've also conducted sessions for children aged 8 to 14. Their energy is pure and vibrant. They enjoyed the crystal singing bowls but disliked the metal ones, as the sound woke them up. I've even alleviated headaches and feverish symptoms in children through these sessions.

As I embraced this process of giving back to the community, I felt compelled to expand my reach. Without external funding, I manifested job opportunities and chose the one that resonated most with my heart, even though it paid less. Living in Houston, I've seen the city frequently impacted by storms and floods. With my background in urban planning, I took a position as a stormwater planner for the City of Houston, addressing issues related to storms, floods, and tornadoes. Being a water lover, I felt a calling to serve the untamed waters. I wasn't sure if this was the right move, but a high-vibration message from the universe assured me it was.

During employee training as a new hire, I was asked to showcase a hobby. I spoke briefly about meditation and sound healing, and HR was intrigued. They invited me to offer meditation sessions for employees, making mindfulness meditation with sound bowls a first for the City of Houston. Initially hesitant to take on this responsibility, I eventually agreed and now host regular lunchtime sessions. This initiative has since been recognized as a stress-reduction program.

Witnessing attendees leave these sessions with a renewed sense of peace and lightness—a look I recognize from my own healing journey—reaffirms my mission. When we serve with the intention of helping others, the universe conspires to assist us. However, this requires taking risks and persevering through challenges.

I have recently begun renting a studio to offer my services regularly, transitioning from the once-monthly sessions I previously held. Over the past year and a half, I've provided healing sessions to 150 attendees. It's not about the number of people who come but about how many welcome this energy at a cellular level. As a Reiki Master, I can sense those who resonate with this energy, those who resist it, and those whose spirit is nudging toward transformation.

Healers and multidimensional beings like us have much to accomplish on Earth. Serving others creates a ripple effect of harmony, elevating collective consciousness for the New Earth. This work transcends nationality and religion, encompassing all sentient beings. When a person becomes internally aware of this truth, they naturally become more respectful of all life.

It's also important to recognize who is ready to receive this energy. If someone's soul isn't open, their body will reject it on a physical level. I've made mistakes by trying to share this energy with people who weren't ready. Don't be discouraged if your favorites don't attend a session—they'll be divinely guided at the right time.

Learning is a joyous, lifelong experience. We are all children on this planet, here to learn our soul lessons. I don't know what the future holds for me—balancing a job, a studio, my 12-year-old twins, and community service—but I am content. If we find happiness in who and where we are, forgive ourselves and others, and stay aligned with our purpose, we can transcend timelines and choose the best path for ourselves and humanity. As the planet transitions to a higher dimension, now is the time to step up and help humankind.

About Mayuri Radha Das:

Mayuri Radha Das is an avid nature lover, a Reiki Master, a certified sound healer, a Hoponoponopono practitioner and a mindfulness teacher. With a Master's in Urban Planning and Geography, she also works as a Storm Water Planner at the City of Houston, while offering mindfulness & sound meditation to City employees and to the community. She is in love with water and the beach. She is a profound believer of galactic consciousness, quantum mechanics, in the miracle of frequency and staying balanced. She can be reached at starheki@gmail.com or www.starheki.com

Trust the Path
By Sylvia P Mason

My name is Sylvia, and I've always had a unique way of seeing the world. *"I SEE THINGS DIFFERENTLY"* is not just my lifetime motto; I consider it much more. It reflects my unique perspective on life—a perspective that has been both a curse and a blessing but always intriguing.

Since I was very young, I have struggled with the realization that I was different from others. It was a challenge that I couldn't comprehend. This was back in the 1970s when topics such as intuition, knowing, and the spiritual world were considered taboo. My home environment was no different. Whenever I tried to bring it up with my parents, I was told, "We just don't talk about that." I would overhear them saying, "She will grow out of it."

As I matured, I began to have experiences where I would intuitively know things and feel certain emotions that others didn't. These experiences often left me intrigued and perplexed, as if I were tapping into another world—a world of mystery and wonder.

I became increasingly fascinated by the mystical and spiritual realms. One day, I stumbled upon a charming store with the scent of herbs filling the air and shelves filled with colorful crystals, oracle cards, and intriguing books. It was there that I had my first psychic reading. After several sessions, the psychic noticed my natural intuition and sensitivity. Her words were both validating and motivating, igniting a desire within me to explore and develop this side of myself further.

After that, I became deeply involved in collecting crystals and studying oracle cards. I also spent a lot of time learning various spiritual practices. However, when I summoned the courage to share my knowledge and abilities with my friends and my significant other, it led to rejection and judgment in those relationships. Sadly, my father's warnings proved correct, and I stopped talking about my abilities and avoided using them altogether.

I never anticipated that suppressing my natural talents would result in such turmoil. The confusion, nightmares, and surreal visions I experienced were overwhelming. However, when one of my visions materialized into reality, it became a pivotal moment that empowered me to make the life-altering decision to leave my husband and embrace the path of a single woman.

This decision brought relief and liberation as I could finally be my true self. I realized that I felt like a stranger to myself, shackled by the need for acceptance and tormented by the belief that I was allowing my true self to wither away.

This journey brought me immense satisfaction as I discovered my true essence and purpose in life. It was an exhilarating time for me. My business was thriving, and I had recently acquired a cozy country home surrounded by beautiful gardens. I felt deeply connected and in tune with the universe, attracting positive things, including meeting the man I envisioned spending the rest of my days with.

When I met his family, I quickly realized I needed to hide my gifts and abilities. This time around, I was older and chose to practice discreetly. At first, I thought it was just a normal part of starting a new life together, building a new relationship, and purchasing a larger home.

It was late fall, and the sun was shining, warming the earth. I felt overwhelmed, stressed, and confused, so I sought solitude by settling next to our serene pond. I sat cross-legged on a lounge chair, gently swaying back and forth. Unintentionally, I slipped into a meditative state, allowing the tranquil surroundings to embrace and soothe me.

Hours passed, and my husband returned home to find me in a meditative state in our backyard, our fur children lying on each side of me. He was startled and concerned; his worry was evident in his voice as he asked if I was okay. I reassured him that I was, and with a request to be left alone, he respected my space.

Later, he returned with a blanket, his concern for me evident in his every move. He gently wrapped me in the blanket, urging me to come inside as the evening chill set in. Overwhelmed with emotion, tears streamed down my face as I admitted that it was time for a change. "Let's continue this conversation inside," he suggested, guiding me back to the comforting warmth of our home. As we nestled into the comfort of the couch, he carefully draped more blankets over me and presented me with a steaming mug of hot soup. Aware that he wouldn't comprehend the events that transpired, we remained silent, immersed in our own thoughts.

For me, I learned an important life lesson:

It dawned on me that I had inadvertently let go of my spiritual practices in the whirlwind of daily life. This realization prompted me to ponder deeply on the impact of this change and consider how it had affected me personally and professionally. I openly began to integrate meditation and other spiritual practices into my daily routine, and within a month, I started to feel a sense of purpose and direction. Six months later, I noticed a significant improvement in my business: the bills were paid on time, and we had a savings account.

Life is painful when your spiritual gifts are turned off, and you live with only half your potential.

The Retreat

A new client invited me to attend a weekend retreat called *Sacred Seasons*. The retreat was scheduled for Halloween weekend, making it the perfect timing for a weekend getaway—something I had never done before.

Our accommodations were in an exquisite eight-bedroom house next to a peaceful lake, surrounded by nature's beauty. During our stay, we were lucky to observe a majestic resident eagle and other captivating wildlife.

It was invigorating to be among individuals who had gone through experiences similar to mine. Our conversations revolved around intuition, its impact on decision-making, empathy, and trusting instincts. These discussions deepened our connections and gave me a sanctuary where I could fully embrace my abilities, feeling empowered and inspired.

As I wandered along the tranquil waterfront, a retreat participant approached me with a warm smile and said, "Your healing abilities are truly remarkable." I humbly replied, "I do not heal anyone." This wasn't the first time I had heard this; the first time was when a native medicine woman expressed the same sentiment when I was in my twenties.

When asked what I did for a living, I elaborated on my profession, explaining the nature of my work. The participant responded, "You're doing healing work every day. You're not just dealing with financial issues but helping people overcome them."

Their words struck a deep chord. "You have tremendous potential that you haven't even begun to tap into because you've been in the spiritual closet your entire life. It's time to take control of your journey, unlock your potential, and witness the incredible impact you can make."

This weekend retreat marked a turning point in my life. During the two-and-a-half-hour drive home, I reflected on the meaningful conversations I had. Each one resonated deeply, stirring profound self-reflection.

The Call That Changed It All

When I returned home from the retreat, I felt lost. I recognized that I was on the edge of a powerful spiritual awakening, more intense and prolonged than anything I had experienced before. Grabbing a notebook, I hesitated momentarily, realizing I was stepping into uncharted territory. Journaling felt foreign—I had always avoided writing things down. At first, the words struggled to find their way, but gradually they flowed, and I realized they were for future reflection.

As the universe works, I soon received an email from a business colleague I had worked with years earlier. The email contained a link inviting me to schedule a one-on-one meeting, which I arranged for the following week.

During our conversation, she posed several questions. Then she said, "Many of the calls I receive are from people who don't believe in themselves as alchemists or manifestors. That's usually the first hurdle. But with you, it's different. You already know this about yourself. However, you're not vibrationally aligned, and your mind pulls you out of that knowing."

She explained that she offered mentorship to teach alchemy and manifestation but added, "You're more advanced than you realize. You could teach what I'm offering."

She advised me to take time for self-reflection, identify areas where I could expand my knowledge, and actively seek opportunities to deepen my expertise.

Following her advice, I embarked on a personal journey to embrace spirituality fully. I dedicated significant time and resources to exploring the spiritual realm, which was no longer a taboo subject but something to be celebrated. The sheer volume of online information surprised me; I had always turned to books for research.

The sheer volume of data was overwhelming, and much of it was contradictory. It was challenging to process and required careful discernment to find the most reliable and accurate details. However, this process became a significant learning experience, leading to personal growth and profound enlightenment.

During this journey, I discovered that meditation and energy exercises aligned my inner vibrations, allowing me to effortlessly draw answers to my most pressing questions. This profound experience deepened my intuition and illuminated various aspects of my life.

As I continued my journey, I pursued accreditation in various modalities, including spiritual life coaching, intuitive energy healing, and sound healing using Singing Bowls (Crystal and Tibetan), Crystal Pyramids, and Drums. These certifications laid the foundation for creating and recording meditations, further solidifying my interest in manifestation techniques.

As I honed my skills, I asked myself how I could effectively share my knowledge and insights with others. Seeking guidance, I entered a deep meditation session. In its infinite wisdom, the universe responded: it was time to share my gifts and make a difference in people's lives.

Feeling a profound shift in my being, I sensed a deeper connection with the universe, signaling the onset of another spiritual awakening. With my journal open before me, I inscribed one word:

A Book.

Despite my love of reading and the power of knowledge, I had never felt compelled to write a book. But once I began, I was amazed by its transformative effect on my life. Writing became a powerful way to openly express my spiritual beliefs and experiences, a transformation I hadn't anticipated. The book is titled:

MYSTICAL SECRETS: A Guide to Powerful Manifestation

This guide outlines steps to align the Mind, Body, and Spirit with the universal flow of energy. By achieving this alignment, readers are empowered to manifest their deepest desires and create the lives they truly want.

The writing process was deeply personal and transformative, fostering significant growth. The support I received along the way was a driving force, teaching me the importance of stepping out of my comfort zone. After keeping my innate talents hidden for so long, this project was my opportunity to embrace them fully.

I've long believed in practicing what I preach, and I've used vision boards as a manifestation tool for most of my life. These boards encompass personal and professional goals, guiding me toward success. A year has passed since I published my book, and the results have been remarkable.

Coming out of the spiritual closet and aligning with the flow has profoundly impacted my life. After my summer vacation, I realized I had accomplished all the goals I set for myself this year. The realization left me in a mix of emotions: shock, bewilderment, and uncertainty about what to aim for next.

Despite the uncertainty, I am deeply grateful for the life I've created and the fulfillment I've found. Over the years, I've uncovered my innermost desires and discovered the elements that bring me true joy.

Discovery

Taking time to reflect, I now stand at a crossroads. I feel called to more and am on a quest to discover my true purpose.

As a lifelong learner, I understand that life is a journey and each step a quest. I decided to deepen my understanding by revisiting the basics of Alchemy and Sacred Geometry.

Imagine stumbling upon a revelation that reshapes your understanding of consciousness. That's exactly what happened to me when I discovered that consciousness is not a singular entity but a complex system with three distinct focuses, each with its purpose and objective.

This revelation reshaped my perspective on aligning thoughts, emotions, and beliefs to manifest and recreate one's life effectively. It revealed the immense power of the superconscious mind and its potential to unlock new possibilities for growth and transformation.

After decades of self-discovery and growth, I've realized that my true purpose lies in sharing my knowledge and wisdom with others. I've studied for a long time and understand how daunting this journey can feel. Nobody hands you a guidebook or tells you what to do, but I'm here to help.

I firmly believe that no one should feel lost or alone on their journey toward creating the life they desire. My mission is to inspire and empower others to unlock their fullest potential, ignite positive change, and provide the confidence and reassurance they need to succeed.

To achieve this, I've created practical workshops, events, and tools designed to empower individuals and help them manifest a life they love. These offerings are built on years of study, experience, and the lessons I've learned through my own trials and triumphs.

I am truly grateful for your interest in my personal journey. I hope that the experiences I've shared resonate with you, offering valuable insights and the comfort of knowing you are not alone on this path.

"Embrace your unique gifts, even if you're misunderstood. Be who you were meant to be."

Create the life you love.

Sylvia

About Sylvia P Mason:

Meet Sylvia. She seeks spiritual truth, and she brings her love for nature and animals into every aspect of her Life.

"I see things differently" is more than a phrase for Sylvia; it's the guiding principle that shapes her unique perspective on Life.

Sylvia, a seasoned Intuitive business mentor and accountant for the past 30 years, discovered her natural ability as an intuitive energy healer during her own spiritual journey. She realized that her secret passion was her ultimate desires.

"I've manifested my ideal life, and now I am living it," she confidently stated.

Now the founder of Eighth Vibration, Sylvia demonstrates the power of manifestation in her debut book, "Mystical Secrets: A Guide to Powerful Manifestation." She is currently working on her upcoming book and also conducts workshops and events aimed at helping individuals manifest the Life they Love by raising their vibration.

These are available at www.eighthvibration.com.

Breathing Through the Pain: My Journey from Barely Surviving to Enthusiastically Thriving
By Karen Lynn Warwick

I vividly remember the day I hit rock bottom. It was a migraine so severe that I questioned whether dying might be a better option. The pain was so intense that, for the first time in my life, I thought if I passed on right then, it might not be the worst thing. On top of the migraine, I had a constant, undiagnosed pain on one side of my head. This pain controlled my life—always present, spiking to excruciating levels whenever I sneezed or moved my head too quickly. It felt as though someone was driving a screwdriver into my skull and leaving it there. I clung to the edge of existence, each heartbeat pulsing with pain, each breath uncertain. My life was slipping away—physically and emotionally—and I had to decide if I was going to fight back.

If you had asked me then if I thought I would become a healer, I would have laughed—if I could have. It's hard to laugh when every breath you take and every movement feels like agony. My reality was one of invisible physical pain beyond what most people could imagine, combined with a deep emotional and energetic void. I couldn't envision a future where I could help anyone, let alone myself.

Growing up, my childhood was marked by emotional neglect. I had the basics—food, water, clothing, housing, and even more than the basics, like an allowance. By most societal standards, I had a life better than many others, and for that, I'm grateful. But what was missing were emotional and attachment connections. No one taught me as a child how to process my feelings or understand the complex emotions swirling inside me. I had a few adults I could rely on, but they weren't nearby, and in the 1970s and 80s, I didn't have a cell phone to call or text when things got tough.

I was left mostly alone to figure out life. Without the emotional support systems that many kids have and with little adult guidance, I relied on pop culture, magazines, and television to guide me. I had no idea how to handle the extreme swings of emotion that were constant in my family—mania, depression, alcoholism, verbal abuse, and physical aggression. The house was an ocean of unchecked emotions. I locked down emotionally and energetically, trying to control everything I could because the world around me felt so chaotic. I became hypervigilant. I was confused and angry. I wanted control, perfection, predictability, and order because that's what I lacked. And yet I was numb. My breath was shallow, barely moving past my shoulders. I felt like I never took a full breath. I thought if I could just keep everything around me controlled, I would be okay. But I wasn't.

What I didn't know at the time was that I was already storing trauma in my body. I've since learned that this is called a somatic response—when your body physically reacts to emotional or psychological stress. Our bodies store emotions, and the anger, fear, and stress I grew up with became trapped, manifesting as physical pain. My body had become my own personal prison for unprocessed trauma, even though I didn't realize it at the time.

In fifth grade, I experienced severe neck pain and couldn't turn my head. My teacher, showing no compassion, accused me of faking it to skip gym class because of my period—in front of the entire class. Humiliated, I felt my neck stiffen further as shame flushed through me, locking into my body. I held my breath in horror, unable to release the hurt—a pattern that repeated over the years, with each moment adding to the unprocessed pain I wouldn't fully confront for nearly 40 years.

As a teenager, I was numb. I had locked myself down so much that I didn't know how to feel. I wasn't a problem child, which meant I was mostly invisible. I did everything I could to avoid conflict, to keep the emotional volatility around me at bay. I didn't want to cause more disruption, so I kept quiet and tried to make myself as small as possible. I didn't receive attention at school because I wasn't a problem student. I didn't have a voice because I was in an impossible home situation that I didn't think I could leave. And I didn't feel. I didn't feel because I hadn't been taught how, because I had been told I was overly sensitive, and because I was supposed to be one of the stable ones in the house. But I was screaming inside. I wanted to be seen. I wanted to be heard. And most of all, I wanted to feel.

But I had never been taught how to feel. And so, the feelings I had buried deep began to bubble up in destructive ways. I started self-harming, desperate to feel something—anything—just to remind myself that I was alive. I was walking through life numb, and the only thing that made me feel alive was pain.

If I could go back to that young girl, I would tell her she's not alone. I would wrap her in the biggest hug and tell her that she doesn't have to navigate life by herself. I would teach her how to breathe—how to inhale completely, regardless of the situation, and then exhale, releasing anything that didn't serve her. I would teach her how to process her emotions in a healthy way. I would show her how to feel without hurting herself. I would help her see that she has the power to heal and that her body knows exactly what it needs—if she could only breathe deeply, fully, and completely enough to listen.

It was in those dark moments when I unknowingly began the path of becoming a healer. I certainly didn't see it at the time. But that little girl who struggled to feel and who lived amid chaos became the woman who eventually became a healer—first for herself and then for others. A healer for myself, most importantly. A healer for my daughter and future generations, for my chosen family and friends, for my clients. I didn't know it then, but today I know I am a better wife, mother, friend, sister, daughter, facilitator, and healer because of those challenging experiences. I had to learn to feel in order to heal. And, in time, I would learn the value of a full, deep, complete breath.

When I was 22, my health took a serious turn for the worse. A medical procedure gone wrong triggered a cascade of autoimmune issues. My body seemed to be falling apart, and no treatments seemed to help. My life became a series of doctor's appointments, healer visits, tests, and treatments that never quite worked. It was an uphill battle. An up-and-down battle. A never-ending battle. My conditions became so exacerbated when I was pregnant that I vomited for seven months straight. I battled brain fog so severe I thought I had dementia at age 35. Extreme food allergies caused never-ending hives, and joint pain prevented exercise. I had stabbing chest pain while I was watching television with my young daughter, wondering if I would see her grow up, graduate college, get married, and have children. And a battle overshadowed by the mystery head pain and extreme migraines. I'd spend days—sometimes weeks—unable to function, lost in a haze of pain. It was a battle that made me feel like a terrible mother, wife, and friend. It was a dark time filled with so much guilt and shame. I wondered daily why I couldn't positively think away and naturally treat the symptoms. Why couldn't I heal when I was surrounded by the natural healing community both personally and professionally? With every new diagnosis and doctor's appointment, my hope wore thin. I felt like I was losing a battle that had started long before I was born. Each ache, each flare-up, was my body's cry for healing—healing from the trauma generations before me had never dealt with, trauma I now carried.

By the time I was 47, I had hit a breaking point. Twenty-five years of health crises had worn me down. I didn't know if I could keep going, but deep down, I knew I wasn't going to give up. I made an appointment with a neurologist, unsure of what to expect but desperate for relief. To my surprise, she diagnosed my constant head pain as hemicrania continua. I had never heard of it; no one I knew had ever heard of it. But finally, I had a name for the pain that had been tormenting me. I felt my body release some of its stored tension for the first time in years. I took a breath in hopeful relief and cried. Breathing and feeling—two things that continued teaching me on my path to becoming a healer. For the first time in years, I allowed myself to hope, which opened a door to new thoughts, ideas, and actions for my healing.

The first day without constant head pain in years was surreal. I kept waiting for it to return, my emotions swinging wildly—elation and giddiness one moment, terror the next. It took four months to get the hemicrania continua under control, and I was deeply grateful to finally be free from the relentless pain on one side of my head. Managing the migraines took over two more years, but my doctor never gave up—and neither did I. I became my own advocate, working closely with this neurologist who respected my preference for natural remedies and remained dedicated to helping me find relief. Healers come in many forms.

Slowly, things started to improve. I wasn't cured, but the pain was finally manageable. It was around this time that I turned 50, and I made a decision: I was going to say "yes" to life. No more holding back. No more saying no to opportunities. If someone asked me to do something new or challenging, I would say yes.

I began lifting weights, taking dance lessons, and pursuing continued healing through breathwork, trauma release, and sound healing. I said yes to everything life had to offer. And in saying yes, I rediscovered myself. I reconnected with parts of me I had long forgotten. On one of these trips, I experienced breathwork in a way I never had before. It was a 90-minute guided session, and it changed everything.

During that guided breathwork session, I had the most extreme healing experience. From the breath that went all the way down to my pelvis and back up to my clavicles, to the beat of the music pulsing through my body, to the facilitator's guiding words, I knew I was healing. I could feel the breath moving up and down my spinal column in a wave-like motion, and I felt my pelvis and hips open in a way I had never experienced. I kept moving my body, however it wanted to, and released so much stored somatic trauma that I felt it rush out as extreme heat, cold, and shaking—

sometimes all three at once. I felt sludge moving out of my throat and coughed out black energy. I rubbed the occiput area of my skull, moving the stuck energy, the somatic trauma, out of my head as I breathed. I was on another plane of consciousness while still fully aware of my body and breath. At one point, the scapula area of my left shoulder released in a huge rush of heat, and the muscles—tense for over 40 years—finally relaxed.

For what felt like the first time in my life, I took a full, deep breath—connecting the inhale to the exhale, feeling it move throughout my body. It truly was a miraculous healing. I was feeling, releasing, and healing, over and over with each breath. I knew I was in the right place, in the right moment, to facilitate a huge change in my life—with my breath. It was as if I had been holding my breath for 40 years, maybe longer, and I was finally able to exhale. For the first time, I could breathe with intent—to heal, to release, to live. With each conscious breath, I felt layers of trauma melt away. I realized I had the power to heal my body, that I could finally let go of the invisible pain that had once defined me.

That session changed my life completely. I started doing conscious connected breathwork regularly, traveling all over the USA and the world to workshops and conferences to deepen my practice. The more I breathed, the more I healed. My migraines became rare. My energy returned. My pain lessened. My brain became quick and sharp again. My body felt stronger, lighter, and more alive. I fell in love with life and knew what the other side of this journey looked like. I was leaving behind the darkness with gratitude and awareness, knowing that I would never take being pain-free or healthy for granted. I knew I would always be grateful for my breath, for my body, for the ability to function without pain, and, yes, for all the experiences that had led me to that point. I wasn't just surviving anymore—I was thriving.

I never thought I'd be a healer. But through my own pain and healing, I discovered the power of breathwork. I learned how to feel, how to release, and how to heal in ways I never imagined. And now, I get to share that gift with others, which, in turn, is such a gift for me. Every time I witness someone finding release, each exhale filled with relief and healing, I am reminded of why my journey mattered and how my suffering became my gift.

I'm deeply grateful that I didn't give up on myself that day when I hit rock bottom. Every painful experience, every held breath, led me to where I am today. I became a healer not despite my pain, but because of it. And now, I help others heal by teaching them how to breathe, how to feel, and how to say yes to life. Each healing breath I take, each breathwork session I lead, serves as a reminder of life's beauty and the resilience we hold within. I finally breathe with freedom from pain, with optimistic joy, and with never-ending gratitude.

About Karen Lynn Warwick:

Karen Lynn Warwick is a compassionate, intuitive healer dedicated to guiding individuals, couples, and groups on their paths to self-directed wellness. After overcoming childhood trauma and years of health challenges, she began exploring natural healing methods. Her journey took a transformative turn when she discovered the power of breathwork, becoming an internationally certified Breathwork Facilitator.

Expanding her healing tools, Karen pursued certification as a Master Sound Healer, recognizing the deep healing potential of sound. She also embraced community connection, becoming a Women's Sacred Circle Facilitator, where she supports women on their wellness journeys and encourages all women to support other women.

Karen's healing experiences fuel her passion to help others in their pursuit of holistic wellness, offering support in relaxation, stress relief, trauma release, and personal empowerment. With clients across the globe, Karen offers both in-person and online sessions tailored to each individual's needs.

For more information, please visit www.breatheagainwellness.com.

Death
Endurance
Rise

By Marie Hamilton

My father passed on April 1, 2023.

My mother passed away just four years before, on April 22, 2019.

It was strange to acknowledge that I no longer had parents, my kids no grandparents, and my grandkids no great-grandparents. Just… no more.

When my mom passed, it felt like I lost an arm. When my dad passed, it was like something was missing—a deep hole, an empty void. The apple didn't fall far from the tree, but now there was no tree, no trunk, no stump—just an empty hole.

My dad was intubated for a month before he passed, suffering greatly. Watching him in pain was so hard. My mother, on the other hand, was killed by a vagrant who beat her in the street. The coroner's report stated blunt force trauma.
There was court, police, sentencing, and news coverage, all of which compounded my grief, pain, and sense of chaos.

How do you cope? Be strong? Not cry at the wrong times and places? How do you stop feeling? How do you explain what's happening in your heart and brain? How do you deal with the first birthdays—yours, your kids', your grandkids'—without them? And the holidays—Christmas, Easter, New Year's, Valentine's?

To be honest, I didn't always have good relationships with my parents. There were times I was estranged from them for years. That pain was already there, but their deaths brought it all to the surface, emotions so overwhelming. I wish those times of estrangement had never happened.

And then there was the family—those terrible relatives who had awful things to say, adding salt to an already deep wound. My parents had been divorced for many years, and I was already 40, an adult with my own life, when they separated. You'd think their divorce wouldn't affect me, but years later, it crept in. Parents are your parents at any age.

I couldn't cope. All of this had been building subtly over time, layering and layering. I recognized these feelings from previous deaths—my mother-in-law and grandmother in 2012, my father-in-law in 2017.

I started cussing like there was no tomorrow—not just a cuss word every other word, but five cuss words every other word, in both Spanish and English. To me, it felt like normal, actual sentences, but it was extremely offensive and overwhelming. My family had to learn to deal with me in their own way. I didn't realize it at the time but recognize it now.

As I tried to go on day by day, I couldn't have known this kind of pain would eventually lead me to a peace that allowed me to function again. I was deeply touched by my son Randy, who stepped up, offering support, raising money, and helping with the funeral arrangements.

I cherished the incredible years I had with my dad—barbecues, vacations, dinners, and fun family moments. He spent his last Christmas at my home. My mom, before her death, had become my best friend. She would stay with us for months at a time over the last several years. We were a family, separate but still together.

I couldn't pick up the phone and ask her, "Mom, I bought some meat today—how should I cook it? What spices should I add?" I remember walking into Walmart with my husband—my mom's favorite place. As soon as we got inside, emotions welled up, and I started crying. I turned to him and said, "I can't be here. Get me out of here!"

There were days when the sadness was so deep that even trying to go back felt impossible. Other days, I couldn't get out of the car. Memories would flood me, leaving me staring, yelling, and crying in the parking lot, grasping for strength. Eventually, I managed to go inside. Walking down the yarn aisle (totally Mom territory), I hoped I wouldn't break down and cry. I mentally forced myself to stay strong, choking up but pressing on.

It did get better. I can now pass that aisle and think of her and smile.

When my dad died, I felt so alone, isolated, and empty—angry, too. More of the same. Instead of waking up by stretching or yawning, I'd spring into a sitting position, wide awake. It was the weirdest thing ever. My body just did it.

The sadness and anger were extreme. I didn't like talking to anyone or having anyone talk to me. I didn't know how to function. My nerves were shot. It was happening again.

I couldn't call my dad and tell him, "Hey, your grandson just graduated high school and got accepted to several colleges." Dad loved hearing about all the sports my son did and seeing pictures.

My husband took me to a brunch, and it happened again. Mariachis were playing. My dad had been a mariachi and professional singer. When one of his songs came on, I started crying. I couldn't cope. A waiter noticed and kindly said, "Don't cry," in Spanish.

I hated this. I couldn't tell when my sadness was anger or my anger was sadness. My emotions intertwined, leaving my head unable to communicate with my heart. My chest felt like a deep, dark void.

I never felt so vulnerable, and I hated it. It was constant. I had to work to appear "normal," but I didn't even know who "me" was anymore. My feelings were numb. Happiness and joy had left my body. They didn't exist anymore. I had to fake it, and it was exhausting.

I felt weak, pathetic, dumb, depressed. I had no purpose. I didn't care about anything. I thought, Why do I exist? I'm awful. I have no purpose here. My home was in disarray, and I was overindulging in food and alcohol. I couldn't breathe. I gained weight and got drunk.

To avoid feeling, I pretended, avoided, didn't talk, and didn't think—especially around holidays or birthdays. But I could see my family hurting, and I couldn't be there for them.

I became stagnant, stuck, living this new, different life. Physically, mentally, emotionally, spiritually—I was affected on every level. Life was speeding past me, and I couldn't catch up.

This was the new me, and I didn't like her. I had always been a driven woman, and my family was everything to me. I knew I had to get well to be there for them. In the middle of all this, Covid hit. Losing friends, family, and people I knew only compounded everything. Our family dog, Luigi, who had been with us for 20 years, passed on December 2, 2020—

the same date my grandmother passed in 2012. The connections were undeniable, and they deepened my pain.

Then I had my own near-death experience with Covid. It felt like the whole world had changed, and I rationalized, "No one is the same, so it's okay to feel crazy."

I joined a Christian grief support class for a few months, but I was still a mess. There was no relief. I tried a Christian female counselor at my church, but the help was limited. It didn't work. I was told that the man who killed my mother had free will and that I needed to forgive him. I tried—truly, I did—but it only led to more regret, resentment, and sadness. It felt like I wasn't allowed to grieve or feel anything. People said things like, "She's in a better place," but it meant nothing to me.

After 20 years, I left the church.

I felt lost. I went to a doctor, who offered me medication. I said no—I didn't like taking drugs. They suggested therapy, and I agreed.

I had three male therapists, but they also pushed medication. I still refused. Eventually, I found a Mexican therapist who I felt understood me—my culture, my background. I thought we would be a good fit, but then she left.

I reluctantly went back to one of the male therapists, continuing because I needed help. Later, the Mexican therapist reached out, offering zoom sessions due to Covid. I stayed with her off and on for 2 ½ years.

Covid had slowed the world down to a pace that matched where I was. For the first time, I didn't feel so out of place.

My healing began with meditation and affirmations. I didn't know if it would work, but I tried. Starting in the morning, by afternoon, I felt something—a spark. My heart tingled and sent a faint wave of happiness through my body.

It was incredible. I told all my therapists about it, but they just let me talk without much feedback. Still, I kept going.

I began to notice two distinct sensations: one of pain, like a dark, sticky, black film clinging to my heart and the other—a spark, small but growing—lifting me out of it, all at the same time!

The affirmations worked. The spark got bigger and lasted longer. The sticky black film began to unstick and fade.

I was intrigued. How could this be happening? How could breathing, meditating, and repeating affirmations create such change? The church had always warned me about practices like this, calling them borderline "woo woo." But I couldn't deny the results.

I found a meditation app and started having whole days of happiness. I told everyone. This was the start of my healing journey.

I took a crystal healing course. My mom loved crystals, and I used to think she was silly. Now, I understood. I felt connected to her through them.

I explored further, taking courses in sound baths, crystal bowls, Tibetan bowls, tuning forks, Reiki, and more. I watched YouTube videos, read books, and researched the science, history, and origins of these modalities. For the next two years, I dove into exploration and learning.

My Mexican heritage celebrates the Day of the Dead with week-long traditions. For their first year, I placed my parents on the altar as passed loved ones. I didn't want to do it, but I had to. To my surprise, it was incredibly healing. Memories and feelings of their presence surfaced, and it was cathartic. Knowing that all of Mexico, other countries, and even parts of the U.S. were celebrating at the same time was deeply comforting.

Through my courses, I met a medium, Joshua Anthony. At first, I had reservations. My religious upbringing had labeled this as taboo. But I was curious and reached out.

On November 2, 2023—Day of the Dead—Joshua connected me to my mother, father, grandparents, and ancestors. It was the first time my dad was on the altar. There was no way Joshua could have known.

The experience brought profound healing and peace. The black cloud began to lift. Sunshine peeked through. I was cautious but open to this new experience, Joshua's accuracy amazed me, and my heart started to restore itself.

I felt my brain unwinding from years of fear and doubt. My clarity was crystal sharp. I finally understood the phrase, "wound tightly." For the first time, I felt free, alive, energized, and at peace.

My first teaching session in crystal healing was powerful. Watching others find relief and comfort moved me deeply. I felt a surge of purpose I had never known. My pain had become a bridge to peace—for myself and others.

I began helping my husband, kids, and friends, from sports injuries to arthritis, broken bones to back pain, I used my skills. I slept better. Life was changing.

I traveled to different states, earning master certifications. My excitement for learning was insatiable. Coming from a business background, this was a completely different path—one centered on healing. I even became a minister to do more.

And at 60, I got my first tattoo: Japanese Reiki healing symbols wrapped in jasmine, my favorite flower, on my forearm. I'm a totally different person in a sense!

I know my parents are with me, guiding me.

Life is a journey, and healing is a constant process. The world isn't perfect, and challenges will always arise. But having tools and modalities for mental, physical, emotional, and spiritual well-being makes all the difference.

Thank you, wonderful people, for taking the time to read my journey and the incredible transformation I've experienced.

Thank you, Joshua, for your role in my healing. Thank you, Life Changing Energy and Vickie Gould, for changing my life in ways no one else could.

Wishing you an incredible, safe healing journey!

With much gratitude Marie. ♥

About Marie Hamilton:

Marie Castro Hamilton is a business woman and entrepreneur, a wife and proud mother of 3 and 5 grand children. Owns her own Mobile Home company, helping families find affordable housing.

Marie continues her intuitive nature of helping others by ongoing studies as a Metaphysical practitioner. She's double master certified accredited by Complimentary Medical association, expert level, in crystal healing, sound baths, tunning forks, Tibetan bowls for varies ailments, traumas, anxiety chakra alignment, and overall wellness in physical mental emotional and spiritual healing. She is a Reiki Master practitioner and Life-changing energy facilitator and teaches all the courses she practices. She continues studies in kinesiology, and other healing methodologies.

Her mission statement and belief, that all have the right to be healed physically, mentally, emotionally and spiritually to live in state of well being, peace, harmony joy and happiness.

Facebook: Marie Castro Hamilton.

Email: gemscrystalslove@gmail.com

A Journey Through Shadows to Light

By Marcella Hutchens

Standing in the kitchen holding the phone, I felt unable to move, shaken to my core. The man I thought I would spend the rest of my life with was calling to tell me that the man knocking at my door was a process server with divorce papers. I refused to answer the door, and they finally left. I then fell to the cold kitchen floor, with my back against the cabinets, knees to my chest, sobbing uncontrollably.

I found myself staring into the abyss of my life—divorced and grappling with the deep, aching sense of loss that had become my constant companion. The echoes of my marriage haunted me like distant thunder, reminding me of what once was and would never be again. But amid the darkness, a flicker of light emerged—a glimmer of hope that came through unexpected channels. Divorce is one of the most stressful life events. I wouldn't wish it on my worst enemy.

My husband, the man I had shared my life with for over a quarter century, sat across from me the next morning, his gaze distant. "We've grown apart, and I want a divorce," he said. Those words shattered the carefully constructed facade of my life. The dreams we had built together crumbled like a house of cards. Grieving the loss of our shared future, I found myself spiraling into despair.

As I sat in a hollow silence, surrounded by the ruins of a life I thought I knew, I couldn't fathom that this very darkness would one day become the path to my brightest light.

The divorce left me emotionally shattered. I had spent years as a homemaker, raising our children while he pursued his career. I was thrust into the harsh reality of financial instability. Over the years, my savings dwindled, and I faced homelessness. It felt as though the ground beneath my feet had eroded, leaving me floating in a void. I was brought up in a strict family with strong religious values, and for me, marriage was for life. I thought he felt the same. I admit I took my marriage for granted and didn't nurture it. I let it wither and die. I focused on our two beautiful children, thinking he could take care of himself. I guess, in a way, he did—by finding someone else who would.

In the stillness of those empty days, the silence was deafening, each hour stretching into the next. I stared at the walls of a home that felt both familiar and foreign, haunted by the echoes of a life that was no longer mine.

I experienced the five stages of grief: denial, anger, bargaining, depression, and acceptance. This was, in every sense, a death—the death of a marriage. I also grieved the loss of the dream I had of marriage. I initially denied the reality of my situation. "This can't be happening to me," I told myself. I replayed our life together, trying to pinpoint the moment everything went wrong, hoping that if I could identify it, I could fix it.

Anger followed quickly, directed at my ex-husband, at myself, and even at the universe. "Why me?" I felt a deep sense of betrayal—not just from him but from life itself.

Bargaining soon crept in. I found myself negotiating with the universe, praying for a sign, a way out, a miraculous solution. I sought solace in self-help books, looking for a roadmap to healing, but the more I searched, the more lost I felt.

Depression came crashing in like a heavy blanket—suffocating and cold. Days blurred together. Consumed by the darkness, I didn't want to leave the house. The thought of facing the world felt insurmountable. I lost touch with friends, isolating myself further in my grief.

But, as years passed, I began to feel a shift within me. Acceptance wasn't instantaneous, but it emerged slowly, like dawn breaking after a long night. I realized that while I could not change the past, I had the power to reshape my future.

I have always been a spiritual person, but I began diving deeper into my ongoing spiritual growth. I started doing the work—the shadow work. Going within and confronting my shadows. Standing in front of the mirror, I whispered, "I am worthy. I am enough." It felt strange, almost uncomfortable, but something began to shift inside me. For the first time in months, I felt a flicker of self-compassion. Each day, I practiced mirror work, gradually peeling away layers of self-doubt and negativity.

As I delved deeper into my spiritual studies, I discovered the power of divination. Tarot cards became a tool of reflection for me. With each reading, I unearthed insights about my past and possibilities for my future. The cards spoke of transformation, urging me to embrace change and let go of what no longer served me.

Another pivotal moment in my journey was discovering sound bowl healing. The first time I heard the bowls resonate, I felt vibrations travel through me, washing away some of my pain. Each sound wave seemed to carry away the heaviness in my heart, creating space for healing. I began attending sound baths regularly, each session bringing me a step closer to releasing the grief that had been holding me captive.

I started to envision a life beyond my current struggles. It was as if I had donned a pair of shades, and the world suddenly appeared brighter, more colorful. I realized that although my past was filled with sorrow, my future held limitless possibilities.

Yet, fear was a relentless companion. The fear of failure loomed large as I considered starting anew. Through my spiritual practice, I learned to confront these fears head-on. I journaled my fears, examined them, and slowly transformed them into affirmations of strength.

"I am the creator of my life," I wrote repeatedly. I began to recognize that my fear was simply a shadow of my past, not a prediction of my future. As I faced my reflection each day, murmuring words of affirmation, it felt as though I was meeting myself for the first time—a fragile, hopeful version of me, hidden beneath years of neglect and self-doubt.

With newfound confidence, the universe seemed to respond to my renewed energy. I continued to nurture my spiritual practice. I joined a community of like-minded individuals who were also exploring metaphysical studies. Together, we shared our journeys, our struggles, and our triumphs. This support system became my lifeline, reminding me that I was never truly alone.

I attended many courses, classes, and workshops, and received numerous certifications. I began to teach some of the techniques I had learned—mirror work, sound healing, and the wisdom of tarot—sharing my journey with others who were lost and seeking direction. It was a full-circle moment that filled me with joy and gratitude. Sharing my journey in a community workshop, I watched as faces softened, as participants found resonance in my story. The realization that my pain—and my healing—could be a source of comfort for others was both humbling and empowering.

Looking back, I can see how the stages of grief were integral to my healing. Each stage, though painful, brought me closer to understanding myself and what I truly wanted in life. I had transformed from a woman crushed by the weight of her past into a woman who embraced the possibilities of her future.

Overcoming fear was truly a breakthrough. By going within and discovering what beliefs were holding me back, I realized that some beliefs weren't even mine but had been passed down. Letting those beliefs go will help me guide my children to release those old patterns too. It opened a whole new world and a new way of existing. I'm here to help heal humanity, and that starts with me.

As I've gotten older, I have struggled with self-confidence, feeling less seen. There was a time I didn't want to be seen, but now I know I do. My spiritual gifts have blossomed and are flourishing. I'm here to be of service to others. We all have gifts we need to share. Step into the light and be seen.

When I started listening to my inner voice and taking consistent action, things began to accelerate at dizzying speeds. By raising my frequency and maintaining that new level—or higher—the possibilities are endless. I wish the same for you.

Today, as I stand on the precipice of a new chapter, my future is so bright. My journey is still unfolding, and while challenges may arise, I am no longer afraid. The lessons I've learned through grief, self-discovery, and spiritual healing have illuminated my path.

My children are my why. By embracing, loving, and accepting my shadows, I became whole again. I love all of me. I accept all of me—the good, the bad, and the ugly. And I know there is no good, bad, or ugly, really. It is just me.

My future is bright, and I am ready to embrace it with open arms. I am more than my past. I no longer care what other people think. I am true to myself. By healing myself, I heal my family too. I have so much fun and joy in my life after finding myself again. I am a testament to resilience and a believer in the power of transformation through this journey of shadows to light.

About Marcella Hutchens:

Marcella Hutchens, M.S. Teacher and Trainer, Certified Psychic, Medium, Healer from the Lisa Williams International School of Spiritual Development, Reiki Master Teacher, Sound Bowl Healer and Shamanic Practitioner. She lives in Florida, has two amazing children, and two beautiful cats. Connect with Marcella through email: Mhutchens1818@gmail.com for readings, sound bowl sessions and divination classes.

The Missing Piece
By Brooke Stone

It all began with a surprise pregnancy. This third baby was completely unexpected and unplanned, but still felt like a blessing. We were sailing into uncharted territory and decided that it would be best if I didn't go back to work after maternity leave, as it was just too much to ask of our support system. So I spent nine months daydreaming of an easy labor and of what life would be like when the baby was born—of the bliss of being able to stay home and tend to my family's every need, envisioning myself as the most perfect version of a mother. Unfortunately, those dreams didn't quite become reality.

Labor with my daughter was extremely difficult, as if she needed to be forced out into the world. But the next two months were wonderful and filled with love. Then one day, she decided she wasn't going to nurse anymore, and my whole world was turned upside down. I was completely focused on doing everything right—why was she fighting me? I explored every possibility, but nothing made sense. Even her doctor was baffled. The bliss I had longed for was replaced by feelings of utter failure, helplessness, and overwhelm.

Not ready to give up, I decided to see if I could get any insight from an intuitive reiki practitioner in town. According to him, connecting with her spirit was the answer. Now, I was raised by hippies—my mom an herbalist—and had been certified to do reiki years prior. I was probably more spiritual than most, but…connect with her spirit? What did that even mean? I wondered. He suggested more reiki classes, and not knowing what else to do, I agreed.

He could clearly see the state of crisis I was in and was kind. As we went through the training, he would facilitate experiences—guided meditations that turned into deeply personal journeys as he held space. I had powerful visions, and during one of them, Jesus led me down a golden staircase of light while the reiki symbols infused into my being. I wasn't sure what to make of it. I had never experienced anything like that before; nor was I religious or familiar with Jesus in any way. The teacher didn't say much, so when our time came to an end, it was all just kind of left there, suspended in my memory. Things hadn't really gotten easier with the baby, but I tried to adjust as best I could, doing what needed to be done in each moment to survive.

Then Covid hit. Of course, this brought fear but also a sense of relief. I had an excuse to stay home and be a hermit, which was exactly what I wanted to do—to hide from the world. I was miserable and so frustrated with myself. Unable to lose the baby weight, I was ashamed and unbearably uncomfortable in my own skin. Convinced that something in my body was off, I would buy every supplement or remedy that came across my path. I was desperate to find something that would make me feel normal again and berated myself viciously for being unable to make progress or figure it out. I had everything I dreamed of—a stay-at-home mom—so why wasn't I happy? What was wrong with me?

While on vacation in the spring of 2021, out of nowhere, I was struck with appendicitis. Alone in a strange ER for hours, I went in circles, trying to make sense of why my life and health seemed to be unraveling. A good friend, Hannah, was my health and wellness guru, and I vowed to see her for NRT (nutritional response testing) when I got home. I had to get to the bottom of what was going on with my body, and how, as a vegetarian who ate well and took care of herself, I ended up with appendicitis. Clearly, something was wrong.

I made the appointment right away and went through multiple rounds of NRT and supplement protocols. Months went by, and the difference I felt was tangible, but something was still off. The stubborn baby weight wasn't budging, and I just felt lost—like there was no hope of ever feeling truly happy again. When it was time to sign my daughter up for preschool, the guilt was unbearable. I still wasn't working, but I knew she needed this—needed more stimulation and socialization than I was capable of, especially given the mental and emotional state I was in. I prayed that with more personal space, I'd be able to make progress and finally feel better.

As my journey with Hannah continued, parts of my body were testing as blocked or not at full function, but the root causes were not physical—they were energetic. Hannah also offered intuitive energy healing sessions, which involved a combination of channeling and energy work. It seemed it was time to try a new approach, and I was stunned at what these sessions brought forth. I was learning so much about myself, peeling back the layers, healing wounds, and getting reintroduced to the world of spirit and energy in a whole new way.

I remember driving to her office one morning. It was an hour away and a lovely, peaceful ride. I always appreciated the quiet time to myself, but there was something different in the air that day. The colorful autumn leaves seemed to be more vibrant than usual, and the sunshine made every body of water sparkle. I was surrounded by magic and found it hard to focus on the road in front of me with so much beauty in every direction. As I drove, it felt like I was going to burst—full of wonder and anticipation. When I sat in the chair across from Hannah, she asked how I was doing, and I blurted out, "I feel like I'm on drugs!" It was the truth. I was finally shifting, and for the first time in years, I felt a glimmer of hope.

I realized that I had blamed my physical body for so long, but the real problem was that I was completely disconnected from my soul. It all clicked into place: that was the missing piece, the reason I never felt right, why it was so hard to find joy. I had been constantly looking for some external thing to fix me, when really what I was searching for was my true self—that powerful connection inside that I had blocked out for far too long.

But alas, the story doesn't end here, happily ever after. As much healing as I had done, there was still this feeling of lack inside, a belief that I wasn't enough. I was sending my kids off to school every day, and doing what with my life? I was tortured by the fear of what everyone in the community might think of me—that I was lazy or unmotivated. In reality, there was plenty to do to feed and keep up with the demands of a family of five. Life was extremely busy, but any time I felt overwhelmed, I would beat myself up all over again. How dare I feel sorry for myself when so many moms work full time and juggle family life?

I also couldn't ignore this gnawing sense that I needed to do more. But what? The thought of going back to my old job made me feel sick, and trying to find a new one that worked for us didn't seem possible. So I left it alone, hoping that the right opportunity would show itself in time. I was grateful for my partner's support, but I felt useless.

Meanwhile, as I continued to see Hannah, my vision with Jesus came up in conversation, and she was blown away. "You need to be doing this!" she exclaimed. "You are a lightworker!" This was not the response I expected since my teacher had acted like it was no big deal. I brushed it off, but every time I went back to see her, my guides would come through saying things like, "You can do this, too. Practice on Hannah." It terrified me and seemed impossible. She was amazing, so gifted—I didn't even know where to start! But eventually, one day she said, "They're telling me you're ready. It's time for you to start doing this for people."

I froze. WHAT? It was never my intention, on any level, to do what she did. I was the one that needed healing! I might have technically been certified to do reiki for over ten years, but that was my best friend Kate's idea. This was not part of the plan!

I went home thoroughly shocked, wondering what to do. In complete denial and not ready to accept what I had been told, I ended up going to see Kate and told her everything. She said, "You're not going to believe this, but my client that just walked out is looking for someone to rent her reiki room. I instantly thought of you—she's wonderful; you have to meet her!" Once again, I was in shock, but it felt different this time. It was like a numbness that flowed through my whole body, whispering, 'Say yes. Don't be afraid.'

So I met with the woman. The space was newly renovated and absolutely gorgeous. She was so sweet, so flexible, so reasonable. As nervous as I was to take this leap, I was more scared not to. I had felt purposeless and inferior for far too long. What if this was what I was meant to do but just never knew? Was I really going to slam the door in the universe's face when it was all laid out for me so perfectly? No, I couldn't. I had to at least try.

So I spent the next couple of months preparing the space, announcing my new venture, and navigating fear and anxiety like I had never known in my life. It was truly paralyzing at times. What if I couldn't deliver? What if I failed? I was so busy gathering all the things I thought I needed, I didn't even make time to practice with anyone, which only added to my worry.

Finally, everything was ready, and I asked my mother-in-law if I could try to work with her. I knew she wouldn't judge me no matter what happened. I felt clumsy and awkward, but during the session, I saw a little girl with long brown hair and big blue eyes dancing around the table. Was this my mother-in-law as a child? I wondered. When we ended, she said she had seen the same little girl dancing around her! How exciting, I thought. Maybe I really can do this?

As I began taking clients, it continued—their inner children participating in such beautiful ways. Soon, I was having so many visions that I had to write them down as I worked. I could sense how important they were, and with so much happening, I didn't want to forget anything. Loved ones were coming through from the other side, angels, ascended masters, galactic beings, planets, stones, plants, animals...there seemed to be no limit to who or what would decide to join us. Each session was like a journey in itself. It was incredible, but also very surreal, and it wasn't easy sharing what I was seeing. I worried that people would think I was delusional, but the more I did the work, the more excited I got, and the less it bothered me.

Another surprise was what my body was doing—spontaneously breaking out in shamanic dances, my hands moving in ways I never learned to move them, rattling rattles and drumming drums that weren't physically there. Clients would sometimes cry as I worked, and I would be holding back my own tears, relaying loving messages from spirit and details of past life scenes that had played out in my visions like a movie. I was bewildered by how much I loved helping people in this way and by all these layers of reality that I never knew existed. I was learning more about who I was and what I was capable of—in ways beyond words, beyond this world, beyond this life.

I was a healer. Flipping on the light switch of my soul illuminated everything around me—how connected I was to all of it. And how I was now to be a lighthouse for others, helping to guide them through the dark, choppy waters, finding their way back home to themselves, too. It was fulfillment and a sense of purpose like I had never known before. The possibility of being able to help someone the way Hannah had helped me fueled my desire to keep going deeper.

Each session was so different, but there were aspects that I noticed coming up time and time again—the release of grief and trauma, seeing who people are on a soul level, what they are capable of, and then watching them activate and rise in consciousness. One day while doing yoga, a visual message plopped right into my head—a spiral-shaped path of releasing, remembering, and rising, a cycle we continue to move through for the entirety of our human existence. Once again, it all clicked into place. I finally had a way to explain what I was doing without sounding like a crazy person or putting my work—so vast and limitless—into a little box.

All I wanted to do was help people, and this realization gave me newfound confidence to share myself with the world.

Looking back on the journey, I can see how spirit was there behind every twist and turn, divinely orchestrating each struggle and putting what I needed to get through it right in front of me. My youngest was sent here to teach me something—how to listen, how to follow the breadcrumbs back home to myself, and see how truly supported I am, no matter what I may be going through. Focusing on external solutions only distracted me from seeing the truth—that I was already whole. Stepping into my power, acknowledging who I am and all I am connected to, changed everything. I finally started treating my body like the sacred vessel that it is, listening to what it truly needs, and my health has transformed.

Navigating this transformation, this awakening of self, wasn't easy but was the ultimate blessing in the end. If we can reconnect with our inner knowing, allowing ourselves to be guided by the trail of breadcrumbs left just for us, and have a whole lot of courage and trust, that's where the magic is—where the healing is. There is so much gold to be discovered when we find the missing piece and reconnect with our true selves, and that gold is what we're meant to share with the world. No matter how big or insignificant it may seem, every single one of us is important and so incredibly gifted in our own way. I'm just a regular girl living a simple life, trying to learn more about who she is and what she's doing here in each moment, but this world needs me, and it needs you.

It needs us to be brave enough to find our light and shine like the divine beings that we are, inspiring those around us to do the same.

About Brooke Stone:

Brooke is a heart-centered intuitive energy healer based in West Brookfield, Massachusetts where she lives with her partner and their three beautiful children. Certified in Usui and Holy Fire Reiki for over a decade, she started her own practice, Heart Stone Healing, in 2022. Brooke offers sacred healing sessions and personalized channeled messages, and finds her greatest joy and purpose in service. Embodying Divine Feminine Consciousness, she creates a nourishing, safe space for those she works with to be held in a womb of unconditional love, as they experience the gentle yet potent rebirthing process. It is her honor to guide others along the spiral path of releasing grief and trauma, remembering who we truly are, and rising to reach our full potential on every level. Brooke's love for all life, all beings, all of creation, pours into everything she does. You can reach her at heartstonehealinglove@gmail.com

Introduction and A Dark Night of the Soul

By Kimberly Measel

A Dark Night of the Soul: A spiritual journey that forces you to shed previous beliefs, habits, and relationships so that you can transition to a more mindful, fulfilling life. *(Patricia Williams)*

As stated, it shakes every aspect of your belief system and makes you question everything in your existence. Basically, you wonder if you're losing your mind.

I will also add here that it is a difficult and painful process. The good news is that there is a purpose behind it, and if you dig deep and ask the bigger questions, you will be rewarded with beautiful transformations and a new, deeper meaning to your life—one that your Soul custom-designs for your greatest expansion.

I remember reading somewhere that most will experience this cataclysmic event when things in their world are not lining up—and in my case, it was more like awakening the sleeping giant within. This is exactly where I found myself on October 3, 2020, as I sat on the church bench I had occupied for the past 25 years.

I grew up in a Mormon household, so technically speaking, the religious narrative provided my foundational perspective for the past 55 years. I had parents who were faithful members—not just attending church every Sunday but creating the framework and structure for the other six days of the week as well. The Mormon lifestyle was definitely a way of life, not only in what was presented over the pulpit but also in the demands of your own inner guidance system. I was no different. I felt safe, secure, and happy.

With no paid clergy, the opportunities to serve God and others were endless. I served in leadership positions for youth and adult organizations, played the organ for church services, served overseas as a missionary in my twenties, and got married "for all time and eternity" to my husband in the temple—a sacred space where a personal level of righteousness is required to enter. I had four children, attended faithfully, served joyfully, and led a fulfilling life.

This wasn't a Sunday-only religion; it required my all. I didn't attend Sunday meetings and leave it at the door when services were over. This was who I was and how I lived. I knew God and had a personal relationship with Jesus Christ. I was optimistic about the future. Everything seemed to be humming along in my world until Covid hit the planet in early 2020.

This is where things began to change for me—really, for everyone. Who wasn't affected in some way by Covid?

I have a science background, with a college degree in Health Science. So, when I saw how the medical, political, and religious communities responded to Covid, well… nothing added up to what they presented, and I had more questions than answers. The scientific part of me could not align with the mask mandate. I had taken the same microbiology classes that physicians take before medical school and knew that viruses were vastly smaller than the materials used in masks. I couldn't understand the narrative around wearing a mask. Intuitively, the information presented felt like lies.

I decided to take a bird's-eye view approach to wait and see. I was also looking for direction to see what our church leadership would say on the matter. How were they going to council millions of church members? I hoped they would draw a line in the sand and guide us to demonstrate faith and prayer in our lives. After all, sacred scripture is replete with examples of how this might look. Apply these principles in your life, and God will show up for you. It might not be in the way you expect, but faith and prayer are powerful, and experience is an undeniable teacher.

I haven't always agreed with how church leadership approached doctrinal points, but if something didn't align in the moment, I would just "shelf" the information for later. However, the Covid situation was adding weight to that mental shelf, and cracks were beginning to form.

The Prophet and President of the Mormon church was a world-famous cardiologist with numerous accolades and accomplishments—a man whose wisdom and knowledge were widely recognized. He was also seen as a Prophet, called by God to lead and direct the members and affairs of the church. Being someone in authority, I waited with bated breath to see how Covid would be handled.

One month into our collective Covid experience, a formal letter was written and signed by the Presidency of the church and was read by local leadership in congregations around the world. I was eager to hear the council they would provide. The letter began by acknowledging the situation and stating that the Covid vaccine was "an answer to our prayers." We were encouraged to be "good global citizens" and to protect ourselves and others.

My jaw dropped open in disbelief. Were they speaking in code? Did we need to read between the lines? The church pew I was sitting on suddenly became uncomfortable. My stomach churned, and I instinctively began taking deep belly breaths—three of them, to be exact. Cognitive dissonance became a very real thing.

I thought of our Mormon pioneer forefathers, who endured extreme hardships and persecution as they traveled westward in covered wagons and handcarts during the late 1800s. When they faced physical and spiritual challenges, they met them with faith, prayer, and fortitude, expecting miracles. Much of our Sunday School curriculum centered around their experiences, teaching modern-day members to apply these lessons in their individual lives and expect divine intervention.

So why, in this modern era, was the response to COVID—a man-made vaccine—being presented as the answer to our prayers? Was this really what faith and prayer had led us to?

My body was in full alert mode. Red flags flew high, and I knew I couldn't ignore them. An action step would be required. My Soul wouldn't allow me to kick this can down the road or sweep it under the proverbial rug.

This was the moment when my dark night of the soul began. Little did I know that this initial questioning would ignite an inner journey, leading me to truths I had never dared to consider before. It felt ominous.

Intuitively, I knew that everything was about to change. I had to take more deep belly breaths just to feel centered. I knew I needed to ask deeper, more profound questions—not of others, but of myself. I could feel that God and my Soul were leading me somewhere new. I had been in transformative spaces before, but never at this magnitude. I was fully aware of the gravity of the choices and decisions that lay ahead. I already felt committed to the journey.

If you are not aligned with where your Soul leads you, feelings of discontent, unhappiness, and dissatisfaction will remain ever-present. Truth and sovereignty were going to be my baseline measurements moving forward. But leaving behind the spiritual safety net I had known since childhood felt like stepping off a cliff. Would I find solid ground, or would I fall endlessly into uncertainty?

My prayers became more like actual conversations. I would ask God a question and then sit quietly, waiting for something to come into my mind. The answers came as words in my own voice, which was confusing at first. How could I be sure I wasn't just making up the response?

I had recently learned that whoever you are calling out to—be it God, Jeshua (Jesus Christ), or your own Soul—communication will come in your voice and manner of understanding. This felt true, and I trusted it. I believed the heavens wouldn't mislead me. Religion had taught me to pray only to God, but my Soul reminded me that I could speak to whomever I wished and would still receive answers.

This revelation shifted everything. The rigid religious box I had been living in no longer confined me. I felt freedom to explore and expand my relationships with those in the unseen world. I began to resonate with the Archangels, learning that there are many of them, each with unique frequencies, vibrations, and responsibilities. I learned to call on them for help, answers, and clarity.

The Archangels are happy to assist but require our permission to intervene so as not to overstep free will. If they are not invited, they work quietly in the background of our lives, gently guiding and supporting us. Religion had never taught me this, but I was ready to embrace these new ideas, though not without difficulty. In the beginning, shame and guilt often accompanied my exploration. Still, I persisted.

Around this time, I began noticing numerical synchronicities. I'd glance at the clock and see 1:11 or 3:33. This happened so often that I couldn't dismiss it. I discovered these numbers carried different meanings and felt that my guides and angels were using them to communicate. It was both exciting and comforting. These signs became guideposts for me, a reassuring indication that I was being led in the right direction. Even now, I notice these signs daily, though they've expanded to include symbols and other synchronicities that feel like breadcrumbs left for me to follow.

This journey also introduced me to the idea of reincarnation—something most Christians don't traditionally believe in. However, I found myself drawn to explore it further. I had been asking, "Who am I?" I had always felt I came from somewhere else before arriving on this Earthly plane, but I had no satisfactory answers.

My Soul led me to the concept of reincarnation, which finally made sense. I came to believe that mastering Soul lessons requires more than one lifetime, and that Earth serves as a school for these lessons. This perspective resonated deeply with me. The box I had lived in for so long was now fully open.

I began exploring modalities like past-life regression. In this practice, one enters a deep theta hypnosis state where the Higher Self facilitates personal healing and reveals the truth of who you are across lifetimes. This remembrance was a catalyst for me. It led me to sacred angelic alchemy symbols, tools that facilitate transformative journeys. I became an A.U.R.A. practitioner through the Rising Phoenix Aurora Mystery School. This modality was unique in its approach, requiring practitioners to be clear channels of love and focus on facilitating self-healing through the Higher Self. It also emphasized the importance of removing negative entities to create space for healing.

My journey didn't stop there. I discovered the benefits of Reiki and Sound Healing, disciplines that align with the idea that the universe is built on sound, frequency, and vibration. The science behind these practices fit seamlessly with the relationship between the quantum field and the metaphysical world. I began to see energy in a whole new way—its connection to humans, the Earth, the universe, and God/Source.

Each new practice helped me reclaim parts of myself I hadn't realized were lost. These spiritual tools acted as keys, unlocking hidden doors within my Soul.

About a year and a half ago, a series of synchronicities led me to a gifted intuitive healer and psychic channeler, Patricia Asaro. At the time, I had been feeling a powerful nudge to travel to Ireland. Aside from my ancestral ties to the region, the call to go there was undeniable. Compelled, I booked a session with Patricia.

During our session, she channeled specific messages about my upcoming trip. She told me I was to go "where the four cities meet." The reading included details about how I work with energy, specifically in building Pillars of Light that connect crystalline etheric grids to the Earth's ley lines. Patricia explained that traveling to Ireland would shift my life's trajectory in profound ways.

I had no idea what "where the four cities meet" meant, so we pulled up a map and discovered that the locations aligned energetically in the center of Ireland. Zooming in, we identified the Hill of Tara. This ancient site, significant since the late Stone Age, housed burial mounds and had been a key location during the Early Christian Period around 600 BC. It was also where Ireland's High Kings and Queens were crowned. This was where I was meant to go.

The trip to the Hill of Tara became a journey of initiation and self-discovery. It opened the door to further exploration of ancient burial sites across the United States. Each site deepened my connection to my Soul and expanded my understanding of who I am. I came to see Earth as a school for Soul lessons, where every experience contributes to growth and healing.

This process allowed me to shed belief systems that no longer served me. I rediscovered the sacred place within myself that I call Home. I also began to recognize the restless energy sweeping across the planet—a collective nudge for humanity to awaken and question the structures we've long accepted.

This journey taught me the importance of curiosity—of being open to the questions that arise rather than judging them or dismissing them outright. What no longer serves us? What truths have been hidden in plain sight? These questions became a source of empowerment, leading me toward freedom from old belief systems. The process was not without difficulty, but it was deeply rewarding.

Around this time, I began to feel a profound sense of peace, one I had only dreamed of before. By embracing the unknown and inviting these experiences into my life, I started to see that there was no limit to what could be discovered. Each step felt like a small victory—a breadcrumb leading me closer to my authentic self.

Today, I help others rediscover their inner truths. I guide them as they open their own boxes, unlocking the light that has always been within them. My own journey reminds me that we all carry a box—a safe space within ourselves where truths lie waiting to be uncovered.

Opening that box takes courage. It requires us to question the systems and beliefs we've inherited and to step into the unknown. But within that space lies liberation—the freedom to live authentically and aligned with our Soul's purpose.

Are you willing to turn the key? Are you ready to step into your own personal empowerment? Your Soul is inviting you to take this journey. The invitation is always there. All you have to do is accept it.

The work doesn't stop once the box is opened. My journey continues to evolve, as does my connection to the unseen world. The signs, synchronicities, and lessons still guide me daily. They remind me that growth is a lifelong process and that every step forward brings me closer to my highest potential.

I am honored to walk this path and to help others walk theirs. Together, we can uncover the truths that will set us free, one question, one breath, and one step at a time.

About Kimberly Measel:

Kimberly Measel is an intuitive healer specializing in unique energy modalities. She is a Reiki Master, CMA Accredited Sound Healer, A.U.R.A and R.A.A.H Reiki Hypnosis Practitioner, Akashic Reader, and Pure Energy Crystal Healer. As a Light Pillar Grid Architect, Kimberly works closely with the earth's energy and often partners with her Chesapeake Bay Retriever, Steele, during sessions.

Trained in the ancient mystery schools of Rising Phoenix Aurora and the House of Huna, where she is remembered as Huna Ta Ra Kuia, Kimberly creates sacred spaces for others to heal and rediscover their true selves. Her intuitive, creative approach reflects her deep commitment to serving Father/Mother God and supporting humanity's ascension journey.

Based in Oxford, Michigan, Kimberly enjoys nature, reading, and meaningful conversations with her community. She is dedicated to inspiring transformational healing for the earth and its people. Learn more at www.energywielder.earth.

From Failure to Featured
By Bobby Gray

When I think back to grade school, the memories are harsh, judgmental, and unforgiving. Cruel words like 'faggot' echoed not only daily in the halls of the schoolyard and on the playground of grade school but also through my adult mind nearly 40 years later. It was no surprise that I hid behind friendships to escape the constant abuse and ridicule of the other kids. My entire school career was more than a struggle; it felt like a dangerous, painful battlefield. I barely made it out alive, let alone thriving and achieving, while dealing with the complexity and survival of just the day-to-day. It's no wonder I gravitated toward anything that offered a sense of connection, freedom, acceptance, or belonging—even if it was unconventional or sometimes unsafe.

Here's the deal: I have always had a major interest in expanding one's mind and exploring various levels of consciousness. The depth and scope of these studies have simply fascinated me. Learning, on the other hand, often left me feeling under-stimulated, undervalued, and unprotected. Maybe the environment just wasn't ideal for growth and development, if you know what I'm saying. As I sit here drafting this contribution, I think to myself: "Wow, there's still such a serious problem." And not just with how broken the system was—but how broken it remains. Don't come for me; I've already served my time.

You see, in grade school, when it was supposed to be fluffy bunnies and teddy bears, field trips, and pudding cups, I was casually met with pet names like 'faggy' daily from what felt like the whole entire student body. This was long before the societal conversations around pronouns, the he/she/they/them movement, and the widespread LGBTQ+ acceptance we see today. Let me tell you: the other kids simply were not my friends. In any way. Ever.

As a child, you don't really know who you are yet, and sexual preference is definitely not even a question. At what point are we so out of integrity that there's a need to refer to someone as 'faggot' all the time? It didn't matter if it was on the playground, in the classroom, in the hallways, or within earshot of a teacher or faculty member. Let's just say it's probably a miracle I'm not actually dead right now. When you're learning as a child—

or even as a person—it's a journey of the self that should be protected and respected.

Think about the Salem Witch Trials. How many innocent people, including children, were burned and tortured to death because of similar, close-minded, ridicule-based thinking? Clearly, their ancestors are alive and well today. Partially because of this constant level of stress and abuse, I did very poorly throughout my entire school career. I relied on the few friends I had to escape the relentless bullying, intense judgment, and harsh criticism. Ever hiding on the sidelines, I tried to blend in just beneath the surface, never really speaking up for myself or claiming what are basic universal rights, moral values, and human decency.

When I got older, I discovered the Area Vocational School program. Think of it like diesel mechanic college. There was a career fair, and some girls from the local beauty school were there answering questions and sharing their experiences. I thought, "Wow, this could be cool and interesting." Eventually, this path would prove not to be easy, but it was a start. It set me on a course of exploring the unconventional, leading me to some of the most profound experiences, journeys, and concepts of my lifetime.

Not really loving school, I saw the vocational program as an opportunity to leave a horrible environment filled with miserable kids. Thank God, this meant I was now in a class full of 35 girls for half the day. Days for this program were split between your home high school (mine was Littleton Options, an alternative high school) and the selected trade campus (Englewood Beauty College). Here, I began to partially bloom into the person I would become later on.

These beautiful leaders eventually shaped my life. I am honored and truly so grateful for the following influential people: Ms. June and her beautiful partner, Ms. Liz. The ever-wild and fun Ms. Kathy, and Mrs. Colleen—the Nail Room Queen. Even Mr. Jerry. Decades later, they remain fond memories. So many bright souls shared their knowledge fiercely, helping young students find their way through life and eventually into their selected careers.

Wow, these would be the days that started changing and shaping my life, my career, and eventually my future and destiny. Learning all the ins and outs of the hair, skin, and nail industries, including licensing, was, to say the least, a lot. So much so that when I had accumulated the hours required for my diploma from beauty school, I simply quit going. This decision would prove unhelpful to my finances, career, or future. After going through two years of night school and summer school—and even an additional senior year—I was just so done with school.

It doesn't take a rocket scientist to figure out why. Being bullied almost daily for 10+ years by your peers can take a toll. Wow, I must really have been a piece of work, let me tell ya. In all actuality, there was nothing wrong with me. On the contrary, the way society is programmed—with corrupted blueprints passed down through generational traumas, systemic issues like racism, alcoholism, and poverty-stricken mindsets—is what's truly mind-boggling.

Now, looking back, so many of those life experiences I struggled with make much more sense to me because of the energetic match between my internal state and those situations. We are truly the masters of our own minds, universes, and environments. If left to our own devices—depending on our education, dedication, and the intention or inspiration—we have the potential to create masterpieces: of thought, artform, word, imagery, solid form, film, print, digital, or sound. Even our energy and healing can be found in peace and silence.

Although life doesn't always give us peace and quiet. The shooting in my apartment felt like the last straw in a long line of traumatic experiences. I was already in a dramatic personal struggle, and now I simply never slept. Nights blurred into days, my job and marriage suffered, and my personal existence became a state of constant anxiety and trigger responses. I felt like life had hit me with more than I could bear, and I didn't know how to find my way out of the insanely crippling darkness.

I went into my normal overdrive—functioning in a highly toxic situation, working 60+ hours a week for far too long. (Again, all another story.) Eventually, there would be a Facebook ad, and the rest was history. I clicked on it and immediately became a lifelong raving fan of LifeChangingEnergy.com and Vickie. I went from the $99 special to becoming a Certified Master Sound Healer in no time at all at a live certification event—which just so happened to be on my actual birthday a few short months later.

What a treat to share with my LCE family and experience all the amazing facets of this three-day adventure. Lifelong friendships, connections, tools, and systems or practices to stay on top of my game and visible in the marketplace, may or may not have also been found.

Life happens—husbands get laid off, and stress takes over again. The balance of life is one that will always be tested and will shift on us many times. What I can tell you from personal experience is that it never stops—the good, the bad, the ugly, and yes, even the amazing! It all depends on where your focus is on the vibrational scale, what you're attracting to yourself, and at what speed. The more intense the feeling, the faster the manifestation or realization travels into your universe.

When a friend suggested a sacred plant medicine tour in Colombia, my initial response was a string of profanity swirled with skepticism and curiosity. Part of me was scared to death, but deep down, another version of myself—one that had been a prisoner for far too long—was desperate for freedom and change. Knowing something had to give deep within my soul, I felt this was a chance, a stirring—this was the call. If it could help me reclaim even a shred of peace of mind or sanity, I was sure as hell going to try!

The first night of the Ayahuasca ceremony felt like a complete unraveling. As the medicine took hold, I had no idea what was going on. Should I swallow it or spit it out? The feelings and experience were all so intense. I became violently ill even before mixing the two kinds of stuff they gave us—a mix of tobacco in a tar-like form and crushed dried coca leaves mixed with ceremonial ashes. I purged violently and then returned to the gathering circle, where curious eyes met me, wondering what exactly I was going through. Hours of intense physical and mental purging followed that first night.

To my astonishment, this wasn't even the real Ayahuasca itself—hold on, wait a minute here! I just barfed my life out for like three to five hours consistently, and that wasn't even the real deal? It was just the pregame. Who in the world—? OK, so the journey consisted of four separate kinds of sacred plant medicine experiences. I had just encountered the first, which was really a combination of two different things.

The following night, it all really began. Nothing in the weeks, days, months, or thousands of miles I traveled could have prepared me for what I was about to experience. I took the shot glass of a dark, earthy, herbal liquid. It was thick and somewhat hard to explain. I'm sure my entire body was screaming, "Don't do this; we're going to die!" Let's say, around five to fifteen minutes later, I really didn't feel all that well.

I ventured toward the toilet, where I found myself outside on my knees behind the outhouse. I remember saying, "Am I going to D I E?!" To my astonishment, what can only be described as the voice of Grandmother Aya softly entered my consciousness: "Only if you really want to." I thought, "Holy shit. I still have so much to do, and I'm not ready yet!" She calmly responded, "Then go ahead. Do what you do." At this point, I felt like I had been spared by the Devil—just way less evil. (Sorry, Sacred Plant Mother Earth Goddess, you are not evil in any way, although the purge may make you feel otherwise.)

I walked back toward the gathering circle, unknowing what was about to take place. Shortly after, people could barely walk and were rushing to the restroom. Boy, did I know how they were feeling. I may or may not have been giggling to myself. I found one of our friends crawling around in the grass. "Are we going to die? Are we safe here?" she asked. I lovingly responded, "No, we're totally fine. I'm here for you, and YES, we're going to make it!"

"How do you know?" she asked. She was clearly on a different level than I was, so how do I tell her what Grandmother Aya had just revealed to me?! If you're not laughing out loud right now with me, that's OK.

The sacred plant medicine opened a door, but the real work began afterward. Meditation, sound healing, and daily energy practices became my constants. Each session brought me closer to a state of acceptance, moving up the vibrational scale from fear and shame toward neutrality and peace. Over time, I came to realize that these practices weren't just tools—they were lifelines and pathways to reclaiming my life, healing, and destiny.

Through many of these experiences, I came to understand that true healing requires more than addressing individual symptoms—it demands a shift in one's personal level of consciousness. It's about learning to live from a place of radical self-care, recognizing that our thoughts and vibrational frequencies shape our mental landscape and eventually our reality. This realization contributed to my creation of the Golden Hours Mastery Program, a system designed to help others break free from limiting beliefs and find their own path to fulfillment and a joyous life.

This program was born from my deep desire to give others the tools I wish I had found sooner. It's not about achieving instant enlightenment but about stringing together small, intentional actions to create profound, noticeable change in one's life. I want others to know that it's possible to go from feeling like a total piece of shit, hiding in the shadows and not standing up for yourself, to completely owning the stage with the poise and beauty of a brilliantly articulated light warrior boldly claiming the entire spotlight.

Life doesn't always give us the circumstances we desire, but it does present us with the rare and defining opportunity to choose how we respond. By embracing holistic practices and committing to daily action based on self-care, I learned to move beyond survival instinct and fight-or-flight mode and step into a life of intentional, divine communication, creation, and daily gratitude. It's a journey I'm still focused on and passionate about sharing boldly to empower and uplift others.

You don't need to fly all the way to the Amazon or experience a sacred plant medicine tour to begin your healing. The real transformation starts when you decide to take the first step—whether it's meditation, journaling, breathwork, or simply realizing that you are enough. Wherever you are in life, remember that you have the power to rewrite your story. Right now, today. Simply take a deep breath and start.

About Bobby Gray:

Simply a Master of Intuitive Transformational Sound Healing and a seasoned expert in communications, emotional intelligence, and the art of personal transformation. With over 20 years of mastery in hairstyling and an elite certification in sound healing, Bobby G has dedicated their life to helping others unlock profound levels of clarity, alignment, and empowerment.

Drawing from a rich tapestry of experiences, including sacred plant medicine journeys, advanced sound healing activations, and international retreats, Bobby channels divine energy to support clients on their journey to self-discovery and cosmic ascension. His work integrates ancient wisdom, universal laws, and cutting-edge techniques to create transformational experiences that go beyond the ordinary.

As a co-author of this book, Bobby shares his unique insights and wisdom to inspire others to embrace their highest potential and step into their authentic power. Their message is one of hope, healing, and limitless possibility.

Embracing The Journey through Spirituality and Sound

By Kristin Whitcomb

In the early morning of December 2, 2019, I was awakened by the frantic barking of my loyal companion, Baxter. His persistent barks signaled a looming crisis, and as I struggled to get up, I realized I was lying face down on my pillow, damp with drool. I wiped my face and got up to let Baxter outside.

Catching a glimpse of my reflection in the bathroom mirror, I was reminded of life's unpredictability. The journey to the emergency room was a blur, and the grim prognosis of impending mortality from the medical team left me in a peculiar fog. I was disoriented yet strangely serene, caught in a limbo between two worlds, my emotions a turbulent sea of fear, acceptance, and determination.

In this profound moment, I faced the possibility of departing from this life. The medical professionals urged me to contact my family, and a barrage of questions flooded my mind: Had I accomplished my earth-life objectives? Did my loved ones take pride in my achievements? How could I effectively communicate my final sentiments to my son and mother? Could this indeed be a manifestation of death? Who would have imagined such an outcome?

As each test result arrived, accompanied by uncertainty, I found an inner resilience forming, challenging the bleak predictions of the medical professionals. I realized the necessity of forging a path forward, which instilled a sense of empowerment amidst the unpredictability of my medical situation. However, my mental state felt unfamiliar and disorienting, adding to the complexity of the circumstances. When the emergency room physician stated, "Your brain imaging is perfect; there is no evidence of a stroke, so we are discharging you as there is nothing further we can do for you," I asked, "Who will assist me now?" A question that nobody could answer.

Trudging wearily back to my new retirement home, my physical health deteriorating, I felt my inner determination begin to glimmer like the lotus flower tattooed on my left forearm, reminding me of my ability to bloom amid prevailing uncertainty. At the age of 57, the prospect of my imminent passing raised more questions than answers. Reflections of my life began swirling through my mind. I recalled how I had spent the majority of my time in a fast-paced, competitive world: as an athlete, an educator, an ex-wife, a mom, a mother-in-law, and a business owner. I was intelligent, quick-witted, sassy, and ready to embark on my retirement status in new and adventurous ways. The world *was* my oyster—until now.

My health challenges encompassed cognitive difficulties with significant physical impairments. The inflammation within my brain resulted in various debilitating physical issues, including an inability to utilize my hands. The mobility on my left side became significantly compromised and my extremities were not receiving brain synopsis, so walking became fragmented and holding or gripping things in my hands was not happening. Excruciating muscle and joint pain accompanied it all, confining my existence into uncharted territory. My thoughts became fragmented, often lacking coherence. My nervous system was unregulated, and the ongoing struggle began to adversely affect my business, making it increasingly challenging to develop plant-based products for my clients—an endeavor I had nurtured with great passion over the years. Consequently, the grand opening of my new company, JusB*LLC, was postponed, and my health continued to decline without any definitive medical explanation.

> I scribed my thoughts in my journal:
> *When I heard my diagnosis—I was angry.*
> *When I lost movement in my left side and dropped weight below 100 lbs.—*
> *I became angrier.*
> *When I lost my life as I knew it on 12.2.2019—I became anger-driven.*
> *And*
> *When I did not die, my anger became RAGE.*

The ferocity of my anger was evident to everyone, including myself. The more I lost—my health, my independence, and my new company—the more I felt life itself had betrayed me. The loss of my independence and the ability to perform simple tasks on my own was a blow I struggled to accept. Confused and exasperated, I found it difficult to comprehend how death could even be possible—but the physical evidence was my new reality.

My thoughts turned to my personal history, where just one year earlier, in October 2018, my doctor had confirmed my "perfect" health at my annual well-woman check-up and prompted me to receive two newer vaccines for women 55+: shingles and pneumonia. One month later, I moved into my newly built retirement home, excited about the freedom it would bring.

It was a villa home where the HOA would handle the lawn and remove the snow, allowing me to travel the world without worry. But after the first rainstorm—and for the following two years—my roof experienced random leaks, despite the builder's attempts to fix the issue. As the leaks persisted, the builder and I argued about the underlying cause. The warranty paperwork stated that if I had any contractual work done on the house or roof, all warranties would become null and void; the builder had to inspect and approve or fix all defects.

My inquiries revealed significant flaws in the city and county building inspection procedures. Rather than implementing standard inspection protocols, they permitted the builder to engage in "self-inspections," a practice extended to the roofer, who conducted their own "self-inspections." Subsequent investigations uncovered substantial evidence of roofing and construction defects in 400 of 520 homes, prompting the roofer to file for bankruptcy protection and the county to engage legally with the builder.

Inevitably, I became increasingly enmeshed in legal disputes involving both individual and collective claims against the builder, the Homeowners Association (HOA), the city, and the county. I needed legal counsel to handle it all, and many neighbors began attributing blame to me for their perceived decrease in property values, leading to an overwhelming sense of despair.

Research eventually revealed that the builder did not comply with approved grading and drainage plans for the community. This deviation resulted in stagnant, swampy water conditions both within the community and on individual properties, facilitating the growth of mold under the siding, roofs, insulation, and other porous surfaces of the newly constructed homes.

When the naturopath doctors diagnosed mold in my lungs, I began to understand how the mycotoxins released from airborne mold spores had entered my bloodstream, leading to inflammation in internal organs and mimicking the stroke-like episode I experienced in the emergency room. My body's inability to combat the toxic mold reaction was attributed to one of the vaccines I received at my well-woman check-up, which had weakened my immune system.

My new retirement home had become a prison of death. Each moment felt akin to existing within a confining and detrimental environment, slowly killing me. As my dreams of traveling unraveled into spiraling darkness, I began to embrace this transformative end-of-life journey. Despite my family's opposition, I decided to move to my 2-acre mountain home, two hours away from friends and family and one hour from the nearest medical facility, seeking peace in nature as my life neared its end.

Amid my indifference to just about everything, I clung to hope for relief from the intense physical pain I was experiencing. As I awaited death, I realized my relationships, especially with my son, deserved my attention. Our relationship had faced many challenges since 2009, when my 31-year marriage to his father ended. His father and I carried the weight of dysfunction from our childhoods, shaped by the families we grew up in. Together, since the age of 16, we both struggled to navigate life without healing from those traumas. Now, a decade after the divorce, I resolved to turn any remaining anger between my son and me into profound and authentic love, choosing healing and connection over past grievances.

I delved deeper into researching my health condition, reminiscent of my journey in 2016 when I sought the healing properties of plants for pain and inflammation relief after a motorbike accident. Grappling with the threat of death was profoundly different from dealing with a shattered leg, yet I was determined to find my way out of the darkness. I wanted to die "in light" of it all.

As minutes transformed into hours, hours into days, and days into weeks and months, I found solace and empowerment in exploring the intricate world of naturopathic studies. While the vast knowledge ahead felt daunting, it ignited excitement within me. I felt drawn to the realms of healing and spirituality and sought guidance from compassionate healers who introduced me to the interconnectedness of body, mind, and spirit, transcending traditional American medicine.

This new journey of self-discovery illuminated the surrounding darkness and empowered me to seek alternative therapies. From meditation to acupuncture, Auric readings to Irigenics, I immersed myself in practices that enveloped me with positive energy and loving support, instilling a profound sense of empowerment. Each day brought new friends, fresh ideas, small victories, and moments of progress, fueling my determination to overcome adversity and thrive, even in the face of death.

Delving into the tactical studies of numerology and astrology, I found solace, wisdom, and connection in their intricate patterns and celestial guidance. Engaging with a wise astrologer from Boulder, I unraveled the enigma of the planetary universe, honing my soul's purpose into clearer focus. Rekindling my fascination with spiritual literature, a world that captivated me as a child, I embarked on a transformative journey where profound insights became powerful catalysts for growth, shaping my understanding of energy's ethereal realms and illuminating my path.

Sundays with my astrologer mentor, Jim, became a beacon of hope throughout the COVID-19 pandemic, a time when the world was gripped by fear and uncertainty. My naturopathic doctors advised against further vaccines after determining the shingles vaccine had triggered a reaction in my body, disabling my autoimmune function. This systemic failure allowed mycotoxins from construction defects in and around my new home to infiltrate my body through the bloodstream.

Reading my natal chart, Jim affirmed that the healing path before me was meant to be. He identified aspects in my chart encouraging me to explore holistic healing, prompting my engagement in Astro-herbalism, Medium/Psychic mentorship, and a Past-Life Regression course to enhance my self-healing. With each mentor who entered my life, I felt the universe guiding me, reassuring me that I was not alone and that I was supported on my healing journey.

My spirit found resilience and optimism in the ethereal world, and my body slowly began to respond. I remember discovering frequency healing at a body, mind, and spirit fair, where I met someone who created tensor rings infused with healing frequencies. When I put the small tensor ring on my wrist, I felt a surge of protection flowing through my body, emanating through my disabled hands. It was an incredible sensation as if electrified healing waves were passing through me, and I could sense that something within me was shifting. I felt this energy surge again when I visited an Aura Psychic Artist who painted my portrait while reading my aura. Her wisdom encouraged me to "dance" from within when I was mourning the loss of my physical abilities to so. Her words radiated into my perspective, and I began to work on a deeper level—from within.

The eventual diagnosis of Chronic Inflammatory Response Syndrome (CIRS) led me to explore naturopathy and embrace holistic healing practices. As I immersed myself in daily frequency healing modalities—techniques that use specific frequencies to restore natural balance—I noticed positive changes throughout my body. These vibrational healing frequencies were restoring inner balance, leading to remarkable results: my memory improved, my hand dexterity was restored, my brain fog diminished, my sleep became more restful, and my communication—both writing and speaking—became controlled, clear, and understandable.

I found solace in the rejuvenating powers of nature's elements. Sunlight invigorated and uplifted my mood; love offered emotional healing and support; starlight instilled a sense of wonder and connection to the universe; and moonlight calmed my mind and helped me sleep better. My relationship with music underwent a transformative shift. I began to concentrate on uplifting lyrics and learned to engage deeply with the essence of the music, allowing me to receive spiritual messages. During sound healing sessions, I successfully released long-held emotions of rage and resentment, as each musical note served to unlock the shadows I had carried for years, leaving me with a sense of invigoration and motivation.

On New Year's Eve 2022, I sat quietly, reflecting on the years gone by. I had lived a whirlwind of experiences—two thousand twenty-two was filled with either chaos or overwhelming love. Each twist and turn held meaning that I was only beginning to grasp. Reflections in my journal captured this:

"Thanks for all you brought to me.

Two oh Two Two

A lot of bullaballooooooo

Or a lot of Lovalooooooos

All of it held meaning:

Growing through deceits

And standing tall in Truth & Love

Tomorrow, I will see

Two oh Two THREE

Can't wait to see

What's in store for me

The energy is worldly and chaotic.

Or wonderfully in a state of change

It's going to be a fascinating year,

So it is.

I will ring you in with cheer."

As I closed my eyes that evening, listening to the steady tick of the clock reaching midnight, I felt a sense of peace washing over me. I was ready to embrace the new year, walking alongside everyone traveling their earthly paths, guided by the light that had ignited my soul. Tomorrow, when the sun rose on two thousand twenty-three, I focused on stepping into the unfolding story of my life with hope, joy, and unwavering love.

The past five years have been a profound exploration of mortality and healing for me. I have come to understand that every challenge I face is a catalyst for recovery, opening my eyes to the extraordinary capabilities of the human body and brain when it comes to self-healing. When I align my internal energies with the world around me, I feel a sense of harmony that I have never known before.

The experiences on this transformative journey led me to achieve expert-level certification in sound healing through the LCE program, unlocking pathways I never knew existed, both for myself and others seeking healing. It has reignited a passion for writing that has long been dormant, inspiring me to share my journey with others and guide them toward illuminating their internal paths.

As I continue to learn and grow, I am determined to live my best life rather than merely exist until the end. I remain profoundly grateful for the guidance and wisdom of my mentors, who lifted me from the depths of darkness and empowered me to help others find the light on their healing journeys. Their support has been invaluable, and I aspire to share the lessons I have learned in deep gratitude.

About Kristin Whitcomb:

Kris possesses a distinguished career spanning three decades in public education, during which she held various positions, including teacher, principal, district data coordinator, and adjunct professor. Her educational background includes degrees in Elementary Education, Educational Administration, and a master's in business administration (MBA).

In 2019, her experience with Chronic Inflammatory Response Syndrome (CIRS) inspired her to pursue the fields of energy and frequency healing. Since then, she has established herself as a recognized expert in sound healing, a master herbalist, an astrologer, and a past-life regression practitioner.

Kris founded JusB LLC, an organization dedicated to empowering individuals on their journey to natural healing. She advocates for transformative healing by integrating ancient wisdom with modern methodologies, instilling renewed hope in those she serves. Through her commitment to building trust and promoting self-awareness, Kris helps individuals reconnect with their authentic selves and facilitates meaningful healing through energetic transformation.

Get in touch:

JusB*Home | JusB* (jusbco.com)

JusB* Facebook Page: https://www.facebook.com/100064176069010/

JusBmindful@gmail.com

Cell Phone: 303.668.9085

Out of the Darkness of Domestic Violence

and

Into Consciousness, Forgiveness, and Compassion

By Joyce Martin

Being in a domestic violence relationship for many, many years led me to recapture my spirituality and eventual healing. There were times when I thought I'd never have the courage to get out of the situation, but I finally did. I want to give courage to those reading this as well—the courage to get through it, no matter what your decision is: to stay or to go. I don't judge you, and I encourage others not to judge you either. I want to support you and help you realize you are not alone. No matter how difficult the situation is, it is possible to overcome—even if, right now, you feel skeptical that it will ever happen. I appreciate your skepticism, but I offer my story about how I overcame it through my spiritual journey, and I hope it helps you too.

I was skeptical too because my entire life has been fraught with obstacles, hurdles, and perils. I didn't know how to get out of the abusive situation I was in or if I would ever be able to overcome the challenges.

Some days, when I reflected on the abuse I had endured in my lifetime, I felt as if I would be stuck in the muck and mire forever. My life felt like a complete failure. I felt depressed, anxious, hopeless, and, at times, suicidal. I once heard that being sick and tired of something is the greatest opportunity for change and growth. So, there I was—sick and tired—and I knew I had to do something about it. As my life was spiraling out of control, a small part of me knew these were life lessons meant for a bigger purpose, and I felt a longing to find out what that purpose was. I later came to realize that this was all put in place by the universe to take me on a spiritual journey, to awaken my spirit so I could heal.

Failure, pain, and obstacles teach us lessons, and those lessons, especially the tough ones, can eventually lead to an awakening if you open yourself to what's possible. I have used these lessons to inspire me, and, in turn, I want to inspire others to see their difficulties as opportunities. I have found that setbacks gave me a chance to stop and reflect, to make corrections to my path, jump over the hurdles, and move forward. I began to think like an Olympic hurdler going for the gold medal and became tenacious. I began to believe there is no hurdle I can't get over. If I can't jump over it, I'll go under it, around it, or just kick it down. I've found that I am strong enough to move through any pain, even the pain of abuse, and I know you can overcome your own difficulties too.

Many of us who become abused as adults don't just walk into an abusive relationship without having some sort of prior history. As was the case for me, it stemmed from something deeper. For me, it began with the abuse that happened in my childhood. The pain stayed with me because I never had the opportunity to talk about it or work through it. Growing up being abused led me to fall back into the same trap as an adult because it was, strangely, comfortable.

The details of the abuse aren't particularly important, and if you'd like to read more, that's a whole other book. But the important part of this story is to demonstrate that it's not only possible to survive but to come out of the darkness and thrive. The biggest part of my survival was becoming awake or spiritually conscious. Through my spiritual journey, I began practicing the concepts of consciousness, forgiveness, and compassion. When I learned these concepts, I discovered there is no need to struggle against what is or what was anymore.

Struggling is a self-imposed hell. Self-imposed hell may seem extreme, but I say self-imposed because there are options you have right now, in this very moment, that anyone can use to stop the struggle.

I know what it is like to experience deep, heart-wrenching pain, disappointment, depression, abuse, suicidal ideation, and anxiety, but I finally came to a point in my life where I just wanted it to stop. These painful emotions were like bad old friends that just kept hanging around me for years, mooching off my sanity and bringing me down.

Pain of any kind is a difficult thing, but when the pain is not brought to conscious awareness, it continues to live in you. It becomes part of your identity, your ego will feed it, and it can come out in very negative ways toward others or yourself at any time.

I knew I had to make a conscious choice to be different. I did not want to live with the pain for the rest of my life. I was miserable but decided I was not going to be a victim any longer. I chose first to get out of the relationship and then get out of the darkness of my own mind, which can be as bad as—or worse than—an outside source of pain. I just didn't want this toxicity taking over my life anymore. It was occupying far too much of my time and energy, and I literally felt drained.

In *The Power of Now*, Eckhart Tolle talks about how the self, or the ego, loves to use pain to feel important, to garner pity, or to get some other reaction. However, for clarification, I want to reassure those of you aware of this concept that I didn't write this to rehash the pain for my "self or ego." Also, I am not writing this to use as a catharsis, as the catharsis has already happened.

The true purpose of this story is not about me but to share a universal story about how our pain is there to light the road to our spiritual journey into consciousness. Being spiritually conscious and using pain as a motivator, instead of having the pain use you, is what I'm advocating for. I have learned that no matter how difficult the pain of abuse, depression, anxiety, or any other type of pain you are going through, it can all be transmuted when you are fully conscious. Then, this consciousness can lead to finding peace within yourself.

I have learned that the pain of my story is simply past history. This is my story, but it's not who I am. Until I wrote the story down, it only existed in my head. Yet even now, as it exists on paper, I have a quiet knowing and a peaceful detachment from the pain, thanks to writers like Tolle, Chopra, Dyer, and others. Their work helped me understand these concepts, and I feel so grateful for such a beautiful gift. My hope is that this will be a gift to you as well, and at least one more person can stop suffering and enter into pure spirit consciousness.

So, how do many of us handle a lifetime of pain that's been inflicted on us by others who are spiritually unconscious? Unfortunately, the way this can manifest is that we become spiritually unconscious ourselves. We try to numb the pain, and we use maladaptive coping mechanisms such as illicit substances, food, restriction of food, video games, social media, TV, love, sex, gambling, etc. This helps us live in a dream or delusional state of mind instead of facing or learning the truth. Then, we give in to desires of the world. In essence, we are covering our pain by desiring external things, not looking internally.

Now, as a practicing licensed clinical psychologist, reiki master, sound healer, and meditation facilitator, I have learned that many of us don't have a spiritual practice. Many are looking for outside sources to fix things, but we often forget to look inside ourselves. The best thing we can do is to be consciously aware of the pain, to feel it, observe it, and not judge it. Don't allow yourself to go back to an unconscious or delusional state; accept what is.

Non-acceptance of what is simply adds to our pain. When we resist the reality of things, we can stay stuck, and that leads us to a dark place. I understand that feeling pain is not most people's first choice, for sure. As was the case for me, I didn't want to accept what was, and I tried to avoid the pain too, just like most people. The problem with that is it doesn't make it go away. I found that when I finally accepted the pain, saw it for what it was, embraced it, and made it fully conscious, I could transform it. But of course, I'm not saying this is done overnight. This is a practice.

The other thing we do that doesn't work is rehashing the pain over and over in our minds like a mixer. Overthinking, beating ourselves up, and churning the contents of our story repeatedly in the hope that it would become smoothed out just doesn't work. In reality, things are never smoothed out just by ruminating on them. No matter how many times we think about the pain, it remains ever strong in our minds. I was guilty of this too. I could go for hours, and before I knew it, weeks were going by as I rehashed my story, but when all was said and done, the pain was still there.

Intellectually, I kept thinking, "Why can't I just snap out of this?" I was a psychology major at that time, but even with knowledge, I couldn't! My thinking mind kept telling me that my brain was filled with neurotransmitters and that if I just got some antidepressants, I would be fine. Yet, that didn't help either.

The pain that I felt was so deep from feeling victimized by what happened to me, I knew I couldn't stand it much longer. I thought, "Either it goes, or I go," and at that time, the only thing that was keeping me alive was my children. Truly, if it weren't for them, I don't know what would have become of me. Fortunately, at that point, I knew I did not want to cause my children suffering and pain and repeat the cycle.

Then, as I was driving to work one day, I thought, "Why can't I get control of my own brain?" This was much like the recount of Eckhart Tolle's experience in *The Power of Now*, even though this thought occurred to me well before I read any of his books. It was then that I began to see a separation from the pain, and for a minute, I felt better.

That realization was like an epiphany, and soon the universe began presenting serendipitous events—one of which led me to *The Power of Now*, and the other to *A New Earth*, both by Eckhart Tolle. I already owned them for a few years but had not read them. The books sat on a shelf for years, but somehow, now I was drawn to them. I was hungry for answers, and these books provided me with exactly what I needed in that moment. This experience was wonderful, and like a snowball effect, I quickly linked to other spiritual books. My spiritual quest bloomed like a lotus flower, and I felt as if I was breaking out of the mud.

I found myself being at ease and not in need of anything. I began to believe that I am okay just the way I am, and I'll tell you, so are you. I have learned along the way that there is no material thing out there that can bring me happiness. Happiness is elusive, but true joy comes from connecting to the source from which all things emanate.

Each day, I look for the passion and joy within. I express gratitude for all the bad experiences because they led me to my spiritual awakening. I express gratitude for the good things I have in my life too—my two wonderful sons, my work, my writing, etc.—and I'm grateful for each thing and each person I encounter.

I strive not to attach myself to anything, as everything is fleeting, and at some point, all will be lost. I am at peace at this time in my journey. My life is still a work in progress, as all our lives are. I know what happened in the past was merely the universe guiding me to evolve my human consciousness exactly to where I am right now. I do not know what the future holds, nor do I allow my mind to worry about it.

I know now that the past does not define me—it isn't me—and I no longer identify with it. In fact, it doesn't even really exist. I stay in the present, so even when my mind may try to lead me to despair, I bring it back to consciousness, observe it, and do not judge it. I work on bringing space between the thoughts and just let them dissipate into thin air.

After becoming conscious, I realized that forgiveness is the next step in the journey. To forgive others as well as yourself is to lift a huge weight off your shoulders. I know many people have probably heard this before, but it is my hope that everyone will be able to take this message to heart this time for good. Forgiving others and having compassion for everyone, including those who have hurt you, is key. It's not an excuse or a free pass for them—it's just the truth. Using forgiveness as a spiritual practice will set you free. Practice is an excellent word for it, because if I didn't practice it daily, I could lose it too.

The story about the wrong someone did to you is carried around in your head, and it's a very heavy burden to bear. Only you have the power to let it go. It's the best gift you can give yourself. Holding onto the pain, frustration, anger, etc., doesn't do anything to the other person. They're off somewhere enjoying their life, not even giving you a second thought, but you're keeping it alive, and it's hurting you.

The only thing I want to feel about those who hurt me is compassion. If it were not for the terrible suffering they endured themselves, they wouldn't have become unconscious enough to hurt others. Their pain was a breeding ground for their actions. When someone unconscious does something to you, it's because they are in such pain themselves that their outward actions mirror what they feel inside.

So, finding consciousness, forgiveness, and compassion are the tools to bring you out of the pain. Feeling grateful for everything that led you here today is the final piece of the puzzle.

Namaste.

About Joyce Martin:

Dr. Martin is a Licensed Clinical Psychologist. She is passionate to work with anyone who is interested in overcoming life's challenges. She graduated from John F. Kennedy University, and UC Berkeley. She has worked in mental health for over 20 years. She has treated patients for a variety of diagnoses, including Depression, Anxiety, Adjustment Disorders, (PTSD) Post Traumatic Stress Disorder, & Grief and Loss, Substance Abuse Treatment, Elder Abuse, Domestic Violence and Anger Management as well as those diagnosed with severe mental illness such as Schizophrenia and Bipolar Disorder. She has a holistic approach and incorporates singing bowls for grounding and relaxation. She offers a safe space in which to heal. She enjoys her work as a therapist, and a sound healer, but is also a speaker, writer, and consultant. Her aim is to combine mind, body and spirit, and to make mental health accessible and accessible to everyone.

Belonging
By Becky Diver

Have you ever been in a room full of people but felt so alone? Have you ever felt like you didn't belong—that no matter what situation you were in or whoever you were around, you felt like an outsider?

I've always questioned my sense of belonging, my worth. My entire life, at least until I was deep into my healing journey, I felt I wasn't enough, like I didn't belong.

Belonging means being accepted for who you truly are—your authentic self—and is essential to a person's well-being. It helps us feel supported and accepted, contributing to our happiness and sense of purpose, which, in turn, impacts our emotional, mental, and physical health.

It was March 2020, and the world as I knew it was coming to a standstill. I had just received the news that my salon had to close indefinitely because of a virus that was spreading. I thought it would be a short closure, a few weeks at most, but I had no idea how drastically everything was about to change. This virus would change the world forever.

Everyone was told to stay home, isolate, and wear a mask when they went out for groceries or other necessities. Wait it out. But as each week went by, I became increasingly concerned. I didn't know how long I could sustain the closure of my salon. I wasn't just facing the loss of income from my business. I was nursing a knee injury and grieving the loss of our beloved dogs, Daisy and Diego, who had recently passed away within months of each other. With my husband still able to go to work, I was left alone in a quiet house with only our cat, Cali, for company. The uncertainty was overwhelming, and it felt like the walls were closing in. Since I couldn't go running due to my knee injury, I needed to find things to keep me busy and active during the shutdown and isolation.

One of the local yoga studios began offering virtual classes since their in-person classes were on hold. I had only practiced yoga a few times before, but I decided to roll out my yoga mat since I was home and needed something to keep me active and busy.

After 12 long weeks of shutdown, I was finally allowed to reopen my salon. Even though I was thrilled to finally get everything back to the way it used to be, I quickly realized that the way things used to be was non-existent. When I reopened my salon, I was met with fear, uncertainty, varied opinions, and judgment. I wanted my clients to feel as comfortable as possible during this trying time, but I felt like I was being pulled in a million different directions because everyone's ideas of how things should be done were different. I was surprised and saddened by how people were reacting to the pandemic and by how the world had changed in such a short amount of time. I didn't know how to find my way in this new world. More accurately, I didn't know if I wanted to belong in a world divided by anger, fear, and judgment.

I continued taking virtual yoga classes as part of my daily exercise. But as I was trying to navigate the changes happening in the world, my yoga practice also began changing. I found myself feeling a sense of calm and peace when I arrived on my mat and moved through the various poses. Sometimes, emotions would arise for what I thought was no apparent reason.

When one of my dear clients, a woman who had considered me the daughter she never had, came in for her weekly hairstyle appointment, I let my guard down and allowed her to go without a mask, even though I had a mask mandate at that time. Later that day, she sent me a text, telling me she had been waiting for her husband's Covid test results and that he had tested positive. A surge of anger and betrayal washed over me. She had exposed me without a word of warning. I never had a chance to tell her how I felt; she passed away a couple of weeks later due to Covid. I felt a deep sense of sadness because I lost someone I had known for decades, but I also felt a sense of shame for the anger I felt.

A few days later, my symptoms began. I couldn't taste or smell—telltale signs of Covid. Then, the symptoms hit me like a ton of bricks! My head throbbed as if it were about to split in two, every breath felt like it was pulled through a sieve, and my chest felt so heavy, like an elephant was sitting on me. I would pace back and forth in the middle of the night because no matter what I did, every inch of my body was in agony. One day, after walking out to the mailbox, I felt completely exhausted. I laid on the sofa, surrendering to the virus, and prayed to God for a sign that I would get through this—or for the pain to end. As I lay in stillness and silence, a few moments later, I felt something in my body, something so difficult to explain, but it was almost like I could feel the virus surging through me, beginning in my head and ending at my toes, like it was making its final run. It was an odd feeling but not scary. There was a peacefulness about it. After that day, I could feel my body slowly starting to heal.

Besides feeling the effects of the virus, I was still grieving the loss of Daisy and Diego, anxious about the uncertainty of whether my business could weather the storm of a pandemic, feeling the sadness and shame from the loss of my client, processing the trauma and grief of losing my father, who passed away about a month before I became ill with Covid, and navigating the changes the world was going through. I hit rock bottom.

I fell into a deep depression, like I was in a dark hole and couldn't find my way out. I felt empty inside. I thought the physical pain from Covid was unbearable, but the mental and emotional pain I was experiencing was even worse. I felt numb. I had spent my life wanting to belong, wanting to matter, but now I was questioning that desire. I didn't want to belong in a world that had become so bitter and angry. I felt like I wanted to die.

At first, yoga was just something to fill the days and keep my body moving while my business was shut down. But as I settled onto my mat, I started noticing unexpected emotions bubbling up during my practice—tears spilling over without warning, then a sense of calm washing over me. It was as if my body was speaking to me for the first time, asking me to release what I had buried inside.

The local yoga studio where I had been taking virtual classes was offering a 200-hour yoga teacher training course beginning in October 2021. I briefly thought about enrolling but quickly pushed the idea out of my head. I have a paralyzing fear of public speaking, including standing in front of a room teaching people, even if it's just a couple of people. Besides, I couldn't take the training because my niece was getting married in October, during the first weekend of the course, and there was no way I was going to miss her wedding.

Still, the thought of yoga teacher training kept resurfacing, like a persistent whisper in my mind. My fear of public speaking and the timing of my niece's wedding gave me the perfect excuses to dismiss it. But on the final day of early registration, I felt an unshakable pull. I called the studio owner, hoping she would confirm my fears and tell me I couldn't miss any of the training weekends. Instead, she encouraged me to join, offering a way to make up for the missed days. I took a huge leap outside my comfort zone, signed up, and immediately wondered what I had just gotten myself into.

My intention for the training was to deepen my knowledge of yoga for my own practice. Since I felt so at ease on my yoga mat, I hoped that by deepening my knowledge, I could better navigate life and the difficulties I was facing. Because of my fear of public speaking, I was certain I had no desire to teach yoga to others.

Training weekends were long and demanding—physically, mentally, and emotionally. Each weekend brought new challenges but also significant growth. Not just in my yoga practice, but in my personal life as I continued to work through my grief. At the end of each weekend, I often questioned whether I had made the right decision by signing up for teacher training. Healing and growth can be very painful. As I progressed, it became clear to me—especially as I would often cry during my practice—that yoga was helping me process the emotions I was feeling. Something transformative was happening.

I hit a breaking point one weekend, ready to quit the training altogether. I felt out of place and inadequate, questioning whether I had made a mistake. But then, the instructor's words during class echoed through me: "You belong here. You are exactly where you need to be." It was as if she were speaking directly to the fractured parts of my soul. From that moment, I began repeating those words like a mantra: "I belong here. I am exactly where I need to be."

I did it! I finished my training. Remember when I said I had no desire to teach yoga to others and that I was only taking the training to deepen my own personal yoga practice? Well, because of the profound impact yoga had on my life and healing journey, I felt a deep desire to share it with others. Yoga had given me something I had spent my life searching for—a sense of belonging that starts within myself. I realized that when we connect deeply with our bodies, we can heal, find balance, and recognize our worth. This transformation inspired me to teach, to help others find that same connection, and to move through their own grief and trauma.

I continue to step outside my comfort zone by furthering my training and doing the uncomfortable to find comfort. I help others through trauma-informed yoga, Grief Yoga®, Energy Medicine Yoga®, and Sound Healing. I believe that by working with movement, breath, and sound, we can deepen our connection with our bodies, bringing balance and nurturing our self-love. When we nurture our love for ourselves, we see our own worth and feel a sense of belonging within. That's where belonging truly begins—with self-love and acceptance. Healing is not linear, and it's not always easy, but the journey will take you closer to yourself. When we learn to accept and love ourselves, we can connect with others and feel at home in the world.

In February 2024, I opened Rising Phoenix Yoga & Healing. It's more than just a studio; it's a sanctuary for those seeking to heal and find themselves, a place where people can feel safe, supported, and know that they belong.

To anyone feeling lost, out of place, or disconnected from yourself or others, I invite you to try the following meditation to bring you back into your body and breath, finding a sense of calm, peace, and connection:

Find a quiet, comfortable place with no interruptions—somewhere you feel safe. Sit or lie down. Close your eyes or set your gaze softly toward the floor. Spend some time just being with your breath. Notice how your breath feels in your body, without judgment. Take several breaths. Then, bring awareness to your body. Notice how your body feels—any sensations or tension—without judgment. Use your inhales and exhales to connect deeper with your body. As you inhale, visualize softness and ease entering your body. As you exhale, visualize tension leaving your body. Release whatever you need to release. If emotions arise, allow them to flow through you, releasing them without judgment. Spend as much time as you need right here. Welcome home. You belong here. You are exactly where you need to be.

About Becky Diver:

Becky began her healing journey as a yoga student looking for variety in her physical fitness regimen but quickly realized yoga is much more than physical postures. Showing up on her mat helped her find connection and a sense of belonging with her body, mind, and spirit. After earning her 200-hour yoga teacher certification and realizing the impact yoga has had on her life, she felt moved to help others on their healing journey. She specializes in trauma-informed yoga, Grief Yoga®, Energy Medicine Yoga®, Expert level Sound Healing, and Mindfulness/Mindful Meditation. She's also certified in Yin, Restorative, Vinyasa, and Chair yoga styles. She feels by finding connection with our bodies through mindful movement, breath, and sound, we can better communicate with and deepen the connection with our bodies. By developing a deeper connection with our bodies, we can live a life of healing and self-love. In doing so, we can develop a deeper connection with others.

www.risingphoenixhealing.com

@becky_risingphoenixyoga

Email: risingphoenix.becky@gmail.com

Unseen, Undetected, and Unbelievable Truth

By Tresa Mazurek

As early as I can remember, I was abused. The details of my abuse really do not matter. It was what the abuse did to me that gave a false belief that I actually deserved what was happening in my life. I felt broken and unwanted. I tried many things over my lifetime to get rid of those feelings, such as multiple suicide attempts, medication, alcohol, sex, drugs, and therapy. I looked everywhere outside of myself to fill the need of being wanted, loved unconditionally, and accepted for who I was, faults and all.

I was raised believing in God, but with the abuse, I didn't completely trust in Him. It didn't make sense to me because of all the struggle. I still kept searching and asking God if this was what life was really about. I was not getting any answers, and my life seemed to be getting worse. Now, I am wondering if I am truly broken or if there is more to my life.

It was Saturday, and I got into another huge fight with my boyfriend. He left our home without saying where he was going or when he was coming back. This was not something new, and I should have been used to it, but something was different. I started to feel like I had no one. I was alone—a failure, unloved, and isolated. All these negative thoughts came flooding in. I felt like my brain was out of control. I couldn't stop it.

I found a moment of hope. Who could I call? I felt like I had used up all my chances with family and friends. There had been continued conflict for the last several years. I really didn't feel truly supported by anyone. I thought if I mentioned any struggle I was having, I would seem weak, judged as a failure, and it would all be my fault again. I continued talking negatively to myself with anger, resentment, and sad disappointment: "Why is it so difficult for people to love me? Was this all my fault? I'm such a fuckin' loser. Nobody wants to be around me. This is why no one really loves me or wants to be around me."

All of a sudden, I got a little moment of clarity: "Stop it! That's enough. I have to talk to somebody. If I don't, what's the point of even trying anymore?" All these negative comments kept playing in my head. I just couldn't seem to escape them. At almost the exact same time, I remembered there was a domestic abuse hotline. Maybe they could help me. A stranger who didn't know my history could direct me to my next step. Anything was better than what I was doing and feeling right then.

I grabbed my cell phone and dialed the number. My body was shaking. I was crying and breathing heavily. I waited and hoped to talk to someone. I got a recording: "We're sorry, we are receiving a high call volume at this time. Please try again. If this is an emergency, please dial 911." After that, all I heard was blah, blah, blah.

I was devastated! My mind started racing again: "See, not even a stranger wants to talk to you. You had no one before, and you never will. Just give up already!" I started yelling out loud: "Are you fucking kidding me? No shit, there is a high call volume! There are a ton of people who are suffering, people need help. I need help! What is going on in this world?"

Tears streamed down my face, and snot ran out my nose. I started coughing uncontrollably. I couldn't breathe. I felt like I was going to puke. I ran to the bathroom. Just as I approached the toilet, I threw up. My heart was racing. Tears and snot continued to slide down my face, all while my body was completely exhausted.

After I finished throwing up, I got enough strength to go to the sink. I turned the water on—cold. I remembered that it was supposed to help me when I felt like my emotions were out of control. I started splashing my face. As I lifted my head, drying the cold water from my face, I saw my reflection in the mirror.

Who was this sad woman? I stared at the stranger in the mirror, someone who looked beaten and broken. Quietly, almost in a whisper, I began to pray. It felt like a final plea: "Help me, Jesus! Help all of us. The world is falling apart. People are fighting against each other. People are suffering in all kinds of ways. I am in so much pain. What am I supposed to do? Why am I even here? Please say something. Send me a clear message. I promise I will do whatever You want me to do. My eyes and ears are open to receive."

The desperation in my hoarse voice seemed to echo through my body. I grabbed my phone. I can't really tell you what gave me the idea, but I turned on KTIS 98.5 FM. The song "Real Help" by Patrick Mayberry started to play.

Out loud, I said, "What? God! Are You speaking to me through this song?" The words felt like a conversation that had been playing out in my head. As I listened, I felt a warm sensation move through my body, as if I was being healed in that exact moment. I had never heard this song before. Is this really happening to me?

"It is an unseen, undetected, and unbelievable truth."

Every step now felt like new territory for me. I felt as if I was standing on new ground. But each prayer, each whispered call for help, became a building block of strength. I said out loud: "Thank you, God. I can hear You. Please keep sending me messages. What am I supposed to do? How am I supposed to handle this? I don't want to be alone. I've always just wanted to belong and be loved unconditionally."

A response came to me: "Tresa, you have never been alone. I have always been here, waiting for you."

Somehow, I eventually fell asleep, crying but trusting that God had a plan and that everything would make sense somehow.

Just before midnight, I awoke startled. I don't know why, but I immediately grabbed my phone and looked at Facebook. The very first post I saw was from my boyfriend's sister-in-law, niece, and her wife, all tagged together about their new cat. I noticed the "add friend" button behind two of their names.

Instantly, I said out loud: "What? I'm not friends with them anymore? Why? What did I do to them?" I became irate and started yelling: "Lord, really? Is this what following You is like? Alone, outcast because I shared the work You were doing in my life and chose healthy boundaries for myself? This is too hard. I can't do this! It was easier to just be like everyone else."

The moment I finished my last word, I felt a wave of remorse. Sobbing, with tears running down my face, I said: "I'm sorry, Lord. Please forgive me. Please help me by giving me strength and courage against these negative and dark thoughts and the actions of others."

Then, it came to me—a knowing, a nudge. I acted immediately. I got out of bed, grabbed my sage, opened every window, turned on all the lights, and lit every candle in my house. I started loudly praying the Lord's Prayer. As I walked through my home, I asked for all darkness, evil, and negativity to flee.

When I finished, a blanket of peace moved over me. I was safe, protected, and loved unconditionally. I had been found, forgiven, and saved. I belonged to someone greater than I ever could have imagined.

"God is real! Jesus is alive! The Holy Spirit, angels, and even evil all exist!"

I can testify to this through my own experience. There was no awareness of time as I went through this. It felt like mere minutes, but hours had passed.

When I woke up Sunday morning, the song "Real Help" was playing again.

"Was this a dream? Was this just coincidental?" I didn't think so. I got ready for church, hoping for more messages to come through songs, people, or scripture. As I walked in, I said to myself: "I will follow You, Jesus. You are leading me, Lord. I trust You with my life and I completely surrender all I have to You."

Again, I was filled with a warm, tingling feeling—a blanket of trust, peace, love, and truth. The messages at church over the past couple of weeks had been about the Armor of God. This was new to me, as I had not read the Bible until this year. Last week's message was about the belt of truth, and today's was about the breastplate of righteousness.

At some point, it was explained that in times of darkness, you can speak the name of Jesus out loud three times, and the enemy will flee. I thought, "Hmmm, good to have that information in my toolbox of knowledge." Everything seemed to align with perfect timing. The answer: "Because that's how God works."

When I got home from church, my boyfriend was there. Our interaction started out fine until I asked him: "What did you do at the golf course yesterday?" He became irritated and responded: "What does it matter what I did? I'm a grown man. I don't have to justify my actions to you or anyone."

I could feel my body getting hot and uncomfortable. I removed myself from the room. As I left, he asked: "Where are you going? What's wrong?" I didn't take the bait and continued down the stairs. Once I cooled down, I joined him again.

We had a pretty good day after that, as long as I didn't ask any questions. Later, he took a phone call. It was one of the guys he partied with last night. They were laughing and carrying on about how much fun they had and how bombed someone was, even falling down the stairs.

Again, I felt like a heater inside me had been turned to max. I went outside. He eventually came out and asked: "What's going on? Why are you out here?"

I didn't answer his question because I believed he already knew. I said: "I really need you to be transparent and forthcoming with information."

He replied: "What do you mean by that?"

Now, my thoughts began flooding: "Seriously, you're an English major, and you're asking me what I mean by that?" Instead of blurting out in anger, I calmly said: "For example, I told you what I did last night—how I was afraid and barricaded the doors after I saged the whole house."

He didn't say anything. The silence felt like hours, but it was only minutes. Somehow, I found the courage and asked: "So, did you smoke pot yesterday?"

He immediately became irate: "Yeah, so what? Do I have to tell you every time I take a shit too?"

Instantly, I said out loud, "Jesus, Jesus, Jesus," with conviction. He got up, didn't say another word, and went back inside.

"What just happened? So, it really works?" I said under my breath. Again: "Unseen, undetected, and unbelievable truth."

When I woke up on Monday morning, I had no idea how my day would unfold. So many things had been happening since Saturday, and my trust in Jesus was growing stronger. I reached out to two women from church and asked if they'd meet me for coffee. I wanted to share what God was doing in my life. They said yes, and I was so excited.

As I talked for an hour straight, one of the women asked: "Would you like something to drink?" Immediately, I felt nudged to stop talking. I said: "Actually, I could use something to drink."

I reached into my purse without looking and grabbed a bill. Being unemployed, I held on to every penny I could, especially now that my boyfriend was moving out and no longer financially supporting my son and me.

Inside the coffee shop, the barista asked: "What can I get you?"

I replied: "I'll have a pumpkin spice latte."

She told me the amount, and I handed her the bill—a fifty-dollar bill. Just as I did, I got a message: "Ask her if you can pray for her."

I had never done that before, but without hesitation, I said: "Can I pray for you?"

She looked at me like I had fallen off the crazy train. "What? Why?" she replied quickly.

I received another message: "Give her all the change." At the same time, words spilled from my mouth: "I don't know what's going on in your life, but God is telling me to bless you with this change. He wants you to know you are loved and to pay it forward."

I didn't know what was happening. "Who tips someone over $40 for a cup of coffee?" I thought. But I didn't question it. I acted.

Her defensive look softened, and she stared at me in disbelief. I then asked: "Can I hold your hand?"

Without hesitation, she put her hand in mine. I asked: "What is your name?"

"Apple," she replied.

At that moment, everything became clear. Again, words poured from my mouth: "You are a seed of God. We all are."

She continued to stare at me. All she said was: "Thanks. Someone will bring out your latte soon." I smiled, went back outside, and never saw Apple again.

I believe all people come into our lives for a reason. Sometimes we know right away, and other times it takes years. This is just a splintered view of my story, but the message needs to be shared.

In the Bible, Matthew 22:37-39 says: Love the Lord your God with all your heart, all your soul, and all your mind. This is the first and greatest commandment. And the second is like it: Love your neighbor as yourself.

Sometimes, the only way forward is through complete surrender. Trust in Jesus, open your heart, and listen to the messages. They are everywhere.

You can also reach out to me, a friend in Christ, at 52tmaz@gmail.com.

Peace, love, and light. God bless you.

About Tresa Mazurek:

Tresa Mazurek has found a sense of purpose in writing from her experiences, both for her own healing and in her desire to help others. A single mom of four, she loves spending her free time with her grandson and three dogs. With the many titles she's held throughout her life, each one has focused on the personal attention of others. Tresa is very intuitive, creative and willing to ask questions to help inform all possibilities. She believes this chapter represents a glimpse of new beginnings for her and hopes the same will hold true for those who read her story. Tresa would love to connect and can be reached at **52tmaz@gmail.com**

Finding My Freedom Through Fasting
By Jazmin Briggs

As I stood in the middle of the Sahara Desert, awe-struck by the Pyramids of Giza and the majestic Sphinx, something stirred deep within me. It should have been a moment of pure wonder, a memory to treasure for a lifetime. But instead, I felt both dwarfed by their beauty and trapped in the vastness of my own insecurities. Everything was clouded by a familiar, cruel voice—the tape recorder in my head that had been playing for years. It whispered that these breathtaking photos would never see the light of day. Why? Because I was ashamed of the body I lived in, a body that felt nearly as massive as the ancient pyramids themselves. In that desert, I knew I couldn't keep carrying the weight of a lifetime of disappointments. I had to rise from these sands anew.

That trip to Egypt in January 2019, which also took me to Dubai and Abu Dhabi, was supposed to be awe-inspiring—a journey to rekindle my sense of wonder. Instead, it became a pivotal moment in my life. I had always been an adventurer, someone who felt deserving of wanderlust and of soaking in all the world had to offer. But as I stood in front of one of the Seven Wonders of the World, all I could think about was how undeserving I felt of this experience. How could I, someone who couldn't even properly care for the temple that was my body, deserve to witness such beauty? The human body, after all, is one of the greatest wonders of the world, and yet I had treated mine with so little dignity or care. I felt profoundly disconnected from myself. Each step I took, every photograph captured, every glimpse of my reflection magnified the self-consciousness I had carried for so long.

Why had these feelings come to a head on this trip? Everything felt magnified, as though a spotlight had shined directly on my deepest insecurities, with the pyramids reflecting back everything I had been trying so desperately to hide. I left a piece of my old self behind in the desert sands. The pyramids, in their spiritual symbolism, represented the integration of self and soul. They reminded me, ever so gently, of my own purpose in this earthly realm—to ground myself and elevate into higher consciousness, to finally fulfill my soul contract. Now was the time.

When I returned home, the exhaustion I had carried for years had deepened. It wasn't just my body that was weighed down but my spirit. I was suffocating. My mind had become a trap, and my body felt like a prison. Despite all the knowledge I had—my Master's degree in Holistic Wellness, countless certifications in health, wellness, and life coaching, and the endless books I had devoured about health—I couldn't embody it. I was a prisoner of my own mind, caught in an endless cycle of failed diets, guilt, and shame. I was a soul drowning in a sea of unapplied knowledge, weighed down by the crushing contradiction between what I knew and how I lived. I had become a woman drowning in information but starving for transformation.

I began asking myself the hard questions. What would it take for me to break free? Would it be a number on the scale? A chronic illness? Rock bottom? My weight had not yet led to severe health issues, but I was lying to myself. The emotional toll was brutal. I wasn't living the life I was destined for—a life where I was meant to teach others about health and wellness and help them manifest their potential. Instead, I was sinking deeper into despair, numb to the excitement of new beginnings. My days were filled with regret, procrastination, broken promises, and unfulfilled dreams. I no longer recognized the woman in the mirror. Worse yet, I had become comfortable with that disappointment. I had reached a point where I tolerated in myself what I would never tolerate in others.

Soon after my travels, at what felt like my lowest point, I turned to YouTube in a desperate search for a final solution. I had tried everything else—diets, exercise programs, self-help books—but nothing had worked long-term. That's when I found what I now recognize as divine alignment. I stumbled upon the *A Healthy Alternative* YouTube channel, and the concept of fasting, specifically water fasting, caught my attention. Could something as simple as water truly have the power to heal not just my body but my mind and spirit as well? I had tried every possible way of eating, so why not try not eating at all?

For the entire month of February 2019, I immersed myself in the channel's content, watching every video and taking meticulous notes. I learned about fasting, hydration, and the incredible power of the human body to heal itself. Something clicked inside me. I wasn't just ready for change—I was ready for radical, transformative change. Armed with newfound knowledge and hope, I decided to embark on a 21-day water fast in March.

I was nervous but determined. The first few days were rough—my body and mind fought back with everything they had. But by day five, something shifted. A calm washed over me, and for the first time in years,

I felt a deep connection with my body. I wasn't just shedding physical weight; I was releasing years of emotional baggage, self-doubt, and negativity that had been stored in my body for far too long.

By the end of the 21 days, I had lost 40 pounds—40 pounds of physical, mental, and emotional weight. But more importantly, I had gained something far greater: a profound sense of freedom. For the first time in what felt like an eternity, I had hope. I had broken through a barrier that had felt impenetrable for years, and I was beginning to believe that true transformation was possible.

Fasting wasn't just about losing weight—it became a process of detoxing and shedding the layers of emotional and mental toxicity that had built up over the years. I was healing from the inside out. I had always heard that the body had an innate intelligence, but fasting made me truly experience it. I realized that I had been using food to avoid facing my deepest pain. And now, I was ready to face it, ready to heal.

As I began to reintroduce food, I noticed that I had changed on a fundamental level. Food no longer controlled me. The cravings and emotional eating patterns that had dominated my life for years were gone. I was more mindful, more present, more in tune with my body. Fasting had opened the door to a new way of living—a fasting-focused lifestyle that allowed me to maintain my weight while continuing to heal my mind and body.

But the journey didn't end there. Life has a way of testing us, and over the next few months, I faced new challenges. My plan to continue fasting and lose more weight was disrupted by the demands of everyday life. I maintained the weight I had lost, but I didn't lose more. For the first time in my life, I wasn't yo-yoing between extreme weight loss and gain. I had found a balance, and that was a victory in itself.

In September 2020, I discovered Restorative Hypnotherapy through another YouTube video, and it felt like the missing piece of my puzzle. I signed up for an introductory class, and everything about it resonated with me on a soul-deep level. Through Restorative Hypnotherapy, I learned that lasting weight release could only happen if I felt safe in my own body. I hadn't realized it before, but my weight had been a shield—a barrier between me and the world. I was afraid of being seen, of being vulnerable, of stepping into my full power.

This was a profound shift in my mindset. I wasn't just trying to lose weight anymore—I was working to heal the parts of myself that had been hurt, abandoned, and neglected for far too long. Once I made that connection, everything changed. I was ready—ready to feel safe in my body, ready to let go of the physical, mental, and emotional weight I had carried for so long. I was ready to make space for what truly served me and to release what no longer did. I was ready to relax into myself fully, deeply, wholly, and expand into the highest version of myself.

By November 2020, I was prepared to take things to the next level with my weight loss. I hired a coach—a coach who truly understood fasting, mindset, and long-term maintenance. I found the perfect coach through the *A Healthy Alternative* community. This coach had walked the path I was on, and I knew he could guide me through the next phase of my journey.

I committed wholeheartedly. My goal was to lose 100 pounds in six months, and I was determined to make it happen. Every day, I showed up for myself, fasting, refeeding with nourishing foods, and working on my mindset. With each passing week, I wasn't just shedding pounds—I was shedding the old version of myself that had held me back for so long. Most importantly, I stopped disappointing myself. I told myself, *This time next year, I refuse to be in the same place. I deserve more, and I owe it to myself to exceed my goals.*

The next six months were nothing short of transformative. I remained consistent and committed throughout the entire process. I alternated between shorter fasts, longer fasts, and refeeding with hydrating, whole foods. My body responded beautifully, shedding the weight that had once felt impossible to lose. But the real transformation wasn't just happening in my body—it was happening in my mind and spirit. Fasting was no longer just about weight loss; it was about freeing myself from the chains of self-sabotage and finally stepping into my full power. I also listened to my Restorative Hypnotherapy scripts nightly, deepening the connection between mind and body as I continued to fast and refeed.

During this time, I poured myself into my business as well. I worked on perfecting my website, implementing systems, and creating a Jazz-Spirations card deck. I was laying the foundation for my holistic health and wellness coaching practice, *Jazz Up Your Life*. Fasting had reignited my passion for helping others, and I knew my journey could serve as inspiration for others struggling with their own weight, wellness, and self-worth issues. I was finally becoming the person I had always dreamed of being—a holistic health, wellness, and life coach who could guide others on their journeys to freedom, just as I had found mine.

By the end of five months, I had reached my goal. I had lost 100 pounds, but more than that, I had gained something invaluable—a deep sense of trust in myself and integrity to my word. I had proven to myself that I could follow through, that I could succeed, that I was capable of so much more than I had ever believed.

After I released 140 pounds through fasting and rebuilt my trust in myself, something incredible happened. My story and journey were featured on *A Healthy Alternative's* YouTube channel. The exposure was life-changing. It brought a new level of visibility to my business, *Jazz Up Your Life,* and it absolutely exploded. My practice grew beyond anything I had ever imagined. I began helping thousands of people not just release weight, but also shift their mindset, rebuild their self-trust, and truly realize their value and worth.

The impact was profound. I had reignited my light, and by shining my light, I was helping others do the same. I had fully stepped into my purpose—guiding people toward their own transformations, teaching them how to live more aligned lives through fasting, mindfulness, and holistic living. I also became a coach alongside the *A Healthy Alternative* coaching and leadership team—the very people who had supported me in my health, wellness, and fasting journey.

All of this was possible because I made one critical decision: I chose myself. When I made that decision, I unlocked a power within me that was unstoppable. It wasn't just about weight loss anymore—it was about empowerment, freedom, and living in alignment with my higher self.

The success of *Jazz Up Your Life* has been nothing short of extraordinary. Through one-on-one coaching, group coaching, teaching, my weekly newsletter *Jazz-Spirations,* my signature course, pre-recorded restorative hypnotherapy scripts, and speaking engagements, I've been able to reach and inspire thousands of people all over the world. They've released the weight—physically, mentally, and emotionally—just as I did. They've learned to trust themselves again, to value their worth, and to pursue their dreams boldly. My journey, though deeply personal, became a blueprint for others to follow, and I couldn't be more grateful for the privilege of walking this path with them.

When you align with your true self and cut out what no longer serves you, the Universe opens doors you never imagined could exist. That's exactly what happened to me, and now I get to spend every day helping others open those same doors for themselves.

Fasting, Restorative Hypnotherapy, and expert coaching were the keys to my transformation, along with radical self-trust and becoming the embodiment of who I always knew I could be. But ultimately, it was the decision to stop being comfortable with disappointing myself that made all the difference. That decision—that commitment to my own well-being—set off a chain reaction that changed my entire life and the lives of countless others.

If there's one thing I've learned, it's this: When you choose yourself, you light the way for others to choose themselves, too. The ripple effect of that one powerful decision is immeasurable.

I am grateful every single day that I made the choice to show up for myself. And now, I get to help others do the same. This journey has been about so much more than weight loss—it has been about elevation, enlightenment, and empowerment while living in alignment with my highest potential.

I can't wait to continue sharing this path with others, as their guide and support, as they step into the fullest, freest versions of themselves. I have created the life of my desires, and I know through the ripple effect of my words, you can and will too.

Thank you, Pyramids of Egypt, for mirroring the ancient strength and wonder within me, reminding me of the grandness I had always possessed.

About Jazmin Briggs:

Jazmin Briggs (Jazz) is a Nationally Board Certified Wholistic Health, Wellness, and Life Coach, as well as a Restorative Hypnotherapist Practitioner. As the dynamic force behind the digital space of Jazz Up Your Life, she delivers paradigm-shifting tools and transformative resources that educate, enlighten, and empower individuals to live a purpose-driven and aligned life. Her personal health journey, marked by the profound power of fasting, catalyzed her transformation and ignited a reawakening of spiritual wisdom, grounding it into practical, actionable steps that transform lives.

Having released 140 lbs of physical, mental, and emotional weight, Jazz now embodies the lifestyle she teaches—a lifestyle of conscious, consistent choices that create lasting change from the inside out. Jazz specializes in inspiring others to take control of their body (for vibrant health), mind (by releasing what no longer serves), and soul (by tuning in for deeper clarity). Visit linktr.ee/JazzUpYourLife for more information!

Reclaiming My Kefi
By Bessy Goulianos

October 2023—another doctor's appointment, another disappointment. As I walked into the silent house, I felt numb…emptier than ever. No matter how hard I tried, I once again found myself in this ever-so-familiar, yet horrifying, vicious cycle that just kept repeating itself over and over again: day after day, month after month, year after F$&@#N year. After I got myself settled, I sat down in my usual spot with a cup of coffee. And as I pointed the remote at the TV, I caught a glimpse of myself on the blank TV screen.

"Is this it?" I asked my reflection. "Is this how you're going to spend the rest of your life? Or are you going to fight and finally make the decision to do whatever it takes to reclaim your Kefi?" (a concept rooted in Greek culture which translates very roughly to "Profound Passion"; joy, excitement, having fun, living life).

The tears came quickly, breaking through the walls I had built to contain my emotions. For years, I had fought to keep my life together while my body kept breaking down. But I could no longer hide the truth—I was exhausted, defeated, and terrified of what the future might hold.

I have battled with chronic illness for half my life. I was diagnosed with Crohn's Disease at the age of 26. That day, June 24, 1999, will forever be ingrained in my memory. The doctor walked into the room and informed me and my now ex-husband that I had Crohn's Disease—there is no cure, but it can be managed with medication. He put me on a medication regimen and sent me on my merry way.

Crohn's Disease? What is Crohn's Disease? I had never heard of it before! So, I did my due diligence and researched what exactly this disease was— what symptoms I might encounter (common and less common), the different types of medication and treatment available at the time, as well as any possible complications I might face. But, to be frank, I just didn't want to deal with it! I had so much going on during that time. I had a six-month-old son who needed me. I had a full-time job. My father had passed away a month prior, so I was helping my mom navigate her new normal. And, I had my own home and husband to take care of. Maybe call it denial or prioritizing others' needs above my own, but I tucked away my Crohn's diagnosis and focused on everything and everyone else.

As the months and years passed, however, it became more and more difficult to ignore my illness, and life not only became harder but my circumstances grew increasingly more complex—eventually to the point where it was life-threatening. In order for me to survive this, I only had one option: I had to undergo a proctocolectomy (removal of the colon, rectum, and anus) and live the rest of my life with an ileostomy (an opening in the abdominal wall to divert the small intestine and allow waste to exit the body). It was live or die. After a whole lot of crying and fear of the unknown, I made the decision and underwent the surgery. The recovery was long and painful, but I felt confident that I had reclaimed my life—or so I thought.

Fast forward to 2016. With this second change in life, I went on to complete one of my life goals of going back to college and earning a degree. I not only earned a dual BA in Sociology and Criminal Justice, Summa Cum Laude, but I also achieved honors in the Chapter of Alpha Phi Sigma, the National Criminal Justice Honor Society, Athenaeum Honor Society, and Dean's List. To top it off, I made the decision to continue my academic studies and was accepted into grad school. This was a huge step for me because, after being on disability all this time and thanks to the Ticket to Work Program offered by the Social Security Administration, I also made the decision to dip my toes in the water and even landed a part-time job on campus aligned with my field of study.

So many great things were happening, and I felt so blessed and excited. But there was something new brewing within my body. Illness was once again slowly creeping in, looking to spoil all my accomplishments, my dreams, and my future. In 2017, I was diagnosed with Hidradenitis Suppurativa (HS), another disease I had never heard of, one that is progressive and has no cure. I, once again, felt defeated.

Once more, I did my research on what symptoms I might encounter (common and less common), the different types of medication and treatment available at the time, as well as the possible complications I might face. It was like déjà vu! And what do you think I did next? YUP! I, once again, plowed through because I had so much at stake—I had grad school to concentrate on, I had a part-time job that I could not lose because child support for my son was soon coming to an end, and I needed the extra income to stay afloat for me and him. There was no room for error or self-care.

As the years continued to tick away, my symptoms got worse and worse. Despite a multitude of medication cocktails I was prescribed, the disease slowly progressed, and within five years, I went from stage 1 to stage 3 (there are three stages of progression for HS).

What once was a sore or two in a concentrated area slowly advanced to multiple ones and spread to other common areas associated with this horrible disease. Living with HS was like being trapped in a body that was constantly betraying me. There were days where I could barely walk or lift my arms because of the large, painful lumps that would appear out of nowhere. Some areas persisted for years, flaring up, draining, spreading, and creating wounds that did not heal.

There were so many moments that I can remember, where simple tasks like sitting, driving, cooking dinner for my family, doing laundry, cleaning my home, or taking a bath were extremely challenging and so excruciatingly painful. Of all the tasks and responsibilities I had on a given day, I remember having to pick and choose one or two tasks—maximum—that were most important and do only them. Can you imagine? I mean, how is that even possible to do when you are running a home, going to school, and trying to keep a part-time job with an ostomy stuck to your belly?

I hate to admit it now, but there were moments when the flares were so bad that I secretly wished I had a urostomy, in addition to my ileostomy, to avoid the excruciating task of having to get up to go to the bathroom. I knew it would be an agonizing and gut-wrenching ordeal. And if that wasn't horrifying enough, I was constantly on high alert because, at any moment, wherever I might be, an abscess could open without warning. The thought of embarrassment and shame I would feel was absolutely crippling.

And it wasn't just the physical pain that took its toll. The weight of anxiety, depression, and social isolation felt like chains dragging me down. Each flare-up brought fresh wounds and deeper scars—both on my body and on my spirit. And despite the numerous medications and treatments, my symptoms only worsened, spreading across my body like a slow-moving wildfire.

So, when I came home on that fateful day last October (2023), systemic inflammation was the issue at hand. Within a year of continuous tweaking of medications, my Sedimentation Rate (a blood test that detects inflammation in the body) went from 67 to 68. Mind you, the safe range is 0 to 10. So, instead of going down, it actually went up by one. My C-Reactive Protein (a protein that your liver makes, which measures the levels of CRP in the blood to check for inflammation) went from 107 to 44. This marker showed significant improvement, but it was still far from the normal range. At this point, I had gone through all the possible medications available in the U.S. for the treatment of HS (pill form and biologics) and was told that the regimen I was currently on was the best I was going to get until something new became available.

Sitting in that empty house, staring into the black abyss on the TV screen, I realized I had one option left—to fight back, but this time with a different approach. I threw myself into researching holistic solutions, desperate to find anything that could help me feel alive again. The more I read, the more I wanted to learn. The more I learned, the more my soul craved to learn even more. Each article, book, and course I found became a lifeline, pulling me out of that dark abyss and despair one piece of information at a time. By the end of 2023, I had compiled a list of courses I planned on diving into headfirst.

I started by learning about meditation and how to properly use meditation for healing. Meditating wasn't entirely new to me; however, when I did meditate, my mind always seemed to resist. But gradually, with practice and sheer determination, something shifted. It was as if the stress began to loosen its grip on my body, making room for a newfound calm. Then I learned about the body's chakra system and how to balance my body's energy centers. Learning about chakras helped me connect the dots between my emotional struggles and my physical symptoms—like my blocked root chakra and the pain that radiates through my lower body. At that point, I took my learning a step further and acquired the use of sound bowls and tuning forks. And OMG! When I first felt the vibrations of a tuning fork resonate through me, I knew I had found a powerful ally in my quest for healing. Next, I discovered the power of mindset and learned simple, easy steps that I could implement into my daily life to improve my mood and frame of mind.

Learning how to meditate and incorporating it as a daily practice did wonders for my overall health. Meditation lowers levels of your body's stress hormone, which reduces stress and, as a bonus, improves your sleep. Let's face it, when you're stressed, it's a challenge to fall asleep. By reducing stress, it also eases psychological symptoms of depression, anxiety, and physical pain related to stress. Over the long term, meditation also helps to improve your immune system because it causes the body to produce more of the immune system's helper cells, which assist in fighting infections.

By educating myself about chakras, I uncovered just how much of an impact they have on our body. Chakras are spinning discs of energy that influence our physical, emotional, and spiritual well-being. There are seven main chakra points located along the central channel of our body (spine) where the energy flows freely, and each has a health focus. When there is an energy block in one or several of them, it can manifest as physical issues. For me, my root chakra was completely blocked, causing imbalances in the other six. The root chakra is all about your basic needs (survival, security, energy). It is the foundation for your physical and energy body, regulating the lower part of your body. When it is blocked, it can lead to a number of issues: a sense of being lost or overwhelmed, difficulty making decisions, depression, anxiety, and lower body pain.

This made total sense to me because I had been in survival mode since my divorce in 2014. Could this be why I woke up one day in 2019 and couldn't get out of bed because putting pressure on the soles of my feet was so excruciating that I had to crawl for a month—and to this day, doctors have not been able to identify the cause? Regardless, by putting in the work and opening the flow of Universal Energy throughout my body, I felt grounded, my energy levels increased, I felt more secure, my focus improved, and I was able to prioritize.

To enhance my healing journey, I added tuning forks and singing bowls to my healing practice. The benefits of vibrational healing, especially with respect to joint pain and boosting my immune system, were amplified. This is why it's so important to check the energy flow of your chakras and keep them balanced—it promotes physical, emotional, and spiritual well-being.

But I didn't stop there! In working with my therapist, she introduced me to Spoon Theory and SMART Goals. This led me to mindset coaching, which uses a variety of techniques, including cognitive behavioral strategies, mindfulness, and positive psychology. Through this experience, I was able to break free from limiting thoughts and behavioral patterns. It helped me cultivate a more resilient and positive approach to my life challenges, giving me the tools and guidance needed to overcome obstacles and learn a new way to reach my full potential.

Through combining meditation, chakra healing, vibrational energy, and mindset coaching, I achieved significant reductions in my inflammation markers. When my Sedimentation Rate dropped from 68 to 32, and my C-Reactive Protein fell from 44 to 19, I couldn't believe the numbers. It wasn't just the lab results that changed—my energy had returned, my mind was clearer, and for the first time in years, I felt hope and a renewed sense of purpose. I realized then that my journey wasn't just about overcoming illness; it was about finding a deeper connection to myself and reclaiming the joy that I had lost.

Healing is not a one-size-fits-all process, and I have learned firsthand that the medical system often treats the body as a collection of symptoms rather than as a whole person. By integrating holistic practices into my daily life, I had found a way to truly address my well-being—mind, body, and spirit. Now, I felt compelled to share this knowledge with others, to help them find their own pathway to healing and discover their Kefi.

No, I'm not cured of HS, but I am healing, and I am stronger than I've ever been. I am on a mission to help others realize that even when life feels unbearable, there are ways to reclaim your joy, to ignite your passion for living. I have found my Kefi, and now, I'm here to help others find theirs.

If you're struggling, remember this: You are more than your illness. Healing is a journey, and it's about embracing every aspect of yourself—physical, emotional, and spiritual. Don't settle for simply surviving; fight for your Kefi and live a life that fills you with profound passion.

About Bessy Goulianos:

Bessy is a passionate advocate for holistic healing and personal transformation. As the founder of *A Pathway To Kefi, LLC*, established in 2023, she has dedicated her life to helping others on their healing journeys. After years of battling chronic illness and facing the frustrations of fragmented healthcare, Bessy sought out holistic approaches that traditional medicine often overlooks. Through certifications in Meditation, Reiki, Energy Healing, and Mindset Coaching, she not only transformed her own health but found her true calling in empowering others.

Today, Bessy's mission is clear: to guide individuals with chronic illness and ongoing mental health challenges toward a more fulfilling, balanced life. She believes true healing encompasses the mind, body, and spirit, and she's dedicated to sharing the tools and knowledge that made a difference in her own journey.

Through *A Pathway To Kefi*, Bessy is committed to helping others reclaim their vitality, resilience, and joy—because everyone deserves to thrive, no matter their challenges.

Email: apathwaytokefi@bessygoulianos.com

Website: www.Bessygoulianos.com

Releasing Cinderella
By Jill Briansky

For as long as I can remember, my mother used to tease me and call me Cinderella. Whenever there was something to do in the house that she didn't want to do, she made me do it and would call me Cinderella. Seemingly harmless and said in jest, yet the message rang clear and deep in my psyche: I am here to serve others. Not being of service, but being in servitude. My mother was a strong-willed human who grew up as a tomboy, playing baseball with the boys. This is not someone you would think would fall victim to society's norms, yet she did.

It was placed upon her, and even though it didn't resonate with who she was, she accepted it and, in turn, placed it upon my shoulders. I, too, accepted it, and I fell—not knowingly, not consciously, but when something is said over and over again, it becomes reinforced, and something shifts.

I was raised to be a wife and mother. It is ironic that I have never been these things, as much as I have wanted to be. As I write this, it seems almost comical, as in the depths of my soul, that is who I am. I am a caregiver, and I enjoy taking care of others. However, what I have come to realize through my years of healing myself and others is that one can be a caregiver with the energy of servitude, or one can be a caregiver with the energy of unity and joy. The action isn't the problem; the intention—the energy behind it—is. The actions we take don't necessarily need to change to align with what we want; we can shift the intention behind the actions instead.

See, when I take care of others from a place of needing to be loved and valued, I am in a space of low-vibration energy, waiting for others to provide my value. When I come from a place of personal alignment and joy, I am coming from a place of strength, empowerment, and high vibration, where I own my value.

The generational customs of keeping women down have led to mothers continuing the narrative as a way of trying to protect and support their daughters. This has created a subconscious belief system that we need to be saved, protected, and provided for. Yesterday, I supported this Cinderella narrative and used excuses that maybe you have used. They included: Why create stress for everyone? They aren't doing it on purpose. It isn't that big of a deal. I don't really care anyway. It has taken me a long time to unwind and unravel this thread, as it has been so deeply implanted in my ancestral line, as well as societal norms. To be honest, I'm not even sure I've completely broken them, but I am choosing to show up in my highest vibration every day.

I have family members who make me feel mute, like I have no voice. When I speak, I am either ignored or talked over, or—my favorite—they walk away as I start to answer a question they asked. I have stopped accepting that my voice only matters when I am of service and have changed my intention to one of empowerment and alignment. As I held onto my new intentions, these lifelong relationships started to transform. To be clear, I fully recognize that my loved ones are part of this embedded narrative and have no desire to cause harm, but the only way for things to change is if someone starts to make a shift. When one person shifts in a relationship, the other has no option but to shift as well. It's as if you're in a tug of war, and when one lets go of the rope, the other is affected by it.

Many men and women are stuck in this dynamic, and most don't even know it, because that's the way it has always been. Unless you are on the losing end of that proposition, you have no need to examine or shift it. In fact, you probably don't even see it. As hard as it has been for me on this journey, I am grateful that I can see it and am choosing a different road.

Seeing the road is the first step, and probably the hardest. When I first saw it, I felt helpless to it. How do you demand to be heard when your voice is continually silenced?

I remember standing up for myself and speaking, but it was as if I was talking to the wind—it just wasn't acknowledged. Each time my voice was ignored or interrupted, it felt like another brick was added to a wall separating me from my true self.

I started to surround myself with people who listened and could hear. Healers who supported me on my path, just as others supported them. For the first time, surrounded by people who truly saw me, I began to understand the healing power of being witnessed on my journey. I have gone through so many phases of healing, and those surrounding and supporting me have shifted as I've healed. That, honestly, has been a bit of a painful lesson, for I have loved many of my friends and teachers. But when someone shifts vibrations, it is hard to hold onto those who are no longer in resonance or for whom our lessons together were only meant to be for a season.

Cinderella's road is paved with tears and seemingly insurmountable obstacles, but she puts one foot in front of the other and continues to climb the mountain because she simply can't stay where she is.

It was not until I fully embraced my whole self and healed many of my accumulated wounds that I realized I was still waiting for my knight in shining armor to show up and save me from my life. As a strong, independent female, this isn't an easy thing to acknowledge, but there it was—clear as day, staring me in the face. I went on a date with someone and realized I had been thinking, *What can you give me? What do you have that would support me?* And then it hit me smack in the face: what I was actually wondering was, *How can you save me?* I was a little horrified… okay, a lot horrified. Then I realized I had been programmed this way. Isn't that what Cinderella is all about? She is the servant who needed to be saved, when in fact, she could probably run the castle better and easier than any of them and with a sense of compassion and kindness. I knew the only way forward was to release the role that was handed to me and step into a version of Cinderella who didn't wait for permission to be seen.

I closed my eyes to go into meditation and clear this narrative, belief system, and ancestral wound. I was struck when my mother and grandmother (both in spirit) showed up—one on each side of me. We stood there, strong and proud, like the Charmed Ones (yes, I'm from the age when I wanted to be Piper Halliwell and freeze everyone—or blow them up, depending on my mood). Hand in hand, they came not only to support me but also to reclaim their power that was lost.

Together, we rise.

The strength of women coming together in solidarity is something that can literally move mountains. Is it any wonder we have been taught to judge each other, be jealous of one another, and focus on irrelevant things like clothes or appearances? It keeps us from our power, our strength—for women in connection are an unshakable force.

For many years, it has been difficult for me to find friends, keep friends, and feel supported by others. People would come and go, to the point where I stopped trying. I was angry and frustrated, and I can't count the number of times I turned to the universe with tears streaming down my face, asking, *Why? Why is this so hard?* As I tried to step into my own power, the voices of "Cinderella" pulled me back, reminding me of all the ways I had been conditioned to stay small.

It wasn't until I stopped asking *why* and took a deep look at my life that things started to change. The universe isn't here to punish, even though our lessons often feel like it. Everything is conspiring for our highest good. I just got stuck in the middle, being angry and frustrated for a long time. My lesson was to stop playing small. I wanted people to hear me, so I needed to put myself out there to be heard. I wanted to be seen, so I needed to show up to be seen. I had a spiritual teacher once who looked me straight in the eye and said, "I see you." And I knew, to the depths of my soul, that she saw every nook and cranny there was to see. I wanted to run and hide but was frozen. I have never felt so vulnerable in my life. This is the paradox of healing: we often are uncomfortable with the thing we strive so hard to obtain because we simply aren't used to it.

But this was where my path had led—to me, showing up fully and completely. I was terrified, but I needed to face my fears. Each time I spoke up, each time I allowed myself to be seen, it was like unshackling another layer of the servitude I'd carried for so long.

Doors started opening. I had just finished a sound healing class and was invited to do a sound bath as my yoga teacher guided everyone through yoga nidra (a guided meditation). I was so nervous, my energy was all over the place. As I set up my instruments, I held the case containing my crystal pyramid, and, as I unzipped it, the pyramid came crashing out and smashed on the floor. I was in shock, but it was also a reminder for me to slow down. I got control of my breath, worked on grounding myself, and settled into the space. The event was so much fun, and I thought to myself, *I can do this!*

The first yoga nidra sound bath I conducted on my own had my nerves tied in knots. I kept checking the attendance weeks before and leading up to the event, so when the day finally came, I was incredibly touched and in awe when people showed up.

I started to feel more and more energy around showing up for groups of people, and I added small group intuitive sound healings (a combination of sound bath and intuitive healing). The first one sold out! I felt confident. As a therapist and healer, I have become very comfortable with sitting with people one-on-one, or even sitting with a couple. How different could seven be? Well, as it turns out, very different. When I looked up at those faces staring at me, I froze. My mind went blank, and everything I had planned to say was lost in the ether. In a half-frozen state, I knew I just needed to start. I guided them into savasana, and from there, the cobwebs faded away. I realigned with my intention, and the words, sound, and healing flowed with ease.

As I continued to connect to my voice through sound and community, I felt a new form of caregiving take root—a gift I could give from a place of abundance rather than lack.

With every new opportunity that emerged, I didn't overthink—I just said yes. Not everything I said yes to manifested, but the act of saying yes and being willing allowed my energy to expand, and more doors opened. This was my simple act of showing up.

With all these changes, I realized I was now focused on the resilience of Cinderella. Her inner strength and faith in herself allowed her to face adversity and overcome difficult circumstances. Cinderella's strength wasn't in waiting to be saved; it was in the quiet resolve to rise above and take ownership of her own story.

So, while I don't think this was the version of Cinderella my mother intended, this is the part of the story I decided to adopt. For me, it was about shifting from blaming others to owning my own circumstances and empowering myself to do it differently—without losing the aspects that made me *me*. I didn't have to be mean or angry to garner connection. I needed to hold onto kindness, love, and self-worth. When that shifted… everything shifted. I focused on what I wanted, not what I didn't. I truly learned how to manifest from a place of peace. This may sound easy, but those narratives that lie deep in our subconscious are strong and need to be healed to allow new narratives to take root.

As I reflect on my journey, I feel compelled to summarize what I've learned about being seen, and it comes down to this:

- **S**: Show up – Show up for yourself every day. Support yourself and allow yourself to take up space. When you show up for you, others will follow.

- **E**: Embrace what makes you *you*. You are unique and have a special gift to offer the world, so let it shine!

- **E**: Expand horizons and go beyond your comfort zone. True transformation happens when we push into areas that makes us uncomfortable.

- **N**: Never give up! You can do this. Change isn't always easy, but it is worth it. Believe in yourself and keep going!

As I sit here contemplating whether to be part of this anthology, this collection of stories that will be shared with the world, I am hesitating. If I show up and am vulnerable, what will that mean? Will people be upset with my story—upset with me? All these fears that I didn't know still resided inside me are coming up and shouting. It takes all my nerve to breathe, settle, and tell the fears that they might be right, but I'm going to take the leap anyway.

I'm stepping off the cliff and owning my voice, owning my story. I put that voice aside—the one that is shaking out of fear—and ask her to become a witness and see what life brings our way. We are creating a new reality, and we don't know what will happen, but we do know what will happen if we don't do this: things will stay exactly the same.

Cinderella needs to move from being a victim of her circumstances to being in total control of her power, resilience, and destiny. I choose to be heard. I choose to be seen. And I hope that in my choosing, whoever feels called to read my story will also feel empowered to choose themselves.

May you be well and embrace the things that make you *you*.

About Jill Briansky:

Jill Briansky is a Licensed Independent Clinical Social Worker (LICSW), with over twenty years of healing experience and the owner of Purple Lotus in Massachusetts. She combines her psychotherapy expertise with holistic modalities like energy work, body work, and intuitive energy healing allowing her to connect with clients on a deeper level.

Jill has been prominently featured in both Boston Voyager and Spirit of Change magazines, for her dedication to holistic wellness and community building. She was also a guest on Soulful Connections podcast.

Jill established a social work program at Watertown Housing Authority in 2020 and has remained on as a consultant. She is an impactful retreat host, conducts captivating sound baths, and multiple sold-out intuitive healing events. Through her work, she inspires individuals to unlock their true potential, embrace their journeys, and cultivate lives aligned with their deepest desires.

Find out more about Jill by going to purplelotus.health.

Something in the Water
By Catherine Devine Zagorski

"Even if you try IVF, you'll never carry past twelve weeks… it's your immune system, it's …YOU. Your best option to become a mother is surrogacy."

The words echoed in my mind as I sat in the empty conference room late one night, working overtime at my advertising office in New York. I had just finished a call with Alan Beers, the top fertility clinic in California. I had hoped that someone three thousand miles away might offer a glimmer of hope as I grappled with the aftermath of my third miscarriage, searching for the next step forward. My husband and I were already consulting with the best doctors in New York at New Hope Fertility Center, four years into trying to conceive and desperate for answers to our suffering.

I felt utterly powerless. The "best" option, surrogacy, seemed like it would shatter me emotionally—watching another woman carry my child. Meanwhile, the second-best option, IVF, came with warnings that it might destroy my body further. Another team of doctors insisted IVF wouldn't work for me due to my overactive immune system and discouraged me from even attempting it. Powerlessness seemed to be a recurring theme in my life, surfacing whenever things spiraled out of control. It felt like my body was perpetually in fight-or-flight mode. Outwardly, I maintained a façade of productivity and success, but inside, my system was screaming in anger and rebellion.

This helplessness took me back to the most vulnerable moment of my life—when I became one of the first people in my hometown diagnosed with an autoimmune disorder in 1997. Doctors initially mistook it for cancer, as my healthy cells were attacking themselves. At sixteen, I spent a month hospitalized, surrounded by doctors pressuring me to undergo colon surgery. They claimed the bleeding and damage to my colon were irreversible, promising "stylish" colostomy bag covers and the option to decorate the hole in my stomach with a rose or peace sign. Their casual suggestions left me feeling dehumanized. For the first time in my life, I felt an electric jolt of defiance as I refused the surgery. I insisted on medication instead, holding onto the belief that I could heal.

Despite ridicule and bullying, I clung to my decision, enduring weeks of monitoring and slow progress. Eventually, three weeks later, I was cleared to go home. After three months of rest and recovery—much of it spent at our neighborhood pool, communing with my favorite willow tree—the doctors admitted that refusing surgery had been the right decision. I made a full recovery from ulcerative colitis, though I remained on medications for inflammation control. At the time, I hadn't yet grasped the significance of inflammation or the connection between healthy anger, boundary setting, and emotional well-being.

That illness marked the beginning of a transformative period of therapy and self-reflection in my family. For the first time, I experienced emotional safety, breaking free from the narcissistic dynamics that had plagued generations of my bloodline. Regaining my sense of personal power and leaving home for college brought a renewed sense of health. I convinced myself I was "healed" and dove headfirst into a hustle-and-grind mentality. By all appearances, I had succeeded: I was the Head of Finance for a global advertising firm, my husband and I owned a Brooklyn building with paying tenants, and we were thriving in the high-energy NYC lifestyle. I envisioned squeezing a couple of kids into that chaotic existence, hiring a Polish nanny, and quickly returning to work.

But life had other plans. The onset of the COVID-19 lockdown changed everything, reshaping my understanding of productivity, rest, and success.

Back in the dimly lit conference room, the weight of my worst nightmare hung in the air. Decades and miles away from the small town where my sixteen-year-old self had fought her first battle, I found myself inflamed and angry once more. My body, subconsciously at war with itself, was rejecting the life I so desperately wanted to nurture. Each miscarriage felt like an exile from my own body, a cruel reminder that something within me was unresolved.

As I stared out the window, the city lights blurred into one another, reflecting the hopelessness I felt. There was nowhere left to run, no one else to blame. The answer lay within me. Whatever unresolved pain was buried in my body, it was my responsibility to confront and release it. How it got there no longer mattered—what mattered was freeing myself. I thought of the words of Jesus: *"The Kingdom lies within."* For the first time in a long while, I felt a spark of power. I stood up, left the empty conference room, and resolved to stop driving myself into the ground in an endless attempt to prove my worth.

I had spent years overworking, leaning into my masculine energy, and neglecting my feminine side. I was out of balance, out of tune with myself. No one could fix this for me—no doctor, no treatment. The realization hit me like a tidal wave: no one could make me a mother but me. Every time I looked in the mirror, I saw a body at war with itself. How could I hope to carry life when I didn't even feel at home in my own skin?

Healing, I realized, doesn't come from the mind alone; it comes from the body. Our bodies hold our stories—the pain, the trauma, and the key to freedom. Whatever we avoid in our minds lodges itself in our cells. Our frequency, our vibration, is uniquely ours, and when we suppress it, we create blockages—fear, shame, guilt. To feel joy, we must raise our vibration. To heal, we must alchemize these stagnant energies and return to love. But how?

For the first time, I felt the power to choose—to let go of the past, forgive my body, and reclaim my life. This was no longer just about becoming a mother; it was about rediscovering myself.

In the days that followed, I felt drawn to make drastic changes. I stopped going to my usual watering hole for whiskeys and instead sought solace in daily mass and prayers to the Divine Mother. I ordered boxes of holy water from the Lourdes spring and began envisioning my body's water molecules crystallizing into perfect geometric shapes, reflecting the Divine Mother's harmony. Though I didn't yet fully understand the concept, I saw her as the Virgin Mary, embodying the divine feminine.

Through my prayers and meditations, I began to see beyond the confines of religion. I recognized that organized doctrines often twisted truths to fit their narratives, but the essence of divine wisdom remained. I remembered a shamanic healing years earlier when Jesus appeared to me in a vision. I had run to him like a child in a field, and he came just for me. That memory stayed with me as a reminder of the divine truth within us all—a truth often obscured by manmade interpretations.

As I drank the Lourdes holy water each night, praying for purification, I had a vision of King David—a past life of mine—his symbol of interlocking masculine and feminine triangles glowing on the Virgin Mary's chest. In my own booming male voice, I heard, *"If you are looking for the One True God, you are missing your Mother."*

Awaking with clarity, I searched for a nearby shrine to the Virgin Mary and discovered one only twenty minutes from my Brooklyn home; on her chest was the Star of David, the symbol for masculine and feminine unity.

On Father's Day, eighteen months after my third miscarriage, my husband and I visited the shrine. Like Anne, Mary's mother, who had prayed for a child, I knelt in the garden and begged with a pure heart for the same. I promised to dedicate this child back to God and vowed that nothing would stand in the way of my mission if my wish were granted.

As I knelt at the shrine, a profound peace washed over me—a deep, lasting calm I hadn't known was possible. The years of pain, rejection, and loss seemed to dissolve in the presence of the Divine Mother. For the first time, I felt truly seen, understood, and embraced. This wasn't about religion—it was about returning home to my soul, meeting myself with compassion instead of anger, and discovering the nurturing mother within me.

She didn't make me wait long. Not even a full moon cycle had passed when my husband shared a dream he had: we already had a daughter and were at home. The moment he spoke those words, I knew I was pregnant. This time, I felt called to have a wild pregnancy and a home birth, guided by intuition. Miraculously, we were led to Richmond Virginia and found the perfect at-home midwife in my third trimester. On March 11, 2021, exactly on her due date, our daughter, Mary Magdalena, was born at home. That night, on our bedroom floor, we became a family of three, holy and healthy in every way.

Exactly one year later, on Father's Day weekend, we returned to the shrine to introduce Mary to Maria Vitolo, her godmother and the shrine's keeper. Maria, the daughter of visionary Joseph Vitolo, had a dream that I would return pregnant again, this time with a little girl. The dream came true. We asked for a son during that visit, and on June 26, 2022, Michael Joseph was born. He arrived swiftly—just three hours of labor—at home, as holy and perfect as his sister.

Tracing back the events that led to this transformation, I saw how they all interconnected. Stopping alcohol raised my vibrational frequency. Prayer and mindfulness helped me process emotions in healthier ways. Drinking holy water with intention began to shift the structure of my body's water molecules, aligning them with harmony and healing. Most importantly, reclaiming my personal power and refusing to rely on external validation or medical interventions shifted my frequency entirely. I had gone from living in fear and victimhood to embodying sovereignty and freedom. I became the woman who could create life, on her terms, and transform her struggles into a guiding light for others.

In my postpartum period, I faced the challenges of breastfeeding and pumping. Determined not to use commercial formulas, I followed my instincts and created my own raw-milk baby formula at home. This formula also nourished me as a nutrient-rich green and chocolate drink. Critics warned me not to "get obsessed," but my intuition told me I was onto something vital. I recognized a gap in the market—just as Amazon identified the need for online shopping. There was powdered milk and breastmilk, but where was the middle ground? What about adoptive parents or others without access to breastmilk? I envisioned a fresh, homemade formula made with love.

I published a cookbook, *Nourished is Best,* and launched a product line under my playful title, *The Raw Milkmaid*®. The flagship product, Magick Milk, combines Amish raw milk with energetically aligned water molecules, formulated to resonate with "heart-opening" frequencies that mimic the love hormones in breast milk. It's not just the milk—it's the water that holds the magic. Babies, I believe, can feel the love imbued in something made just for them.

My ability to see and perceive differently than others felt like a gift—something truly "in the water." Just as quartz crystals store memory in technology, I saw how the water in our bodies acts as a vessel for consciousness. The more precise and harmonious our molecular structure, the higher our frequency, the clearer our perception, and the closer we come to activating our original, divine blueprint. Healing practices like yoga, sound healing, and breathwork became essential for me, as I realized they were tools for elevating the sacred geometry within our bodies, crystallizing our cells to vibrate at higher frequencies of love and bliss.

Motherhood brought a new level of empowerment. I became adept at setting razor-sharp boundaries, shedding toxic and stagnant relationships, and creating a life filled with beauty and balance. I saw how many years I had spent letting others define my body and my choices. Reclaiming my power felt like stepping into the woman I was always meant to be—a woman unafraid to heal on her own terms. Faith, I learned, wasn't just belief; it was action. It was the daily choice to rise above every "no" and every doubt until my heart and mind aligned with my truth.

This newfound inspiration led me to create elixirs sourced from the purest waters in the world. These elixirs are designed for spiritual awakening, personal growth, and divine embodiment, available exclusively through my work as *The Water Priestess,* where I offer other sacred services. The water carries not only healing properties but also consciousness—Goddess Herself resides in its depths. She led me back to myself, showing me that my personal power and sovereignty were the ultimate cure-all.

Through this journey, I've learned the importance of trusting your heart and speaking your truth without fear or shame. Your health, vitality, and destiny depend on it. Healing is not something that happens to you—it's something you claim for yourself. The Goddess within us all is waiting to be rediscovered, ready to guide us back to love, balance, and the fullness of life.

Yes, there *is* something in the water.

About Catherine Devine Zagorski:

Catherine Devine Zagorski is the founder of Veda Ventures Malkoota D'Shmeya, LLC, a company devoted to the rising Divine Feminine. After her personal journey through recurrent miscarriages and infertility, Catherine experienced a miraculous awakening, resulting in two 'wild' pregnancies and home births at 39 and 40, defying medical odds. She now shares this wisdom with others, empowering women to embrace their divinity.

As the creator of two collaborating brands, @the_raw_milkmaid (Magick Milk, a raw cow milk-based baby formula, postpartum & post workout recovery nutrient drinks) and @the_water_priestess (handmade elixirs and spiritual coaching), Catherine blends her passions for healing and creativity.

She is a best selling author of two cookbooks (Nourished is Best & Leftovers to Luxury), a poetry collection (Love: Through the Looking Glass) and a children's book series (The Power of the Rose and its accompanying animation).

Trained in Mystery Schools, including with a High Priestess of the French Gnostic Church, Catherine is a ceremonialist, speaker, and healer. Her mission is to guide others back to their hearts, inspiring them to embody their truest, most divine selves.

www.catherinedevinezagorski.com

www.water-priestess.com

www.therawmilkmaid.com

Finding my Light
By Laura Degelmann

"Darkness will always give you an opportunity to create your own light." (Iain Thomas, *I Wrote This For You* (2011)).

The light and energy of our soul is a powerful thing. It can bring us strength, confidence, motivation, and love. Some individuals are lucky enough to be cognizant of their essence and use it to empower their lives, while others fail to connect with the light within them. These individuals don't recognize the light or understand its purpose until it has diminished. I used to be one of those individuals who didn't see the light and the power I had within. At the time, I was in a place of stress, worry, guilt, and fear— my own darkness. I found the darkness to be overwhelming, all-consuming, and sad. Back then, I could never have imagined that any good could come from being in such a place.

This concept of darkness means different things to different people, and we use a variety of adjectives to describe its impact on our lives. For some, darkness falls upon us quicker than we can blink; for others, it's a gradual sinking we don't even realize until we are waist-deep. I was a gradual sinking person. It wasn't that I didn't recognize the darkness that had come over me; in truth, I was just good at ignoring it. I didn't want to admit that I had taken up residence in a place that drained my energy, motivation, and happiness—mainly because I wasn't quite sure how I was going to get myself out. But I did recognize the events that had led me there.

I really shouldn't have had anything to complain about. I had a roof over my head, great friends, a family who cared for me, and a job I had dreamt about since I was a young girl. I am a teacher. All I had ever wanted to be was a teacher, and I truly feel to this day that I was put on this Earth to teach. I remember myself as a young child, setting up my stuffed animals and playing school with them. I can still picture those animals, all sitting in a row, watching me explain a math problem on my chalkboard or reading a book. I loved it. And here I was, an adult in my 40s, living my dream.

I can wholeheartedly say that teaching has brought me so much joy and fulfillment over the past 20-plus years of my career. I love working with students and teaching them skills they will use their whole lives. I enjoy inspiring them to think about how they can change the world around them. I work hard to create the best lessons possible and don't think twice about spending the last ten dollars in my bank account on something needed for the classroom. I can't tell you how many Sunday outings I've missed because I "needed" to prepare lessons. I've given everything to my teaching, and I'd like to think it showed. I'd like to think that the countless hours of personal time I spent in my classroom made enormous impacts on the students I taught.

But with any relationship, when you give more than you get, there is no way to sustain a healthy balance. You quickly find yourself depleting faster than anything can replenish you. The walls start to crumble, and the darkness begins creeping into your peripheral view. After over 20 years of giving all of myself—emotionally, physically, financially, mentally—it took a toll on me, whether I was ready to admit it or not. I had such an unhealthy work-life balance but couldn't face it. I felt it in my body, I felt it in my mind, I felt it in my soul—something was off. The signs were there, signaling a major shift had occurred. Deep down, I knew I couldn't keep putting myself last. I knew I couldn't keep spending my last few dollars on my classroom. But at the same time, I felt incredible guilt—a massive weight on my heart.

How could I feel trapped in a career that I loved? How could I not continue to give this profession—and ultimately my students—everything I had given in the past? I just couldn't imagine that the thing I had dreamt about since I was a kid wasn't nourishing me in the same way. Worse, that dream was at the root of my life's imbalance. My light and my purpose had faded into darkness.

But out of the darkness will come light, and my light did come. It was during the COVID-19 pandemic that I began to realize change was necessary. In the isolation of the pandemic, I faced the truth I had been fighting so hard to ignore—I was not taking care of my physical, emotional, mental, and spiritual well-being. I was sinking lower and lower into a well of unhappiness, and the fear was real and double-sided. I was afraid that if I failed to find new happiness, I would get stuck in the darkness of stress, worry, guilt, and sadness forever. But on the other side, what was I to change? It couldn't be my career—teaching was what I was meant to do. Even if I wanted to change careers, I couldn't picture myself doing anything else. I had spent so much time (and money) improving my skills that it seemed unthinkable to walk away from this career, which I still loved at its core. But the veil of darkness that had crept into my life was now uncovered, and I could no longer deny that I was sacrificing my well-being. Something needed to change.

Some say the world is full of coincidences. I believe there are no coincidences in life—things come your way when it is time. As the world began to move on from COVID, I had an opportunity to step out of my comfort zone. I had always wanted to learn Tarot cards, and when a local shop started offering an online Tarot card class, I knew this was my chance! I was going to create change by learning something new. My friend and I signed up for the classes and spent the next few months studying the cards and their meanings. I loved the class—it felt great to be a student again! I began to feel a new spark of motivation, and it felt wonderful. Tarot card classes then led to astrology classes, and astrology classes led to the discovery of my mediumship abilities, which, in turn, brought me to the religion of Spiritualism.

Developing my spiritual side gave me so much joy and clarity. I not only felt like I was digging myself out of the dark place that once held me captive, but I could feel my light starting to shine again.

As my spiritual self developed, I became aware that I also had to focus on my physical and mental well-being. I accepted that it was time to leave the school district I had taught in for 14 years. I reached the point where I refused to let the fear of starting over hold me back from achieving the improved work-life balance I knew I needed. I was fortunate enough to get a new teaching position similar to what I had been doing. It wasn't easy to leave the community I had been a part of for so long, but I knew the time had come. Little did I know how much leaving that job would change my life. As soon as I made the job change, I immediately felt lighter and happier. I had more energy and was beginning to feel like my old self again.

The worries and stress that had consumed me in my previous job were gone, and I started setting healthy boundaries between work and my personal life. I was overcoming the darkness and seeing my true light shine again. This newfound happiness and clarity allowed me to recognize the signs that would lead me down my next path—the discovery of sound healing.

I had heard of sound healing before, but I can't say I truly understood what it was. As I started the school year in my new district, I began seeing advertisements for sound healing certification multiple times a day. Each time I saw one, I felt a strange connection—a feeling in my stomach that told me this was important. But how could that be? I didn't even know what sound healing involved. After weeks of seeing these ads, I realized it wasn't just some algorithm at work. This was a sign from my guides, and it was time to listen.

I clicked on one of the ads and began reading about sound healing. From the very first sentences, I was hooked. Something inside of me clicked, and I knew this was a gift that would significantly impact my life. I signed up for certification classes even before I had ever attended a sound bath in person. I just knew! Sound healing combined so many of my passions—music, science, healing, and connection to spirit. As I started the classes, I wondered whether I could see myself playing for others. It would require an investment of time, money, and more of myself. Did I have all of these things to give?

I weighed the pros and cons, consulted friends, meditated on it, and asked my guides for clarity. In the end, I had no doubt this was my path. I made the investment to purchase a set of crystal singing bowls, and my business, **Soul-full Notes Sound Healing**, was born.

It's amazing to look back and see how naturally sound healing fit into my life. I had been a music kid growing up, so playing instruments wasn't new to me. The movement, the flow of sound, the timing—it all came naturally. To prepare, I conducted a few sound baths with friends first so I could get feedback on my playing. Within a few months, I felt ready to begin my sound healing journey with clients.

I started attending wellness fairs to make connections in the health and wellness field. I joined a local women's entrepreneur group and sent countless emails to yoga studios and other spaces where I could conduct sound baths. The Universe ultimately brought me so many amazing connections that helped set me on my way. To this day, I'm amazed and grateful for the incredible people I've met—business owners, colleagues, and clients. Everyone I've come into contact with has been kind, supportive, and encouraging.

I realized that I had surrounded myself with people whose light shines brightly. They are individuals developing their light just as I am, people using their light to help others, and people choosing to spread their light across the Universe. Being around them helps my own light shine even brighter. By the time I had been conducting sound baths for a year and a half, I felt I was living my brightest life.

Then, in May 2024, I encountered a dramatic curveball—I was diagnosed with thyroid cancer. Suddenly, my life was filled with medical appointments and decisions, all while juggling my teaching job, my sound healing business, and an unrelated decision to undergo abdominal surgery. While I could write paragraphs about the emotional roller coaster I faced, I can say that my unwavering feeling throughout it all was that I would be okay. I knew I had the mindset and resources to heal from this disease.

How fortunate I felt that this diagnosis came at a time when my light, the strength I had worked so hard to build, was strong enough to face any new darkness—even cancer. I knew my light would not dim; in fact, I was certain it would shine brighter. Had this happened years earlier, I don't believe I could have said the same.

I immediately knew that sound healing would be at the core of my recovery, along with a variety of other healing modalities. While I experienced pain, soreness, and other physical symptoms, my recovery was fairly straightforward. I truly believe that the healing work I had done before surgery and in the months following made a significant impact on my mind, body, and soul.

Going through this experience made me stronger. Not only do I feel like I know myself better, but I also believe I can now relate more closely to individuals who have faced diagnoses and treatments that took a toll on them.

So when people ask if I believe light can come from darkness, I say absolutely! We may not be able to see the path we will take to move from darkness to light (I certainly didn't), but it's our obligation to ourselves to start walking a path toward change. I look back at my life's journey—the twists and turns, the surprises and accomplishments—with amazement. It is certainly not the life I envisioned for myself when I was younger, but I am so proud of the person I am today.

I am proud of taking those small steps that led to bigger changes because I am so much more than I ever thought I could be—a direct result of the life I have lived. I am proud to have gone through my times of darkness because I feel that the light that has emerged from them is extraordinary.

Everyone's story is their own. It can be bumpy and scary, reflective and beautiful. No two stories align perfectly, and that's the beauty of life—your story is unique to you. This is why you experience darkness in your own way, and it's the same reason why the discovery of your light will also be unique.

I encourage you to learn about and recognize both your light and your darkness—how they feel, what feeds them, and what doesn't. The more you identify with your light, the more you will honor and protect it. I wish you all the best in your journey to find your light. It, too, will be amazing!

About Laura Degelmann:

Growing up, music had always been a big part of Laura's life. Through elementary, middle, high school, and even college, Laura was involved in musical activities. In the aftermath of college, through the hustle and bustle of trying to establish herself in her teaching career, Laura's involvement with music decreased and eventually disappeared- but it never left her heart. In recent years, through her own personal healing journey, Laura turned her attention back to music. She began to study sound healing and immediately knew this was her second calling. Laura became a certified sound healer in 2022 and started her business, Soul-full Notes Sound Healing. She is thrilled to have music and instruments back in her life, and is honored to be able to help others through the music she shares. She continues to teach full time as an Elementary STEM Teacher, and currently lives in Salem, Massachusetts.

www.soulfullnotes.com

Facebook: Soul-full Notes Sound Healing

WARRIOR GODDESS
By Carla Cunningham

Life is not easy, that's for sure! Not for anyone. Everyone is fighting battles others are not aware of. I was fortunate to grow up in a home filled with love. My home life shaped me into a deeply empathetic and compassionate person. I believe that is why I feel so compelled to help others heal.

Intuition has always been my compass, guiding me through the unseen currents of life. For as long as I can remember, I've had a deep sense of knowing—a way of feeling the energy that flows between people, places, and moments. When I was a young woman, I enlisted in the US Army and served in Operation Desert Storm. Serving my country during such a pivotal moment in history gave me a sense of purpose, but a part of me longed to make a more intimate impact on others lives. A deeper, more personal connection. This innate sensitivity eventually led me to become a massage therapist.

As much as I valued my service in the military—a rewarding battle in its own right—I continued to feel that deeper calling to help people on a more personal level. After leaving the military, I sought a path that would allow me to connect more profoundly with others. This desire led me to become a massage therapist, where I discovered the transformative power of touch to help others. In those first years as a massage therapist, I realized I had found the beginning of my true calling.

Four years into my practice, I decided to explore Reiki, intuitively knowing the gentle flow of energy would resonate with me. I quickly became a Reiki master, embracing this new path with a heart full of hope and a desire to help others.

While I felt that I had found my purpose, life took a challenging turn. Life has a way of testing the things we hold dear. During this time, my previous marriage became a dark chapter. What should have been a safe haven for me and my three children became a place of fear and uncertainty. The man I once loved became a source of pain, and I lost touch with the light I used to channel through my hands. Reiki felt distant, like a language I could no longer speak. How could I heal others when my own spirit felt broken?

The energy that had once flowed so freely seemed to retreat, leaving me feeling alone and powerless.

Yet, even in those shadows, a quiet voice inside me remained—a reminder of my purpose. I continued my work as a massage therapist, finding solace in the small moments when I could offer others relief from their pain, even if I couldn't yet soothe my own.

Then came the diagnosis that would change everything: cancer. A word that carries the weight of a thousand fears. For me, it also brought an unexpected clarity. Faced with my mortality, I knew I had to fight—not just for my life, but for the chance to rediscover the part of myself I had lost. During this time, I learned that others with my type of cancer often had a life expectancy of five years. It was a sobering "what if" moment, forcing me to confront my deepest fears and uncertainties.

After completing my initial treatment and being deemed cancer-free, I spent the next year living as if "this could be one of the few short years left." The treatments were grueling, and the uncertainty was overwhelming, but amid the physical battle, I felt myself drawn back to the practices that had once brought me peace.

After enduring chemotherapy and intense radiation, my worst fears came true—the cancer recurred a year later. This time, I had to make a life-altering decision. I chose to undergo not one, but two major surgeries, knowing they would forever change my life. Still, I chose life.

Although the aftermath of those surgeries brought difficult days, I am happy to say that, for now, I am cancer-free. Even so, going through that diagnosis and recurrence has left a lingering sense of vulnerability. I'm not sure I will ever feel 100% safe from cancer—maybe one day. I truly believe that sound healing and energy work, both for myself and others, are vital to my continued healing and to fostering confidence in a lifetime of recovery.

The surgeries left scars on my body, physical reminders of my survival and resilience. Yet, they also marked a turning point—a chance to start over with a renewed sense of purpose. Amid the physical struggle, I returned to the practices that had once grounded me, seeking new forms of healing to reach the depths of my weariness.

It was during this time that I stumbled upon sound healing—almost by accident. The soothing vibrations of sound and singing bowls washed over me, filling the empty spaces within with a gentle hum. The experience was unlike anything I had ever felt before. The sound seemed to reach parts of me that words and touch couldn't, offering a release I hadn't realized I needed.

Intrigued, I began studying sound healing, learning how different frequencies could soothe the nervous system and bring the body back into harmony. I started experimenting with singing bowls, tuning forks, and every other instrument I could get my hands on.

At first, sound healing was something I did quietly, for myself—a private dialogue between my soul and the universe. But as my confidence grew, I began sharing it with others. The results were astonishing. People came in carrying emotional pain, anxiety, and tension, and left with a sense of peace that went beyond the physical. It was as though the vibrations were speaking directly to their spirit, just as they had spoken to mine.

Sound healing felt like a missing piece—a way to blend my years of experience with a new form of expression. Where Reiki had taught me to flow with the currents of energy, sound healing allowed me to create new waves. It became a bridge between my own healing and the healing I offered to others. For the first time in years, I felt truly whole—both as a practitioner and as a person.

Now, when I reflect on the journey that brought me here, I see a tapestry woven from threads of pain and resilience, darkness and light. The challenges of my past no longer feel like weights holding me down but rather stepping stones that led to a deeper understanding of what it means to heal. I am grateful for every moment that brought me to this place, where I can blend the wisdom of personal pain, the power of Reiki, the touch of massage, and the resonance of sound to help others find their way back to themselves.

There is a quiet joy in knowing that I am doing exactly what I am meant to do—helping others find peace in a world that can be so noisy and painful. My journey has shown me that healing is never a straight line; it is a spiral that carries us deeper into ourselves. In that depth, I have found my true calling—guiding others through the echoes of sound back to the heart of their own being.

As I reflect on the winding path my life has taken, I am filled with gratitude. From my time serving in the Army to my years as a massage therapist, through the struggles of living in a violent home and facing cancer, each chapter has shaped me into who I am today. My journey brought me back to the healing practices that had once felt out of reach, like Reiki, and introduced me to the transformative power of sound healing.

I have discovered a special joy in working one-on-one or with small groups in sound baths, where the intimate connection fosters deeper healing. These experiences have taught me that even in the darkest moments, there is a light within us that never goes out. Embracing that light has allowed me not only to help others find their own but also to rediscover my own strength.

Today, I continue to share the gifts of touch, sound, and energy. I have learned that life is not defined by the hardships we face, but by the strength we find to rise again and the love we extend to ourselves and others.

Life is a river with unpredictable currents, and I've learned to follow its flow, even when the waters became turbulent. From my time in the Army to discovering the healing power of touch and sound, each twist and turn brought me closer to the calm within for which I am so grateful.

I can't even put into words how much joy sound healing provides me and the people I share it with. My now-forever and loving husband, who happens to be a huge supporter of my journey, always says, "You always come home a different (happier) person after sharing sound healing." So true!

Sound healing has become a way for me to connect more deeply with myself and others, offering peace and relief in a world often filled with noise and pain. Each session, whether for myself or others, is a reminder of the power we all have to heal and transform.

I am grateful for the path that brought me here—a journey filled with challenges and triumphs, light and shadow. And I am endlessly thankful to share this light with others, helping them find their way back to themselves through the beautiful vibrations of sound, touch, and energy.

About Carla Cunningham:

Carla grew up in the Pacific Northwest with deep rooted connections as a Longmire decent. She chose to enlist in the Army a couple years after high school. She served from 1986-1991. She served in Germany, Fort Stewart, Georgia, and Desert Shield/Storm in Saudi Arabia. After her decision to discharge from the Army she continued to live in Germany working civil service for 5 yrs. She then returned to the United States and decided to attend massage school where life definitely changed. Her passion called her to become a Reiki master. And much later a certified sound healer. She is a mother of three young men she that adores and 1 granddaughter (apple of her eye) and has been happily married since 2011. Carla loves her family very much and has a great passion for the work she does to help others through their journey.

My Healing Journey
By Jennifer Morris

The journey began probably when I was in the sixth grade. I had fallen and injured my knee. When I went to the doctor, he said that I would be lucky if I could walk again, and I would always walk with a limp. The doctor said I would no longer be able to ride horses, swim, do track, or anything physical that I liked to do. Hearing the doctor's words, my world shifted—I couldn't imagine a life where I couldn't run, swim, or ride horses. I was faced with the loss of everything I loved. I was training horses at the time, on the swim team, and one of the fastest people in PE class for track. This was in the early 1970s, and back then, people liked to talk about other ways of doing things besides what we had always been told. In my case, I saw on television the idea of being able to heal with our mind. I was not sure what to do. Should I listen to the doctor and follow his advice? Was I at risk of never being able to walk again?

I remember one day at school my friend Linda came up to me and said, "My momma can make something for your knee." When she offered to help, I felt a spark of hope reignite within me. Every day she encouraged me to keep going, to believe in something beyond what I had been told was possible. I agreed to try it, and the next time I saw her, she brought something stinky into the classroom. "She says we're supposed to put it on there every day," she said, "and I'm going to help you walk." I said, "OK."

It was not easy to say OK though, because the thing that she had brought was a poultice, and it smelled horrible. The kids in the class teased us day after day because of the awful smell. It smelled like Bengay and mustard. She repeated this process every day, putting on the poultice, and then when we were on the playground, she would help me by having me walk with my crutches and not put any weight on the injured leg. At first, I could not move it physically, so she would move my leg for me and then tell me to move forward on my crutches. She would move the injured leg to take the step, and I would move my other leg forward not putting any weight on the injured leg, but on the crutches while I moved the other leg forward. She helped me go through the process of walking without walking. We did this daily, and I noticed that I was beginning to get feeling in the foot. She would also gently massage it. I was still swimming daily for the swim team, just dragging the leg at first.

After six weeks or so, when the break should have healed, she started having me practice moving it. Then one day, when we went out to the playground, she said, "Let's try to put a little weight on it." I did, and it did not hurt! Since I had started to feel the leg again below the knee, I knew the nerve damage was healing. I could move my leg without any help, then move my leg forward on my own, and put a little bit more pressure onto it every day. Before I knew it, I was practically walking again. When my dad took me to the doctor for the next visit, I got out of the car, grabbed my crutches, and I crutched into the doctor's office. The doctor examined me and said, "OK, it's looking good. Why don't you try putting some weight on it now?" I said OK, and crutched out of the office. When I got out to the car, I promptly took my crutches, threw them in the trunk of the car, walked to my seat, and never went back. Something changed in me that day on so many levels. I will never forget Linda Hall, because she was the one who helped me every day and taught me that there are other ways to heal besides the ways that we had been taught.

My journey turned to martial arts the next year, and that was very key in my ability to manage this body. I learned that I could exercise and make myself strong, mind over matter, and the power of meditation. I started martial arts because I was hazed, harassed, and beat up every day at school. I was at a new school now, and the kids were not so nice. I asked my mom to sign me up for Karate so I could have some way to protect myself from the bullies. I was already practicing the moves I saw on the TV series *Kung Fu*. I was glad that I did the martial arts training because it did help me with that goal, but it also helped me with the goal of making my body stronger. I took the lessons from that fateful day when I fell and hurt my knee playing an innocent game of King of the Hill and decided that I wasn't going to look back or stop living just because the doctor said I wouldn't be able to. Every day since then has been this journey.

Martial arts training was the first thing, and I found that learning about mind over matter, meditation, and how to control my reactions really helped my body immensely. I incorporated nutrition into what I was doing because food is medicine, and we should be using food as medicine. Staying calm rather than getting excited when things are not working right and channeling that energy into my exercise and my training made it much more effective than just feeling angry all day because of the kids at school or whatever happened. I continued my martial arts journey for many years. I became a fifth-degree black belt in Ju-Jitsu. I also held top brown in Go-Soku Ryu Karate as well as an orange belt in Karado Karate.

Then there came a time when just building the body, exercising it, and doing the mind, body, spirit exercises became less effective. Coaching gymnastics became my career along with martial arts, and doing that was a lot of wear and tear on the body. There was only so much I could do with Ki (the unseen energy martial artists use for strength and power beyond the physical body) and only so much I could do with the training. No matter how much I trained, ate healthily, and practiced meditation, my body seemed to be breaking down faster than I could repair it. Over the years, my body began to break down, mostly from overuse. I was diagnosed with degenerative joint disease in my late 20s. I was told I exercised too much. So, I started looking for that balance. Resting and not exercising brought more pain.

I was having pain in my back and my legs. I saw the doctors, and I also worked with my karate instructor, Shihan Tom Serrano. He used a combination of Shiatsu, Okazaki massage, and what he had learned from chiropractic. It did help with being able to move again, but I still had chronic fatigue, and all the nutrition that I had worked on in my early 20s in order to balance that mind, body, spirit work wasn't helping. I have always used food as medicine, and I've always known that food is intended to heal us and make us strong. I avoided anything that had to do with processed foods. I ate fruits and vegetables, whole and raw, good lean meats—chicken and fish mostly—and still I was struggling.

Then, in 2001, I had something happen in my brain. A neurologist told me it was a transient ischemic attack (TIA). Unfortunately, it was never fully diagnosed because my healthcare denied a request for an MRI, and the doctor was leaving the medical group. I always take that road, not wanting to cause trouble for people, and I backed down at a time when I really should not have. I did insist that we get the MRI, but by that time, there was no evidence related to my symptoms.

After years of hearing, "There's nothing more we can do," I was left feeling like I was losing a battle I'd fought my entire life.

Not long after, I had a friend, Patti, who was helping me with the classes at my work. At the time, I was teaching gymnastics, martial arts, cooking, science, art, and a cotillion class. I was also teaching Boy Scout merit badge classes: Citizenship in the Community, Nation, World, Camping, Hiking, and First Aid. Add a little bit of archery to that, and I had a full plate.

My journey shifted when Patti had an aneurysm. I immediately wanted to help and do anything I could. I offered my help, and her family accepted, asking me to help homeschool her daughter. As she recovered, the doctors told her that what she needed to do was something totally new and different to help rebuild the pathways in her brain. Her mom worked with Roberta Stanley, who was taking a crystal healing class and thought this would be good for her, so we went. It was amazing.

Our teacher greeted us with such warmth and joy. I felt safe in the class, but I still did the thing I always do with something that is new, and that is an attitude of "show me this works." I hold back until I can see for sure. I do not just accept when someone says this is blue. I am going to say, "Are you sure it's blue? Let me see if it is blue." That is how I connect and learn.

That first day of class was amazing. I was fascinated by the idea that we could put crystals on our body, and it could somehow affect the change in our being, in our health, and who we are. I remember when it became my turn on the table. I had gone in with a terrible toothache, which I told no one about, not even my friend knew it was happening. At one point, someone used a quartz crystal point and aimed it right at the toothache. I felt like a little explosion. Like something just went POW on that side of the mouth and then suddenly my pain was gone. Oh, I still had the tooth problem, but not to the degree that it was. It started to heal over time, and I finally saw a dentist and got it taken care of, but the infection was gone. That blew me away. I am a scientist. Show me that it is real, and I will believe you, but I do not take anecdotal evidence as fact. At first, crystals and energy healing seemed abstract, maybe even a little far-fetched, but when I felt my own pain dissolve under the touch of a quartz crystal, I knew I had discovered something profound. I felt a change while I was on the table and then I had a long-term effect from that change. I found that remarkably interesting, so I signed up for the class. I looked forward to it every week, my time with my friend going to and from class. We studied for over a year, Patti, Roberta, and I, and became good friends with our teacher, Victoria Arkell Colette, an amazing healer, teacher, and human being. I learned so much from her. She incorporated not just crystals, but also taught us to incorporate other modalities of healing: color therapy, aromatherapy, sound therapy, and energy healing.

Being surrounded by others who believed in these alternative methods gave me a renewed sense of purpose and community, something I hadn't realized I had been missing.

An opportunity arose for us to create a healing space. Sounds like the end of the story, but it was more of the beginning of the hard work. The lessons learned, mistakes made, and earth-shattering realities rocked my world every day. Upheaval in my daily life due to circumstances beyond my control kept me focused on becoming a healer.

I became a Reiki Master with my long-time friend and teacher Diane Newton. It was one more key to the puzzle. I also took an ordination at the encouragement of Victoria, and coupled with the Reiki Master certification, I was on the path to greater growth than I had ever dreamed of. One of Diane's friends, Sandy Snyder, played crystal bowls. I had never experienced such bliss. When she performed the healing with the crystal bowls, I felt a shift in my consciousness, not to mention my body at ease.

Eventually, I pursued the bowls, and my good friend, Rich Bertram, encouraged me to take Vickie Gould's online classes. At last, I had a way to finally pursue my long-time dream of working equally with all my chosen modalities. We co-founded *Flowing With Crystal Sound,* an immersive sound healing experience.

All my life I have had to deal with chronic pain, mostly due to conditions I inherited. Sure, I would blame it on something I did in martial arts or later coaching gymnastics, but now I can get through the day and live like a normal human being. Oh, the pain is still there, but it is no longer debilitating. Every healing session feels like a celebration of everything I've learned and endured; it's a testament to the power of perseverance and the miracles within alternative healing.

In my daily practice, I treat clients with the knowledge I have gained over my lifetime, incorporating the lessons learned with all the methods I spoke of here. Every day there are clients who are impressed by their experience with me. Witnessing others find relief and joy in the same way I did fills me with gratitude beyond words—I feel honored to guide others on a journey of self-discovery and healing.

I have so much gratitude for this amazing journey and the things I have seen, done, and accomplished. Wherever you are on your journey, know that the possibilities are endless! I encourage you to start your own journey and enjoy it!

About Jennifer Morris:

Jennifer (Jenn) Morris has over 30 years of experience in martial arts and healing arts, blending traditional disciplines with modern therapeutic techniques. She holds a bachelor's degree in psychology and is a certified Expert Sound Healer, Master Crystal Healer, and Usui Reiki Master. As a 5th-degree Black Belt in Ju-Jitsu and a Tarot practitioner and teacher, Jenn offers a unique, multidisciplinary approach to wellness and self-discovery.

Her passion lies in empowering individuals to overcome barriers and unlock their inner potential. Through sound healing, crystal therapy, Reiki, aromatherapy, and chakra balancing, Jenn creates a nurturing space for transformation and growth. Her sessions inspire students to explore the depths of their hearts for more abundant, joyful lives.

Outside of her professional work, Jenn enjoys writing, hiking, gardening, horseback riding, and crafting. Her connection to nature and creativity enriches her holistic approach, helping others achieve balance and peace.

Unapologetically Auténtica: On a Journey to Empowered Radiance

By Karen L Ramos

For my birthday in June, as I closed my eyes and blew out the candle on top of my birthday cake, I made myself a promise: "I will no longer play it small. No more dimming my light to make others comfortable. I promise myself to be unapologetic in my authenticity." As I blew out the candle, I felt an electric charge within, as if everything in my being knew that an old version of myself had vanished in that flickering flame. I knew I was stepping into my power like never before and changing the trajectory of mi vida. I would be unapologetically authentic in every aspect of my being.

As I reflected on this newfound commitment to radical self-acceptance, I knew it was time to make moves on the dreams I had been pushing aside for far too long. Just a few months prior, in November, I had made the bold decision to launch my own digital marketing agency, Alumbramos Digital. The name itself holds deep personal significance—a nod to mis raíces, with "Alumbramos" translating to "We illuminate" in Spanish. I envisioned a business that would help others shine brighter by working together to achieve their goals.

Before I could celebrate all the clients I would sign, the money I would make, and the difference in the world I would create, _**Bump brakes**_ I had all these big ideas, but I found myself plagued by self-doubt. ¿Quién soy yo to think I could succeed in such a crowded and competitive industry? What made me any different from the throngs of other marketers vying for clients' attention? "Who would want to listen to me? Hear my ideas and think they were good enough to let me help them?"

Launching Alumbramos felt like standing on the edge of a cliff, peering into a vast unknown. I knew I'd found my calling, but I wondered if I was truly equipped to bring it to life. As a former "Jack of all trades and master of none," it had taken me **YEARS** to look at my resume and not feel an ache of unworthiness because none of those experiences had really panned out. Each role I'd held in the past seemed like a stepping stone to nowhere, leaving me wondering if I'd ever feel a true sense of purpose. I went from wanting to be a manager to wanting to be a nurse, vet tech, and in BioTech. I thought that continuing to succeed and grow in my highest-paying job yet would bring fulfillment, but each role only clarified what I didn't want to do.

It was becoming increasingly clear that I didn't want to be an employee anymore. I was on a mission to find my purpose, my mission in life. Where did my passion truly lie? All I knew was that I wanted to make a difference in the world and leave a legacy of prosperity, abundance, and positive impact. The question was, ¿Pero cómo? How could I possibly position myself as an expert worthy of trust and investment?

Before I could spiral into a realm of self-doubt and pity, the answer came to me in an unexpected way: "Do something with that light, that energy that you have always felt within you." A lightbulb went off, and I thought, "¡Ya sé! I'll focus on my healing, and through my healing, I'll figure out how to get rid of those limiting beliefs and do great in my business!" The dream was BACK on track!

I embarked on a profound healing journey, determined to shed the limiting beliefs and emotional baggage that had held me back for far too long. I started immersing myself in personal growth events, workshops, and coaching programs, hungry to uncover my true power and potential. It was at one such summit that I experienced a pivotal breakthrough. As I listened to a parade of inspiring, successful women share their stories, I found myself captivated. But something was nagging at me—¿where were the Latina voices? The representation of women who looked like me, who shared my cultural heritage and life experiences? The lack of diversity was glaring, and it struck a deep chord within me.

"Be the change you want to see," was a mantra I often used to inspire the various groups and teams I had been a part of. And now, more than ever, I knew that I had to heed my own advice. As I reflected on this realization, I heard a whisper from deep within: "¿Por qué no tú?" If I wanted to see more Latinas stepping into their power and making their mark on the world, then I had to be one of them. "Why not me?" I had to share my story, my struggles, and my triumphs in a way that would inspire others who had been marginalized and overlooked. I had to trailblaze a path for future generations to know that if we could do it, they could too.

"Do something with that light, that energy that you have always felt within you." It was something I often said out loud, but within my exploration to really get to the root of a deeply resonating WHY, I realized it was my family's voice, the voice of my ancestors and my guides. It was as if my ancestors were calling out, urging me to carry their legacy forward, transforming their sacrifices into a future of abundance and strength. Even though I hadn't quite tapped deeply into it at that point in my journey, I knew I had their support—even if I had kept them in the dark about many of the challenges I had faced, the odds I had overcome. They were passing me the torch, whether I was ready to take it or not.

What had once started as a search to help my father, who had suffered a stroke, recover after doctors said he wouldn't improve beyond a certain point, became another soul revelation. I had to heal. I had to be that first spark—the one to stand at the gate of future generations of my family and lovingly give back the decades of unresolved suffering that had caused such trauma. I had to heal to create a ripple effect, helping (key word: helping, assisting—not taking on the responsibility to heal for them, as people must want healing for themselves; a tough lesson I had to learn) my family, our community, and beyond. Within that healing, I envisioned opening up opportunities and transitioning from generational trauma to generational wealth.

My family's encouragement was the final piece of the puzzle. I knew then that my healing journey and the launch of Alumbramos were inextricably linked. I couldn't fully show up for my clients until I had done the deep inner work to heal myself. I've always embraced my cultural identity and heritage. I had to loudly claim my roots and weave them into every aspect of my work if I truly wanted to uplift others like me. By showing that through healing, we can be proud of who we are and where we come from, we can ultimately get to where we're meant to go.

As a proud Latina, I take immense pride in my parents' journey. Originally from El Salvador, they came to this country and, through their own challenges, were able to establish Café Costa del Sol, which has been open since 1997. That's a fact I'm so proud to mention when asked about my family. I was lucky to have witnessed that entrepreneurial and resourceful spirit from my parents. I thought if I could integrate parts of myself into my brand, I'd give people a glimpse of who I am and how I want to help us—especially Latinas—grow and flourish. Keeping our vibras on glow, I wanted to walk the talk and elevate our voices. No more playing it small, remember?

So, I dove headfirst into the process of self-discovery and transformation. I peeled back the layers of trauma, self-doubt, and societal conditioning that had kept me small for far too long. I explored a wide range of healing modalities—from reiki and meditation to sound healing and breathwork.

Each new practice unlocked a deeper understanding of myself, my strengths, and my purpose. There is so much out there, and you have to do your research to really find what calls to you. This may be the Jack-of-all-trades talking, but if I hadn't tried and invested in myself—my healing and growth—I wouldn't have come across the different modalities or found my various tribes among them. As a collective, these experiences shaped my purpose in this life a bit more.

As I began to shed the weight of my past, I felt a profound shift within. The once-whispered dreams I had tucked away now roared to life, demanding to be heard. I realized that my initial vision for Alumbramos—a traditional digital marketing agency—was only the beginning. What I truly yearned to create was a holistic hub of healing and empowerment, where women could not only elevate their businesses but also their inner light.

I was so full of ideas, and it was while I sat telling a "business coach" about my vision—so ready to take off—when I was told that I wouldn't be successful. That I couldn't integrate both and would have to choose between digital marketing or spirituality. Now, she wasn't being mean about it; she was just sharing her perspective. From what I could see, this was a successful person in her field, so she had to know what she was talking about, right?

Heartbroken and unmotivated, I spiraled. I decided to drop the digital side and became all about healing. I became a certified Master Sound Healer and completed other energy and business courses. As things were taking shape, I felt like something was missing. I was fortunate to have great mentors on my journey, and when I shared with two of them how I had started Alumbramos as a digital marketing agency but was now rebranding to focus entirely on healing, they both asked the same question: "Why not integrate both sides, since they both speak to you? Go ahead, create your own lane."

That was my turning point. I had let myself be influenced by someone whose name I don't even remember! The real soul revelation came when I realized I DID have good ideas and that these dreams could be as big as I wanted them to be! Not everyone would understand them, but that was okay. I decided to build it anyway and intuitively call in those who would appreciate the vision. The decision to combine marketing and healing was a revelation—no longer did I have to choose. I could embody both, serving others with authenticity and depth. By integrating my marketing expertise with a suite of transformative healing services, I could now offer my clients a truly comprehensive approach to personal and professional growth. I was determined to help women entrepreneurs, especially Latinas, heal the wounds that had been holding them back while amplifying their unique voices and messages.

It was then that Alumbramos - Empowering the Glow was born. I envisioned working with women from all walks of life who were hungry for holistic support, tired of one-size-fits-all solutions, and weary of cookie-cutter marketing tactics that left them feeling inauthentic and unfulfilled. I wanted to attract those who craved a deeper level of connection—a partnership that would nurture their spirits as much as their bottom line.

In my vision, I see women who once felt invisible and undervalued now stepping into their power, owning their worth, and making waves in their industries. I can't wait to watch them shed the weight of past traumas, reconnect with their authentic selves, and reclaim their right to shine. As they do, their businesses will thrive in ways they had never imagined possible.

You see, Alumbramos is not just a marketing agency or a holistic practice. It is a movement—a rallying cry for women to reclaim their power, their voices, and their right to shine. It is a sanctuary where the wounded can find solace, the doubting can rediscover their worth, and the visionaries can bring their sueños to life.

> As I look to the future, my vision for Alumbramos is growing ever bolder and more ambitious. I see it becoming a global hub of healing and transformation, a place where women from all corners of the world can come together to uplift, support, and empower one another. I envision innovative new programs and services that will address the unique challenges faced by Latina entrepreneurs, providing them with the tools, resources, and community they need to thrive. At the same time, Alumbramos will be a welcoming space for women entrepreneurs of all backgrounds who align with our holistic, empowerment-focused approach. I dream of forging powerful partnerships with like-minded thought leaders, collaborating to amplify our collective message of self-love, authenticity, and unstoppable resilience. I am committed to using my voice and my platform to advocate for greater diversity, equity, and inclusion within the entrepreneurial space, ensuring that no woman ever feels unseen or unheard again.

It's a lofty vision, for sure. As I reflect on my own journey—from self-doubt and limiting beliefs to breakthrough moments and the unwavering support of those who believe in me—I know that anything is possible. I am living proof that when you dare to be unapologetically authentic, when you commit to your healing and growth, the world opens up in ways you never could have imagined.

So to the Latina entrepreneurs out there who are ready to illuminate their light, to the women yearning to reclaim their power and purpose, I say this: ¡Tu tiempo es ahora! Your time is now! The world is waiting for you. Together, we will rewrite the narrative, shatter the glass ceilings, and create a future where our voices, our stories, and our brilliance can no longer be ignored. This is my promise to you and to myself. I will continue to blaze this trail, to be the change I wish to see. And I invite you to join me—to let your light shine so brightly that it illuminates the path for all who follow. Because when we come together, when we support and uplift one another, there is NO LIMIT to what we can achieve.

Remember to believe in yourself. Dream those BIG dreams! Don't let anyone tell you that you can't. The world needs your light. You have a story worth sharing. ¡Dale, que tú puedes! WE. GOT. THIS!

About Karen L Ramos:

Born in Boston to proud Salvadoran parents, Karen L. Ramos has always celebrated her Latina heritage and entrepreneurial roots. After earning her BA in Marketing from Johnson & Wales University, Karen explored careers from retail to Biotech before discovering her true passion: entrepreneurship and empowerment.

Her transformative journey through workshops, coaching, and healing modalities inspired her to create *Alumbramos: Empowering the Glow*, a holistic hub for women entrepreneurs. Alumbramos combines marketing expertise with transformative healing, fostering a supportive community where women reclaim their power and amplify their voices.

Karen is committed to uplifting Latina entrepreneurs and advocating for greater diversity and inclusion in business. With a vision to establish Alumbramos as a global sanctuary for healing and empowerment, she encourages women to embrace authenticity and dream boldly. Passionate about creating change, Karen is dedicated to inspiring future generations to shine their light and thrive personally and professionally.

Dear Reader,

Thank you for sharing this journey with us. Each story in The Call Within was written with the hope that it might reach someone who needs to feel seen, understood, and reminded that they are not alone. If even one story resonated with you, then this book has fulfilled its purpose.

We know that healing and transformation can feel like solitary paths at times, but the truth is, we heal in connection with one another. By holding this book in your hands, you've become part of something larger—a collective of people answering their own inner call, one step at a time.

We encourage you to take a moment to read through the author bios at the end of each story. If someone's story deeply touched you, consider reaching out, following their journey, or exploring the work they share with the world. Many of the contributors offer healing services, workshops, retreats, online resources and have social media pages. Transformation often begins with a single connection and you may find that the healing you seek is already within reach.

We also invite you to continue exploring your own path. Life Changing Energy and Brighter Healing Foundation are here to provide resources, community, and support for your healing journey. You can learn more about our mission, upcoming events, and how to get involved by visiting www.lifechangingenergy.com and www.brighterhealingfoundation.org. We have a section with our course selections to help you deepen your spiritual journey and self-discovery.

Your voice matters. Your story matters. And when you feel ready, we encourage you to share it—whether through writing, speaking, or simply holding space for someone else. Perhaps you'd even like to be part of our next co-authored book. You may write us at support@lifechangingenergy.com to find out when the next one will be and how you can be a part of it.

Our paths have crossed for a reason. There are no accidents, and we believe you were meant to hold this book in your hands at this moment. Transformation grows when we pass it on, and your story could be the light someone else is waiting for.

Thank you for being part of this moment with us. May you continue to trust your path, knowing that the call within you is always guiding the way.

With love and gratitude,
The Authors of The Call Within

www.ingramcontent.com/pod-product-compliance
Lightning Source LLC
Chambersburg PA
CBHW061926220426
43662CB00012B/1822